STATES AND POWER IN AFRICA

PRINCETON STUDIES IN INTERNATIONAL HISTORY AND POLITICS

Series Editors
Jack L. Syder, Marc Trachtenberg, and Fareed Zakaria

RECENT TITLES

STATES AND POWER IN AFRICA

COMPARATIVE LESSONS IN AUTHORITY AND CONTROL

Jeffrey Herbst

PRINCETON UNIVERSITY PRESS   PRINCETON, NEW JERSEY

Written under the auspices of the
Center of International Studies, Princeton University

Library of Congress Cataloging-in-Publication Data
Herbst, Jeffrey Ira.
States and power in Africa : comparative lessons in authority and control /
Jeffrey Herbst.
p. cm. —(Princeton studies in international history and politics)
Includes bibliographical references and index.
ISBN 0-691-01027-7 (cloth : alk. paper).—
ISBN 0-691-01028-5 (pbk. : alk. paper)
1. Africa—Politics and government. 2. Power (Social sciences)—Africa.
I. Title. II. Series.
JQ1875.H47 2000
303.3′096—dc21 99-41736

This book has been composed in Galliard

The paper used in this publication
meets the minimum requirements of
ANSI/NISO Z39.48-1992 (R1997)
(*Permanence of Paper*)

www.pup.princeton.edu

Printed in the United States of America

10 9 8 7 6 5 4 3 2 1

10 9 8 7 6 5 4
(Pbk.)

To our children

MATTHEW, SPENCER, AND ALANA

For now when we are close and
for when we are apart

Contents

List of Illustrations

Figures

Maps

Tables

STATES AND POWER IN AFRICA

AFRICA

Introduction _____

THIS BOOK examines state creation and consolidation in Africa over the last several hundred years. It does so by examining the fundamental problem confronting leaders of almost all African states: how to broadcast power over sparsely settled lands. The topic is easy to justify. As James Fessler wrote, "Distribution of governmental authority is one of the oldest and most abiding problems of society. By our solutions of this distributive problem we determine whether the government will be stable or unstable; whether it will be a dictatorship . . . whether we shall have the rule of law, the rule of men, or the rule of men under law."[1] The African experience is particularly important to developing a truly comparative perspective on state consolidation because a plurality of the world's states are in Africa. However, African states have been omitted from the developing scholarly literature on state creation and consolidation. Instead, this literature is dominated by writing concerned with the small number of states on the European landmass. The failure to account for the African experience is unfortunate because state creation and consolidation in Africa, and in many other parts of the world, proceeded in a radically different manner than it did in Europe. In particular, as chapter one makes clear, African political geography poses a completely different set of political challenges to state-builders compared to the problems European leaders faced.

At the same time, the consolidation of states in Africa remains a central political issue. The fundamental assumption undergirding this study is that states are only viable if they are able to control the territory defined by their borders. Control is assured by developing an infrastructure to broadcast power and by gaining the loyalty of citizens. The failure of many African states to consolidate their authority has resulted in civil wars in some countries, the presence of millions of refugees throughout the continent, and the adoption of highly dysfunctional policies by many leaders. Yet international society, by dint of the granting of sovereignty, still assumes that all African countries are able to control all of the territory within their boundaries. The gap between how power is exercised in Africa and international assumptions about how states operate is significant and, in some cases, growing. State consolidation in Africa is not merely an academic issue but is, instead, critical to the future of tens of

_____

[1] James Fessler, *Area and Administration* (Birmingham: University of Alabama Press, 1949), p. 1.

millions of people who are at risk from the insecurity that is the inevitable
by-product of state decline and failure. Therefore, this book discusses not
only the history of state creation and consolidation but also evaluates
different policy alternatives that might address some of the fundamental
political challenges African states face today.

The method adopted by this book is, by necessity, much more contro-
versial than the topic. To answer the questions posed regarding the nature of state-making, it is important to examine the entire sub-Saharan
region. Of course, this is a vast area that contains different peoples, regions, and states. However, sub-Saharan Africa has a large number of
entities that still can be compared because they share similar, although by
no means identical, population structures, levels of technological development, and stocks of material wealth. Sub-Saharan Africa also has been
organized as a particular international regime for more than a century
and the rules adopted by colonialists and independent African leaders
have had a profound effect on how states have been consolidated. Thus, I
am making what Charles Tilly has called "huge (but not stupendous)
comparisons" within a particular state system.[2]

At the same time, it is necessary to analyze the problems of state consolidation in Africa over several hundred years: from the precolonial period, through the short but intense interlude of formal European colonialism, to the modern era of independent states. In particular, it is
critical to understand the continuities in state consolidation over the centuries. Here I am responding to Harry Eckstein's challenge to return to
historically grounded comparative politics.[3] Of course, an argument in
favor of historical depth would be banal if the subject was European state
development given the obvious continuities over time in that region.
However, a similar argument regarding Africa is unconventional because
of the almost universal assumption that colonialism changed everything,
for the better or worse, depending on the biases of the individual author.
I argue that it was impossible for the Europeans to have changed "everything" in the few decades that they ruled Africa. They also had to take
Africa's political geography as a given because they were unwilling and
unable to change the landscape.

Therefore, this book spans a vast geographical landmass and hundreds
of years. Inevitably, it glosses over or misses the nuances that differentiate
various regions, societies, and countries. Put another way, I ignore a vast
number of trees in order to see the forest. I am aware of these costs. I
have spent much of my career arguing for a greater appreciation of the

[2] Charles Tilly, *Big Structures, Large Processes, Huge Comparisons* (New York: Russell
Sage Foundation, 1984), p. 74.
[3] Harry Eckstein, "Unfinished Business: Reflections on the Scope of Comparative Politics," *Comparative Political Studies* 31 (August 1998): p. 520.

increasing heterogeneity of Africa and have suggested that more care be given to understanding the particular problems and opportunities that individual states must confront. Throughout this book, wherever possible, I have tried to qualify the argument to take into account the enormous variations across both time and space in Africa. I have also tried to develop new sources of information and new ways of looking at African politics (e.g., by mapping countries, by classifying relationships between states and chiefs, and by delineating citizenship regulations) in order to understand the variations within the processes I am analyzing.

Further, in order to make the comparative work viable, "Africa" in this study refers to the countries south of the Sahara. While much of the analysis also applies to Egypt, Tunisia, Algeria, Libya, and Morocco, those countries have radically different precolonial and colonial histories, operate predominantly in the state system of the Middle East, and are significantly richer.[4] South Africa also does not feature in the sample of countries under study because of its different history, although I occasionally make reference to it. Finally, I exclude island Africa (Comoros, Madagascar, Mauritius, São Tomé, and Seychelles) because an understanding of the role of land boundaries in the consolidation of states is critical to the study.

However, there is not enough space to make all of the qualifications necessary to completely describe every region, society, and country, and to do so would fatally distract from the central argument: that African leaders across time and space have faced certain similar issues when trying to rule and have often come to similar conclusions on how to solve the problems they have faced. I focus on "the forest" partly because I believe that the structural argument regarding state consolidation is both powerful and relatively well defined. Finally, I believe that the benefits of such an approach outweigh the costs. I agree again with Tilly when he counsels against despairing that we will never have enough knowledge to accurately describe long-term social processes: "Historically grounded huge comparisons of big structures and large processes help establish what must be explained, attach the possible explanations to their context in time and space, and sometimes actually improve our understanding of those structures and processes."[5]

The unwillingness of many Africanists to generalize has its origins in the need to differentiate countries on the continent in the face of racist perceptions that Africa is a homogenous region that is in constant tur-

---

[4] Average per capita income for the five North African countries is approximately (there is considerable uncertainty concerning Libya's income) $1,827. Per capita income for sub-Saharan Africa averages $500. World Bank, *World Development Report 1998* (New York: Oxford University Press, 1998), pp. 190–1, 232.

[5] Tilly, *Big Structures, Large Processes*, p. 145.

moil. I understand the regionalists' desire, after the analytic disasters caused by the homogenizing tendencies of both modernization and dependency theory, to hew closely to the empirical facts. However, failure to examine the broad continuities over space and time has meant that Africa has been excluded from the political science mainstream because overarching arguments about the trajectory of the continent do not exist to compare with the well developed models of how political order was constructed in Europe, Latin America, and other regions. By attempting to describe the African state-building experience, I hope to join the ambitious academic project well described by Wong: "those of us who spend most of our time laboring on so-called non-Western parts of the world should make greater efforts to offer analyses that engage arguments about historical change in European history systematically . . . to generate the elements of well-grounded comparative history that can . . . create a new basis for building social theories to replace the great nineteenth-century efforts limited in large measure to European foundations."[6]

The failure to develop more powerful generalizations is also increasingly hurting the study of Africa itself. For instance, the effort that came to full life in the 1960s to study the history of Africa before the Europeans has not had the impact that it should have had because commentary almost always has been devoted to one polity or one region. Similarly, the study of relations between capitals and chiefs has, but with a very few exceptions, been developed on a country-by-country basis with no hint of a comparative effort. As a result, the study of African politics has sometimes been in accord with the critiques of area studies: more a jumble of accumulated facts than a clear scholarly project that has sought to continually test facts against hypotheses. It is possible to answer those critiques without abandoning the study of African states *qua* African states. To do so requires the development of an analytic perspective that allows the African experience to be understood in comparative perspective.

This book does not provide all of the answers to the big questions posed herein. However, I do hope that it initiates a debate that is long overdue about state consolidation in Africa and in other parts of the world. Such a debate should flourish if it is possible to recognize both the enormous variation within Africa and the possibilities of overarching similarities. To understand, then, what is apparent to anyone who goes to Africa.

Soon after taking power on 17 May 1997, Laurent Kabila changed the name of Zaire to Democratic Republic of the Congo. This book refers to

---

[6] R. Bin Wong, *China Transformed: Historical Change and the Limits of European Experience* (Ithaca: Cornell University Press, 1997), p. ix.

the country as "Zaire" while it was ruled by former President Mobutu Sese Seko and as "Democratic Republic of the Congo (D.R.O.C.)" for the post-May 1997 era.

This book has its origins in 1982 when I went to Nigeria to research my senior thesis as an undergraduate in Princeton University's Woodrow Wilson School. I woke up in the morning when my plane was over West Africa, looked out the window and remarked to myself that there appeared to be very few people on the land. That observation has, to one degree or another, haunted me for the last fifteen years and is the original impetus for this book. As a student, I was fortunate to have as teachers Henry Bienen, Michael Doyle, and Robert Tignor, among others, who cultivated my growing interest in African politics.

While teaching at Princeton, I have been thinking about this book's central argument for over a decade and writing it for the last two years. While writing, I have incurred many debts as I exposed numerous colleagues to iterated versions of the manuscript. Robert Tignor continues to tutor me in African history and Michael Doyle is still teaching me the intricacies of international relations theory. Sheri Berman and Gideon Rose provided me with an especially searching and comprehensive critique of the draft manuscript. I also received helpful comments from Robert Bates, Christopher Clapham, Kent Eaton, Antoinette Handley, John Harbeson, Tony Hopkins, Atul Kohli, Emmanuel Kreike, Donald Rothchild, Martin Stein, Kathryn Stoner-Weiss, John Waterbury, Deborah Yashar, and Crawford Young. Research assistance for the book was ably provided by Elizabeth Bloodgood and Amanda Dickins.

Research for this book was supported by Princeton University's Center of International Studies and the University Committee on Research in the Humanities and Social Sciences.

John Bruce of the University of Wisconsin's Land Tenure Center was kind enough to give me permission to quote from the country profiles the LTC had produced for Africa.

My greatest thanks goes, as always, to my wife Sharon, who manages the roles of partner, friend, and constructive critic with love and good cheer.

Maps 3.1, 3.2, and 3.3 are reprinted from Ieuan L. L. Griffiths, *The Atlas of African Affairs*, 2nd ed. (London: Routledge Press, 1994). © 1994 by Routledge Press. Used with permission of the publisher. Parts of chapter nine originally appeared in Jeffrey Herbst, "Responding to State Failure in Africa," *International Security* 21(Winter 1996/7). Used with permission of the president and fellows of Harvard College and the Massachusetts Institute of Technology.

Part One

THE CHALLENGE OF STATE-BUILDING IN AFRICA

One

The Challenge of State-Building in Africa

The history of every continent is written clearly
in its geographical features, but of no continent
is this more true than of Africa.
  Lord Hailey, *An African Survey*

THE FUNDAMENTAL PROBLEM facing state-builders in Africa—be they pre-colonial kings, colonial governors, or presidents in the independent era—has been to project authority over inhospitable territories that contain relatively low densities of people. Sub-Saharan Africa, with roughly 18 percent of the world's surface area, has always been sparsely settled. Africa had only 6 to 11 percent of the world's population in 1750, 5 to 7 percent in 1900, and only 11 percent in 1997.[1] Relatively low population densities in Africa have automatically meant that it always has been more expensive for states to exert control over a given number of people compared to Europe and other densely settled areas. As John Iliffe wrote, "In the West African savannah, underpopulation was the chief obstacle to state formation."[2]

In only a few places in Africa, including the Great Lakes region and the Ethiopian highlands, are there ecologies that have supported relatively high densities of people. Not surprisingly, these areas, with the longest traditions of relatively centralized state structures, have been periodically able to exercise direct control over their peripheries.[3] However, ecological conditions throughout most of the continent do not allow high densities of people to be easily supported. More than 50 percent of Africa has

---

[1] Calculated from John D. Durand, "Historical Estimates of World Population: An Evaluation," *Population and Development Review* 3 (September 1977): p. 259 and World Bank, *World Development Report 1998*, p 191.

[2] John Iliffe, *Africans: The History of a Continent* (Cambridge: Cambridge University Press, 1995), p. 70.

[3] While hampered by very poor data, Robert Bates found that, in the African polities he was able to code, "the higher the population density, the greater the level of political centralization." See his *Essays on the Political Economy of Rural Africa* (Cambridge: Cambridge University Press, 1983), p. 35. See also Robert F. Stevenson, *Population and Political Systems in Tropical Africa* (New York: Columbia University Press, 1968).

inadequate rainfall; indeed, contrary to the popular imagination, only 8 percent of the continent has a tropical climate. Approximately one-third of the world's arid land is in Africa.[4]

In Africa, two other factors have aggravated the cost of extending power in the face of low population densities. First, African countries have quite varied environmental conditions. Ecological differences across provinces of a country in West Africa, which can be coastal, forest, savannah, or near-desert, are greater than in any European country.[5] Therefore, the models of control an African state must develop for these highly differentiated zones are more varied, and thus more costly, than what a government in Europe or Asia must implement in order to rule over their more homogenous rural areas. Second, it is expensive to project power over distance in Africa because of the combination of a peculiar set of geographical features. As Ralph Austen notes,

> The geography of Africa also presents serious barriers to long-distance transport. Water travel is limited by the small amount of indented shoreline relative to the size of the interior surface of the continent, as well as the disrupted navigability of most rivers, due to rapids and seasonal shallows. The wheel was introduced into northern Africa for overland travel during ancient times but then abandoned because the terrain and distances to be covered could not feasibly be provided with the necessary roads.[6]

The daunting nature of Africa's geography is one of the reasons the region was only colonized in the late 1800s despite its proximity to Europe. The Europeans found it easier to colonize Latin America hundreds of years before despite the much greater distances involved.

Why the particular pattern of population density occurred, given Africa's geography, is not within my competence to explain.[7] Rather, this book examines how successive sets of leaders in Africa responded to a political geography they were forced to take as a given. This is not an argument for the kind of geographical determinism that has captivated scholars from Ibn Khaldûn to Montesquieu to Jeffrey Sachs.[8] A variety of paths were open to African leaders as they confronted their environ-

---

[4] W. Bediako Lamousé-Smith and Joseph School, *Africa Interactive Maps*, CD-ROM, (Odenton, Md.: Africa Interactive Maps, 1998).

[5] W. Arthur Lewis, *Politics in West Africa* (London: George Allen and Unwin, 1965), p. 24.

[6] Ralph Austen, *African Economic History* (London: James Currey, 1987), p. 20.

[7] For a provocative thesis, see Jared Diamond, *Guns, Germs and Steel: The Fate of Human Societies* (New York: W. W. Norton, 1997), chapter 19.

[8] See Ibn Khaldûn, *The Muqaddimah*, trans. Franz Rosenthal (London: Routledge and Kegan Paul, 1967), p. 63; Montesquieu, *The Spirit of the Laws*, vol. 1 (Cincinnati: Robert Clarke, 1873), p. 255; and Jeffrey Sachs, "Nature, Nurture, and Growth," *The Economist*, 14 June 1997, pp. 19–23.

ments. However, the challenges posed by political geography, especially low population densities, could not be ignored by any leader. Such an approach offers a tremendous methodological advantage: by holding the physical environment "constant," I can focus on the precise political calculations of different African leaders over time as they sought to design their states.

In this book, I argue that leaders confront three sets of issues when building their states: the cost of expanding the domestic power infrastructure; the nature of national boundaries; and the design of state systems. Understanding the decisions made regarding each is critical, and there are profound trade-offs inherent to different approaches. Africa's political geography helped structure the responses that leaders adopted to each set of issues just as European decisions were influenced by the structural features of that region. The following two sections provide a comparison of Europe and Africa's political geographies. I then develop the analytic tools that are central to this study.

The European Experience of State Consolidation

The African experience of politics amid large supplies of land and low population densities while confronting an inhospitable physical setting is in dramatic contrast to the European experience of state-building. In Europe, through the fourteenth century, population densities were not high enough to put immediate pressure on land and compel territorial competition. As Mattingly notes, "In the fourteenth and fifteenth centuries, the continental space of Western Europe still impeded any degree of political organization efficient enough to create a system of continuous diplomatic pressures."[9]

However, starting in the fifteenth century in Italy and later elsewhere, population densities increased. As a result, European nations began to compete for territory, a tendency that only makes sense if population densities are relatively high and vacant land is limited or nonexistent, so that the value of conquering land is higher than the price to be paid in wealth and men. In turn, there was significant pressure to strengthen states in order to fight wars. Charles Tilly notes that one of the central reasons for the creation of relatively centralized state apparatuses in Europe was the "continuous aggressive competition for trade and territory among changing states of unequal size, which made war a driving force in European history."[10] Wars of territorial conquest, as chapter four notes in much greater detail, have been central to the formation of particular

[9] Garrett Mattingly, *Renaissance Diplomacy* (London: Jonathan Cape, 1955), p. 60.
[10] Charles Tilly, *Coercion, Capital, and European States, A.D. 990–1992* (Cambridge, MA: Blackwell, 1990), p. 54.

types of states because they create, quite literally, a life and death imperative to raise taxes, enlist men as soldiers, and develop the necessary infrastructure to fight and win battles against rapacious neighbors.

Because European states were forged with iron and blood, it was critical for the capital to physically control its hinterland. Tilly notes, "as
rulers bargained directly with their subject populations for massive taxes,
military service, and cooperation in state programs, most states took further steps of profound importance: a movement toward direct rule that
reduced the role of local or regional patrons and places representatives of
the national state in every community, and expansion of popular consultation in the form of elections, plebiscites, and legislatures."[11] In particular, the constant threat of war and the need to protect valued territory
meant that the physiology of the state forced leaders to place particular
emphasis on control of remote areas that could be lost in battle. Again,
Tilly notes: "Europeans followed a standard war-provoking logic: everyone who controlled substantial coercive means tried to maintain a secure
area within which he could enjoy the returns from coercion, plus a forti-
fied buffer zone, possibly run at a loss, to protect the secure area."[12]
These border defenses protected the state from its external competitors
and, simultaneously, completed the job of internal consolidation. Thus,
frontier fortifications have been, according to Frederick the Great, the
"mighty nails which hold a ruler's provinces together."[13] Lord Salisbury—
a critical participant in the scramble for Africa, and the eponym for the
capital of Southern Rhodesia—even said, in exasperation, that if his military advisers had their way, they would garrison the moon to prevent an
attack from Mars.[14]

Successful European state development was therefore characterized by
profound links between the cities—the core political areas—and the surrounding territories. Indeed, the growth of states was closely correlated
with the development of significant urban areas. As Tilly has argued,
"The commercial and demographic impact of cities made a significant
difference to state formation. . . . The existence of intensive rural-urban
trade provided an opportunity for rulers to collect revenues through customs and excise taxes, while the relatively commercialized economy
made it easier for monarchs to bypass great landlords as they extended
royal power to towns and villages."[15] Critically, for this study, he goes on

---

[11] Ibid., p. 63.

[12] Ibid., p. 70.

[13] Quoted in John H. Herz, "Rise and Demise of the Territorial State," *World Politics* 9
(1957): p. 477.

[14] Michael Howard, *The Lessons of History* (New Haven: Yale University Press, 1991), p.
23.

[15] Tilly, *Coercion, Capital, and European States*, p. 49. Similarly, Michael Mann notes that

to note, "Cities shape the destinies of states chiefly by serving as containers and distribution points for capital. By means of capital, urban ruling classes extend their influence through the urban hinterland and across far-flung trading networks."[16] So profound have been the ties between the major cities and the countryside that the roster of great cities that have dominated the western world (Venice, Antwerp, Genoa, Amsterdam, London, New York) stand as excellent proxies to the rise and fall of national powers.[17]

Understanding African Politics

However, Europe's demographic history is not shared by many other parts of the world. It is quite remarkable that by 1975, Africa had only reached the level of population density that occurred in Europe in 1500. Nor is Africa's population density unusual. Many other regions of the world are also sparsely settled. As is clear from table 1.1, Latin America, North Africa, and the areas of the former Soviet Union have population densities that are historically much closer to Africa than to Europe.

The ramifications of lower population densities can be seen in the very different history of relations between capitals and their hinterlands. In Africa, in contrast to Europe, the current states were created well before many of the capital cities had reached maturity. Addis Ababa appears to be the only example of rapid urban growth in a designated capital not under the control of Europeans.[18] Elsewhere in the precolonial period, even royal villages moved periodically as "soil become exhausted or buildings deteriorated or as bad fortune indicated that the old site had lost its virtue."[19] Even most of the storied towns of West Africa were quite small until after colonial rule began. For instance, in 1901, Lagos had only eighteen thousand people and Accra about twenty-one thousand, while as late as 1931 only ten thousand people lived in Abidjan. At the turn of the century, only Ibadan, with two hundred thousand, had what could be considered to be a large population. Similarly, in 1906, the

---

for Europe, "The state loomed rather larger in the urban sector." *The Sources of Social Power: A History of Power from the Beginning to A.D.1760*, vol. 1 (Cambridge: Cambridge University Press, 1986), p. 423.

[16] Tilly, *Coercion, Capital, and European States*, p. 51.

[17] Ibid., p. 47.

[18] Richard Pankhurst, "Menelik and the Foundation of Addis Ababa," *Journal of African History* 2 (1961): p. 103.

[19] Elizabeth Colson, "African Society at the Time of the Scramble," in *Colonialism in Africa, 1870–1960*, ed. L. H. Gann and Peter Duignan, vol. 1 (Cambridge: Cambridge University Press, 1969), p. 42.

TABLE 1.1
Comparative Population Densities over Time (People/Sq. Km)

Region	1500	1750	1900	1975
Japan	46.4	78.3	118.2	294.8
South Asia	15.2	24.1	38.2	100.3
Europe	13.7	26.9	62.9	99.9
China	13.4	22.2	45.6	91.1
Latin America	2.2	0.8	3.7	16.3
North Africa	1.6	2.2	9.4	14.1
Sub-Saharan Africa	**1.9**	**2.7**	**4.4**	**13.6**
Former U.S.S.R. area	0.6	1.6	6.1	11.6

Sources: Calculated from John D. Durand, "Historical Estimates of World Population: An Evaluation," *Population and Development Review* 3 (September 1977): p. 259; World Bank, *World Development Report 1992* (Washington, D.C.: 1992), p. 219; and Food and Agriculture Organization, *Production Yearbook 1993* (Rome: FAO, 1994), pp. 3–14.

Table was calculated using the midpoint of the population estimates that Durand presents.

two largest towns in East Africa were Dar es Salaam with twenty thousand and Mombasa with thirty thousand people.[20]

The Europeans, after formally colonizing Africa in the late-nineteenth century, did create many urban areas. However, these cities did not serve as the basis of state creation in the same manner as occurred in Europe because the colonizers were not interested in duplicating the power infrastructure which bound city to hinterland in their homelands. Rather, the cities were mainly designed to service the needs of the colonizers. Particularly telling are the location of the capitals the colonialists created. By 1900, twenty-eight of the forty-four colonial capitals were located on the coast, demonstrating the low priority of extending power inland compared to the need for easy communication and transport links with Europe.[21] Rather systematically, Europeans created capitals that moved power toward the ocean and away from the interior centers of power that Africans had slowly created and that had managed to exert control over parts of their surrounding territories. Thus, Lagos became the capital of Nigeria rather than Ibadan, Ife, or Sokoto; Accra the capital of the Gold Coast (Ghana) rather than Kumasi; and Bamako (with its good links to the Senegalese coast), the capital of Mali instead of Timbuktu. Some colonial capitals, including Lusaka, Nairobi, Salisbury (now Harare), and

[20] Walter Elkan and Roger van Zwanenberg, "How People Came to Live in Towns," in *Colonialism in Africa, 1870–1960*, ed. Peter Duignan and L. H. Gann, vol. 4, (Cambridge: Cambridge University Press, 1975), p. 655.

[21] A. J. Christopher, "Urbanization and National Capitals in Africa," in *Urbanization in Africa: A Handbook*, ed. James D. Tarver (Westport, CT: Greenwood Press, 1994), p. 411.

Windhoek were created de novo outside of preexisting polities in order to service the logistical and health needs of the white conquerors. Many others, including Abidjan, Banjul, Dakar, and Kinshasa, were also newly established by the colonialists but quickly acquired an African veneer because they were not in settler colonies.[22] In extreme examples of how African capital cities did not follow the European pattern of extending power, Mauritania and Bechuanaland (now Botswana) were actually ruled by capitals outside their nominal boundaries during the colonial period (Saint-Louis and Mafeking, respectively).

Accordingly, once the capitals were created, they did not immediately begin to effectively extend power throughout their extensive but sparsely settled territories. Catherine Coquery-Vidrovitch finds that "as of the beginning of the twentieth century, the colonial penetration had barely begun."[23] W. Arthur Lewis concluded that prior to World War II, "The countryside had no continuous politics."[24] Tellingly, it was only in the limited number of settler colonies, almost entirely in southern Africa, that the colonial state's reach was extended in a comprehensive manner. In Southern Rhodesia (now Zimbabwe), the presence of a relatively large number of white settlers who saw themselves living permanently in Africa, in contrast to most colonialists who were transients, propelled the creation of a remarkably efficient and brutal state that protected the settlers from market forces while dispossessing many Africans of their land.[25] The fact that wars of liberation had to be fought in Africa's settler colonies (e.g., Zimbabwe, Angola, Mozambique, Namibia) was in good part a reflection of the simple fact that unlike the rest of Africa, where the transfer of power was astonishingly peaceful, those colonial states had the motivation and the ability to fight for power.

During the terminal colonial period, politics become national in many countries as nationalist movements emerged. However, neglect of the rural areas by colonial governments over decades, combined with organizational problems posed by a large peasant population atomistically dispersed across a vast hinterland that had few roads or telephones, deterred most politicians from investing heavily in mobilizing the rural areas. As a result, nationalist politics in the 1950s and 1960s were very much urban affairs. As Aristide Zolberg concluded:

[22] See David Simon, *Cities, Capital, and Development: African Cities in the World Economy* (London: Belhaven Press, 1992), pp. 24–5.

[23] Catherine Coquery-Vidrovitch, *Africa: Endurance and Change South of the Sahara* (Berkeley: University of California Press, 1988), p. 174.

[24] Lewis, *Politics in West Africa*, p. 14.

[25] See Jeffrey Herbst, *State Politics in Zimbabwe* (Berkeley: University of California Press, 1990), chapter 2.

But it is difficult to believe, on the basis of the evidence available, that under existing circumstances the capacity of these [nationalist] movements for "mobilization" extended much beyond intermittent electioneering and the collection of more tangible support in the form of party dues from a tiny fraction of the population. Although their ambition was often to extend tentacles throughout society, they were creatures with a relatively large head in the capital and fairly rudimentary limbs.[26]

The nationalists received states that were appropriate to the way they had conducted their politics: primarily urban, with few links to the surrounding countryside where most of the population lived. In turn, they furthered the urban bias of their states by marginalizing peasant populations and by providing urban groups with privileged access to many of the resources allocated by the state. As Robert H. Bates documented, African politicians traditionally equated their political survival with appeasing their urban populations via subsidies even if the much larger, and poorer, rural populations had to be taxed.[27]

After independence, many African countries made significant progress in extending administrative structures over their territories. However, African leaders still find physical control over substantial parts of the population to be a difficult issue. For instance, Goran Hyden argues that because African peasants depend primarily on rain-fed agriculture rather than on cooperative techniques of production, such as irrigation found in more densely settled areas, and because smallholders are less integrated into the cash economy than elsewhere in the world, the peasantry in Africa is "uncaptured."[28] Hyden argues that because "the state does not really enter into the solution of his [the African peasant's] existential problems" there is "a definite limit . . . to how far enforcement of state policies can go in the context of peasant production."[29] Similarly, Michael Bratton has argued that "The essence of the postcolonial history of sub-Saharan Africa is therefore an unresolved political struggle: On one hand, political elites wish to extend the authority of the state over scattered populations, most of whom live in rural areas; on the other hand, peasants remain determined to preserve a realm of authority within which to

---

[26] Aristide R. Zolberg, *Creating Political Order: The Party-States of West Africa* (Chicago: Rand McNally and Co., 1966), pp. 34–5.

[27] Robert H. Bates, *Markets and States in Sub-Saharan Africa* (Berkeley: University of California Press, 1981), p. 33.

[28] Goran Hyden, *Beyond Ujamaa in Tanzania: Underdevelopment and an Uncaptured Peasantry* (Berkeley: University of California Press, 1980), pp. 9–18. See also Stephen G. Bunker, *Peasants against the State: The Politics of Market Control in Bugisu, Uganda, 1900–1983* (Urbana: University of Illinois Press, 1987), p. 5.

[29] Hyden, *Beyond Ujamaa in Tanzania*, pp. 23–4.

make decisions about their own lives."[30] It is hardly surprising that in a United Nations' survey, African governments were more likely to express unhappiness over their population distributions than governments in any other regions of the world.[31]

Further, the long economic crisis that many African countries have experienced since the late 1970s has caused a profound erosion of many governments' revenue bases and, consequently, their ability to project power. Instead of African states gradually consolidating control over their territories as time progresses, even the most basic agents of the state—agricultural extension workers, tax collectors, census takers—are no longer to be found in many rural areas. The Economic Commission for Africa lamented that, because of the poor state of the road systems, "whole areas are practically cut off from capital cities."[32] This is an especially important problem in Africa because about 69 percent of the population, on average across the continent, still live in rural areas compared to 61 percent for all low and middle income countries.[33] Some states are increasingly unable to exercise physical control over their territories. William C. Thom, U. S. Defense Intelligence Officer for Africa, has written that

> Most African state armies are in decline, beset by a combination of shrinking budgets, international pressures to downsize and demobilize, and the lack of the freely accessible military assistance that characterized the cold war period. With few exceptions, heavy weapons lie dormant, equipment is in disrepair, and training is almost nonexistent. . . . the principal forces of order are in disorder in many countries at a time when the legitimacy of central governments (and indeed sometimes the state) is in doubt.[34]

For instance, a parliamentary report of Zimbabwe's army—long thought to be one of the more competent militaries on the continent—found that the force had only 5 percent of its vehicles in working order, monthly pilot training had been abandoned, and 70 percent of the troops in one brigade had been off duty for a year or more, on forced leaves in order to save money.[35]

[30] Michael Bratton, "Peasant-State Relations in Postcolonial Africa: Patterns of Engagement and Disengagement," in *State Power and Social Forces: Domination and Transformation in the Third World*, ed. Joel S. Migdal, Atul Kohli, and Vivienne Shue, (New York: Cambridge University Press, 1994), p. 231.

[31] United Nations, *Concise Report on the World Population Situation in 1993* (New York: United Nations, 1994), p. 36.

[32] Economic Commission for Africa, *Survey of Economic and Social Conditions in Africa, 1991–2*, (Addis Ababa: Economic Commission for Africa, 1994), p. 117.

[33] World Bank, *World Development Report 1998*, p. 231.

[34] William G. Thom, "An Assessment of Prospects for Ending Domestic Military Conflict in Sub-Saharan Africa," *CSIS Africa Notes* 177 (October 1995), p. 3

[35] "Zimbabwe: Report Cites UK Paper on 'Ominous' State of Defense Force," *Harare*

Even the wave of democratization that swept Africa in the 1990s has not breached the center-periphery divide. The revolts since 1989 against African authoritarianism were largely urban affairs, with little participation by any organized rural group.[36] Not surprisingly, few if any of the political parties that have come into existence since 1989 have strong rural roots.[37] It still appears too difficult to organize the peasants qua peasants, despite the fact that spatial location is an excellent determinant of life chances in much of Africa.[38]

An appropriate capstone to the comparison between Africa—pre-colonial, colonial, and independent—and Europe is their strikingly different traditions involving the most dramatic action typically associated with a state: warfare. Due to low population densities and the large amount of open land in Africa, wars of territorial conquest, as chapters two, three, and four will discuss at length, have seldom been a significant aspect of the continent's history. In precolonial Africa, the primary object of warfare, which was continual in many places, was to capture people and treasure, not land which was available to all. In contrast to European states that, at least at some points in their histories, needed to mobilize tremendous resources from their own populations to fight wars and were therefore forced to develop profound ties with their own hinterlands, precolonial African leaders mainly exploited people outside their own polity because the point of war was to take women, cattle, and slaves.[39] Thus the slave trade, especially in the eighteenth century, should be seen

---

Zimbabwe Standard, 11 May 1998, cited in Foreign Broadcast Information Service, *Daily Report: Sub-Saharan Africa*, 12 May 1998.

[36] Michael Bratton and Nicolas van de Walle, "Toward Governance in Africa: Popular Demand and State Responses," in *Governance and Politics in Africa*, ed. Goran Hyden and Michael Bratton (Boulder, CO: Lynne Rienner, 1992), 1992, p. 31.

[37] Henry Bienen and Jeffrey Herbst, "Economic and Political Reform in Africa," *Comparative Politics* 29 (October 1996), p. 36.

[38] In Ghana, 80 percent of the poor and almost all of the poorest are in the rural areas outside of Accra. Similarly, in a survey of Côte d'Ivoire, researchers found that while 59 percent of all Ivorians live in the rural areas, 86 percent of the poorest 30 percent of the population and 96 percent of the poorest 10 percent of the population live outside the cities. See respectively E. Oti Boateng et al., *A Poverty Profile for Ghana, 1987–1988*, Social Dimensions of Adjustment in sub-Saharan Africa Working Paper no. 5 (Washington, DC: The World Bank, 1990), p. 14, and Paul Glewwe and Dennis de Tray, *The Poor during Adjustment: A Case Study of Côte d'Ivoire*, Living Standards Measurement Survey Paper no. 47 (Washington, DC: The World Bank, 1988), p.13.

[39] The classic statement is by Catherine Coquery-Vidrovitch, "The Political Economy of the African Peasantry and Modes of Production," in *The Political Economy of Contemporary Africa*, ed. Peter C. W. Gutkind and Immanuel Wallerstein (Beverly Hills, CA: Sage Publications, 1976), p. 105. Compare to Charles Tilly "War Making and State Making as Organized Crime," in *Bringing the State Back In*, ed. Peter B. Evans, Dietrich Rueschemeyer, and Theda Skocpol, (New York: Cambridge University Press, 1985), 183.

as part of the process by which African states grew: by capturing people rather than by gaining control over territory.[40]

In the colonial and independence periods, Europeans and Africans have gone to elaborate lengths to prevent wars of conquest from occurring in Africa, a series of efforts that were strikingly successful compared to the war-torn history of Europe and other regions throughout the twentieth century. The consequential role that war played in European state development was not replicated in Africa, or in Latin America for that matter.[41] In particular, African states have never had the security imperative to physically control the hinterlands in the face of competition from hostile neighbors. Since the external imperative for capitals to consolidate authority was largely absent, African leaders have had to devise an entirely different set of strategies to exert control over their territories.

The Extension of Power in Africa

How those who sought to create African states responded to the continual problem of extending authority over distance, given a particular political geography, is the focus of this book. This question goes to the very essence of politics because, as Weber and others have repeatedly noted, the signal characteristic of a state is its monopoly on the legitimate use of physical force in the territory it is said to control.[42] It is also an issue that has been analyzed almost entirely by focusing on Europe.[43] Scholars have concentrated on the European experience when trying to understand state development despite the fact that Europe contains only a small percentage of the states formed throughout history. In part, this myopia is due to the fact that the rise of European states is well documented. Of course, concentrating on Europe, the taproot of the nation-state, appears logical because today all states worldwide do have the form of the nation-

[40] James L. Newman, *The Peopling of Africa: A Geographic Interpretation* (New Haven: Yale University Press, 1995), pp. 129–130.

[41] See the paper of my colleague Miguel Angel Centeno, "Blood and Debt: War and Taxation in Nineteenth Century Latin America," *American Journal of Sociology* 102 (May 1997): pp. 1565–1605.

[42] Max Weber, "Politics as a Vocation," reprinted in *From Max Weber: Essays in Sociology* ed. H. H. Gerth and C. Wright Mills (New York: Oxford University Press, 1958), p. 78.

[43] Representative books include Tilly, *Coercion, Capital, and European States*; Brian M. Downing, *The Military Revolution and Political Change: Origins of Democracy and Autocracy in Early Modern Europe* (Princeton: Princeton University Press, 1992) Mann, *Sources of Social Power*; Barrington Moore, *Social Origins of Dictatorship and Democracy: Lord and Peasant in the Making of the Modern World* (Boston: Beacon Press, 1966); and Hendrick Spruyt, *The Sovereign State and its Competitors* (Princeton: Princeton University Press, 1994).

state as theorized and executed by the Europeans. Indeed, the analysis of the creation of many third world states is, by necessity, intertwined with accounts of European imperialism and colonialization.[44] There was also a long-term western project of delegitimating nonwestern sovereignty that was critical to the colonial project and that, inevitably, seeped into the academic literature.[45]

However, the European experience does not provide a template for state-making in other regions of the world. As S. E. Finer has noted in his monumental work on the history of government, "the development of states in Europe is—in a world-historical perspective—highly idiosyncratic."[46] Many other regions of the world share the African experience of having significant outlying territories that are difficult for the state to control because of relatively low population densities and difficult physical geographies. For instance, Gledhill notes that in Mexico, "The hills are associated with wildness, violence, and political freedom, the plains with docility, pacification, and susceptibility to repression, a contrast which contains an element of truth."[47] Similarly, the idea of the anarchic northern frontier that presented the opportunity to escape from the state is an integral part of old Russian political mythology.[48] In Southeast Asia, the divide between center and periphery is also often pronounced: "In many senses, the capital *was* the state, and its power radiated from center to the periphery."[49] Of course, there is also a long historical tradition of examining the American frontier and the political consequences of open spaces.[50]

Similarly, the study of international relations, which has much to say

[44] I am grateful to Deborah Yashar for this point.

[45] David Strang, "Contested Sovereignty: The Social Construction of Colonial Imperialism," in *State Sovereignty as Social Construct*, ed. Thomas J. Biersteker and Cynthia Weber (Cambridge: Cambridge University Press, 1996), p. 34.

[46] S. E. Finer, *The History of Government from Earliest Times*, vol 1. (Oxford: Oxford University Press, 1997), p. 5.

[47] John Gledhill, "Legacies of Empire: Political Centralization and Class Formation in the Hispanic-American World," in *State and Society: The Emergence and Development of Social Hierarchy and Political Centralization*, ed. John Gledhill, Barbara Bender, and Mogens Trolle Larsen (London: Unwin Hyman, 1988), p. 317.

[48] David Z. Scheffel, " 'There is Always Somewhere to Go . . .' Russian Old Believers and the State," in *Outwitting the State*, ed. Peter Saklník (New Brunswick, NJ: Transaction Publishers, 1989), p. 115.

[49] Emphasis in the original. Donald G. McCloud, *Southeast Asia: Tradition and Modernity in the Contemporary World* (Boulder, CO: Westview Press, 1995), p. 71.

[50] See, for instance, Frederick Jackson Turner, *The Frontier in American History* (New York: Henry Holt, 1920), and Howard Lamar and Leonard Thompson, ed., *The Frontier in History: North America and Southern Africa Compared* (New Haven: Yale University Press, 1981). Of course, both these books examine how colonialists or whites have dealt with the frontier, rather than the perspectives of the indigenous populations.

about the nature of state development, has had an almost exclusive focus on Europe despite the presence of state systems elsewhere in the world that have had radically different operating assumptions. The focus on Europe has been continually bemoaned in the international relations literature although little has been done to correct the problem that almost the entire study of international relations is really an extended series of case studies of Europe. As Gilpin notes, "There is a need for a comparative study of international systems that concentrates on systemic change in different types of international systems."[51]

However, to understand the extension of power in Africa, the traditional tools of political science that stress leadership decisions, institutional structures, and systemic considerations can continue to be used. In the analysis that follows, I suggest that state consolidation in Africa can be understood by examining three basic dynamics: the assessment of the costs of expansion by individual leaders; the nature of buffer mechanisms established by the state; and the nature of the regional state system. Only by understanding all three levels is a complete analysis of the consolidation of power in Africa possible. I disregard the boundaries between comparative politics and international relations because a more holistic analysis is necessary to understand the consolidation of power in Africa, or other areas for that matter.

Costs

All leaders face costs when trying to expand their writ of authority. Given the lack of a security imperative, which forced European state-builders to place assets at the frontier at a loss, African statemakers were able, within certain constraints and given historical circumstances, to make much more nuanced calculations about the costs and benefits of broadcasting power. Of course, the extension of authority always costs something given the need to deploy soldiers and administrators. The exact nature of the costs leaders face depends, in part, on how far power is being broadcast: if a state is making an incremental step beyond its central base that can be achieved using existing capabilities, costs will be lower than if authority is being projected to an area far beyond the base, as this requires mobilization of an entirely new set of resources. Of course, consolidation of rule is also a function of how the state system defines territorial control. Consolidation may only be the investment in enough security assets to secure an area physically, while other states may have to make extensive investments in such areas as roads, telecommunications, and

---

[51] Robert Gilpin, *War and Change in World Politics* (Cambridge: Cambridge University Press, 1981), p. 43.

local government in order to integrate a peripheral area into the overall economy. Thus, African leaders seeking to extend their power face a variety of costs: some inescapable in the short-term associated with conquest; some that are contingent on the scale of the changes being brought about; and some that can be postponed to the long-term that are largely associated with the consolidation of authority.[52]

The implications of understanding, from the perspective of the statemaker, the extension of authority as a series of different types of costs that have to be met are significant. For instance, the cost calculations of African leaders were radically different than those made by Europeans: in Africa, conquest and consolidation must be understood as different processes, with different cost structures, because wars were primarily not over territory and the end of wars did not leave the organizational and infrastructure residual that was typical in Europe. As a result, as chapter five discusses at length, the desired characteristics of a state in Africa are different from those traditionally valued in Europe.

Boundaries

The second major dynamic the book examines is the politics of boundaries. Understanding boundary politics—broadly defined as attempts by states to mediate pressures from the international system through the use of buffer mechanisms to maximize their authority over territory—is obviously an important component of analyzing the extension of authority. States can and do lower the costs of controlling a territory by developing a set of boundary institutions that insulate them from possible economic and political threats while enhancing the capabilities of the center. As William J. Foltz has noted, "Who studies systems studies boundaries" because effective boundaries "increase the collective power of those within them by providing the potential for organization and preventing the diffusion of effort and energy."[53]

The particular institutions that mediate the pressures from the international system become of special concern to weak rulers who do not have clear control over their territory; therefore, examining them may be especially informative in understanding the politics of African state development. In many ways the most consequential buffer mechanism is the

---

[52] Here I am borrowing from W. Arthur Lewis's excellent discussion of fixed costs in his *Overhead Costs: Some Essays in Economic Analysis* (New York: Augusts M. Kelley, 1970), p. 9.

[53] William J. Foltz, "Modernization and Nation-Building: The Social Mobilization Model Reconsidered," in *From National Development to Global Community*, ed. Richard L. Merritt and Bruce M. Russett (London: George Allen and Unwin, 1981), p. 39.

territorial boundary that mediates political pressures, including threats of intervention, from rivals. The traditional view of African boundaries is that they are a critical weakness of African states because they have remained unchanged despite the fact that the original colonial demarcations were done in a hurried manner that often did not account for local political, sociological, economic, or ethnic factors. As Jackson and Rosberg argue, "The boundaries of many countries, particularly but by no means exclusively in French-speaking Africa, were arbitrarily drawn by the colonial powers and were not encouraging frameworks of unified, legitimate, and capable states."[54] Similarly, Davidson regrets that those who recognized that "the colonial partition had inserted the continent into a framework of purely artificial and often positively harmful frontiers" did not come to the fore at independence.[55] Or as Bentsi-Enchill argues, "the nineteenth century partition of Africa by the European colonial powers was not made with any attention to the boundaries of these traditional polities . . . the newly independent African states, are, in general, territorially composite and have inherent problems of domestic boundary demarcation and maintenance between the traditional polities and jurisdictions of which they are composed."[56]

In fact, the system of territorial boundaries, as this book demonstrates in detail, has been critical to the particular patterns of African state consolidation and has been seen as a tremendous asset by African leaders, both in the colonial and independence periods. Far from being a hindrance to state consolidation, African boundaries have been perhaps the critical foundation upon which leaders have built their states. In addition, the territorial boundaries help shape other buffer institutions that also insulate polities from international pressures. These other buffer institutions vary considerably but include currency exchange mechanisms (which define the means of conversion between domestic and international units of money) and citizenship rules (which determine the difference between citizens and foreigners). Chapters seven and eight demonstrate that these boundary systems have also had significant effects on African state consolidation.

Understanding the precise manner in which pressures from the international system are mediated by state structures offers a way to move

---

[54] Robert H. Jackson and Carl G. Rosberg, "The Marginality of African States," in *African Independence: The First Twenty-Five Years*, ed. Gwendolen M. Carter and Patrick O'Meara (Bloomington: Indiana University Press, 1985), p. 46.

[55] Basil Davidson, *The Black Man's Burden: Africa and the Curse of the Nation-State* (New York: Times Books, 1992), p. 163.

[56] Kwamena Bentsi-Enchill, "The Traditional Legal Systems of Africa," in Property and Trust, vol. 6, *International Encyclopedia of Comparative Law*, (Tübingen: J. C. B. Mohr, 1976), pp. 2–138.

beyond grand theorizing to developing concrete propositions that analyze the relationship between the international and domestic systems. There is today something of a scholarly consensus that the international system is important to understanding politics in African countries, but that even third world states have a degree of autonomy, which necessitates examining purely political factors and avoiding the economic determinism that characterizes dependency theory. Accordingly, the next logical step is to better specify how international pressures are mediated by state institutions to affect domestic politics. Such a specification will be especially useful at the end of the millenium because international forces—be they international financial institutions such as the International Monetary Fund (IMF) or the even more impersonal forces of international capital markets—are perceived as having an increasingly profound effect on the domestic decisions of leaders in Africa and elsewhere in the developing world.[57] The analysis that follows demonstrates that much of this conventional wisdom is incorrect.

State Systems

Finally, the study will concentrate on the state system that successive African leaders constructed in order to further their own efforts at state consolidation. One of the reasons that Tilly's analysis is so successful for Europe is that he develops a convincing picture of the international context of state development by focusing on the continual threat of war that all nations faced. There is a similar need to understand the international context African states face, although it is radically different from Europe. It is particularly important to recognize that the international system was not simply a given for even the weak leaders who successively ruled African states. Repeatedly, this study will report that rulers in Africa created a particular type of state system in order to help them confront the peculiar difficulties they were having in exercising their authority across the territories they were said to control. Cooperation, rather than continual conflict, has characterized Africa during the last century of state-making, a vision that directly challenges traditional realist assumptions about the anarchical nature of international society and the importance of the threat of force.

An appreciation of the importance of being able to manipulate the state system immediately allows for an understanding of why simple cost models of state expansion are wrong. For example, Richard D. Auster

---

[57] Barbara Stallings, "International Influence on Economic Policy: Debt, Stabilization, and Structural Reform," in *The Politics of Economic Adjustment* ed. Stephan Haggard and Robert R. Kaufman (Princeton: Princeton University Press, 1992), p. 43.

and Morris Silver develop a model of state development where the state expands until average costs are rising, an adaption of venerable cost models in economics.[58] However, this model ignores the fact that by changing the nature of the international system, states can profoundly alter the costs of gaining and consolidating control over land. Since international society determines what state control actually means, to not investigate the nature of the state system is to fail to grasp the fundamental dynamics of state consolidation. Of course, pure economic models of state expansion cannot incorporate such overarching design considerations because they are based on the assumption that states are system-takers, just as firms are assumed to be price-takers, and therefore unable to affect the economic system within which they operate.[59]

That African states, perhaps best known in the literature as colonial creations and among the weakest in the world, were still strong enough to affect the state systems they operated within is critical to note because scholars have too often taken the international system as simply the background to the drama of domestic state development. One of the unfortunate implications of the division between comparative politics and international relations is that while scholars in the latter discipline have been quick to point out the effect of international forces on domestic politics, the impact of state development on international relations has sometimes not been fully appreciated. In examining how leaders affect the design of the state system, this book thus examines what Robert Gilpin has called the most fundamental type of change in the international system: "change in the nature of the actors or diverse entities that compose an international system."[60]

Costs, Boundaries, and State Systems

Maximum analytic leverage is gained when the interplay between the cost of state expansion, boundary mechanisms, and the state system can be understood. For instance, the cost of territorial expansion can be manipulated by states by changing the international understanding of what it means to control territory. Similarly, particular types of buffer mechanisms increase or reduce the cost of territorial expansion. Likewise, the nature of the international system affects what kind of buffer mechanisms

---

[58] Richard D. Auster and Morris Silver, *The State as a Firm: Economic Forces in Political Development* (Boston: Martinus Nijhoff, 1979), p. 30. See also Gilpin, *War and Change in World Politics*, p. 106.

[59] See, for instance, Robert O. Keohane, *After Hegemony: Cooperation and Discord in the World Political Economy* (Princeton: Princeton University Press, 1984), p. 27.

[60] Gilpin, *War and Change in World Politics*, p. 39.

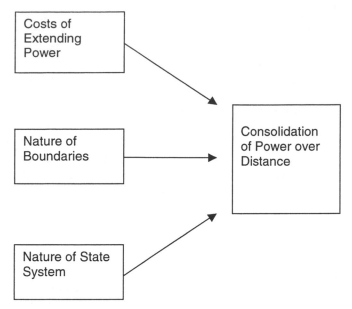

Figure 1.1. Possible Paths to State Consolidation

states can establish. Chapters two, three, and four explain the overall development of African states in the precolonial, colonial, and postindependence periods using this model. Chapters five and six then examine internal design questions to illustrate in greater detail the ramifications of the cost calculations that leaders have made. Chapters seven and eight explain the impact of different types of boundaries on state consolidation. Finally, chapter nine explains the overarching trajectory of African states and develops alternatives to the status quo that might allow states to broadcast power in a more effective manner.

Continuities in African Politics

By examining the different answers that leaders over centuries have given to the dilemmas of state consolidation, I am also offering an approach to confront the fundamental problem of studying African politics. The major difficulty scholars have is that almost all would agree with Patrick Chabal that the colonial interlude was relatively brief and that it is necessary to study lines of continuity between precolonial politics and the modern era.[61] At the same time, attempting to place colonialism within the context of the continuities of African history has been stressed by

[61] Patrick Chabal, *Political Domination in Africa: Reflections on the Limits of Power* (Cambridge: Cambridge University Press, 1986), p. 3.

historians who note colonial rule's artificiality, Africans' role in modifying it through protest, and the long history of intergroup conflict in Africa that predates the Europeans.[62] However, most scholars would also agree with Crawford Young that the imposition of colonial rule changed everything:

> The colonial state in Africa lasted in most instances less than a century—a mere moment in historical time. Yet it totally reordered political space, social hierarchies and cleavages, and modes of economic production. Its territorial grid— whose final contours congealed only in the dynamics of decolonization—determined the state units that gained sovereignty and came to form the present system of African polities.[63]

Similarly, Naomi Chazan and her colleagues justify beginning their study of modern African politics with the creation of the colonial state by stating simply: "The basis of the postcolonial state in Africa is the colonial state."[64] Or, as the manifesto of the Belgian-Congolese elite claimed in 1956, "In the history of the Congo, the last eighty years have been more important than the millenniums which have preceded them."[65]

Faced with the intuition that African politics must have deep continuities but aware of the profound disjuncture in form and practice caused by colonialism, scholars have generally been unsuccessful in developing a view of African politics that takes the precolonial period seriously while still acknowledging the traumas created by white rule. Thus, most textbooks on African politics begin their substantive discussions with the colonial state while only making the briefest of acknowledgments regarding the possibility of continuities with the precolonial era.[66]

However, the continued failure to fully understand the course of African politics is unacceptable. As is argued in the following chapters, there are broad continuities in African politics that become apparent when the approach of successive leaders to the same political geography is exam-

[62] See, for instance, J. F. A. Ajayi, "Colonialism: An Episode in African History," in *Colonialism in Africa, 1870–1960*, ed. L. H. Gann and Peter Duignan vol. 1 (Cambridge: Cambridge University Press, 1969), p. 508.

[63] Crawford Young, *The African Colonial State in Comparative Perspective* (New Haven: Yale University Press, 1994), pp. 9–10.

[64] Naomi Chazan et al., *Politics and Society in Contemporary Africa* (Boulder, CO: Lynne Rienner, 1988), p. 40.

[65] "Manifesto of the Belgian-Congolese Elite, 1956," reprinted in *The Political Awakening of Africa*, ed. Rupert Emerson and Martin Kilson (Englewood Cliffs, NJ: Prentice-Hall, 1965), p. 99.

[66] See, for instance, Chazan et al. *Politics and Society in Contemporary Africa*; William Tordoff, *Government and Politics in Africa*, 2nd ed. (London: Macmillian Press, 1993); Richard Hodder-Williams, *An Introduction to the Politics of Tropical Africa* (London: George Allen and Unwin, 1984).

ined. Given that, as chapter three discusses, the colonial and postcolonial states are such recent creations, it is also hard to believe that the political traditions developed over the centuries have not had an effect on politics since 1960. It would seem, for instance, relatively easy to make the case that precolonial traditions, still vibrant in the early part of the twentieth century in most parts of the continent, have a resonance in modern Africa compared to the rather heroic efforts Robert Putnam undertakes in order to suggest that developments in the Italian peninsula beginning around 1100 A.D. structure modern Italian politics.[67] Thus, one of the operating assumptions of this study is that Pliny the Elder was wrong: there is often nothing new out of Africa.

As some African states break down and the facade of sovereignty that was erected in the early 1960s begins to crumble, it also becomes more important to understand the past in order to foresee a better future for Africa.[68] This is not to engage in misty-eyed nostalgia, believing that somehow political formations developed hundreds of years ago can be replicated today. Basil Davidson is correct in arguing that "the precolonial past is not recoverable."[69] Nor should it be. However, it does seem reasonable to understand what the colonialists did and did not change several decades ago if a more indigenous alternative to the nation-state as theorized, designed, and imposed by the Europeans is to be developed. Certainly, such investigations are already beginning. For instance, Ali Mazrui looks to the African past in proposing models of dual sovereignty that would include both civilians and representatives of the security forces in a new type of parliament.[70]

Conclusion

For a truly comparative study of politics to develop, the great but incomplete drama of African state creation must be understood. This drama is as important to analyze as the processes that led to the creation of France, Germany, and their neighbors. By examining both the environ-

---

[67] Robert D. Putnam, *Making Democracy Work: Civic Traditions in Modern Italy* (Princeton: Princeton University Press, 1993), p. 121. For another argument that state structures are highly path dependent, that is, they reflect events that occurred hundreds of years ago, see Thomas Ertman, *Birth of the Leviathan: Building States and Regimes in Medieval and Early Modern Europe* (Cambridge: Cambridge University Press, 1997), pp. 317–8.

[68] Christopher Clapham, *Africa in the International System: The Politics of State Survival* (Cambridge: Cambridge University Press, 1996), p. 30.

[69] Davidson, *Black Man's Burden*, p. 315.

[70] Ali A. Mazrui, "The African State as a Political Refugee," in *African Conflict Resolution: The U.S. Role in Peacemaking*, ed. David R. Smock and Chester A. Crocker (Washington, DC: United States Institute of Peace Press, 1995), p. 18.

ment that leaders had to confront and the institutions they created in light of their own political calculations, the entire trajectory of state creation in Africa can be recovered. I will demonstrate that, fundamentally, there is nothing exotic about African politics. Rather, as elsewhere, political outcomes are the result of human agency interacting with powerful geographic and historical forces. And, as is the case in other parts of the world, the viability of African states depends on leaders successfully meeting the challenges posed by their particular environment.

Part Two

THE CONSTRUCTION OF STATES
IN AFRICA

Two

Power and Space in Precolonial Africa

The limit of one's strength, that was the
boundary.
  A Yardaji villager quoted in
  William F. S. Miles, *Hausaland Divided:*
  Colonialism and Independence
  in Nigeria and Niger

PRECOLONIAL RULERS in Africa struggled over the centuries to extend
their power. While few were as direct as Emperor Haile Salaisse, who
named his son Asfa-Wasen (Amharic for "expand the frontiers"),[1] the
desire to expand control over people (in particular) was as much a constant in precolonial Africa as it was elsewhere in the world. It is thus
hardly surprising that "among the Yoruba kingdoms, and most West African states, campaigns were so frequent as to be a normal, though sea-
sonal activity."[2] However, precolonial Africa was a world where the extension and consolidation of power meant something very different from
the broadcasting of authority in Europe or in postcolonial regions of the
developing world.

This chapter explores the theory and practice of broadcasting power in
precolonial Africa. It focuses on the nonterritorial nature of power and
how African rulers in the time before the Europeans conceived of their
boundaries. While the political organizations in precolonial Africa do not
resemble today's states, I argue that the different ways of broadcasting of
power in precolonial Africa are eminently understandable. Thus, while
the state system was radically different from the modern set of international norms and practices, there was a system of relations across polities
that could be understood. The final section returns to the model developed in chapter one so that precolonial practices can be placed in comparative perspective.

---

[1] Christopher Clapham, "Boundary and Territory in the Horn of Africa," in *African Boundaries: Barriers, Conduits and Opportunities*, ed. Paul Nugent and A. I. Asiwaju (London: Pinter, 1996), p. 239.

[2] Robert Smith, *Kingdoms of the Yoruba*, 3rd ed. (London: James Currey, 1988), p. 99.

Conceptions of Power

Precolonial political practices do not figure in almost any analysis of African politics because the operations of states before the Europeans are seen as too exotic to be relevant. The critical problem for most current scholars is that power in precolonial polities was not, in the first instance, based on control of land. Unfortunately, the very basis of the modern understandings of states and state systems are tied to the control of territory. As Samuel E. Finer noted, "Tell a man today to go and build a state; and he will try to establish a definite and defensible territorial boundary and compel those who live inside it to obey him."[3] The focus on control of land as the basis of state authority is not surprising in Europe where, due to population densities, land was in short supply. Indeed, an assumption that land was scarce, and therefore control of territory was an important indication of power, underlies much of Weber's own analysis.[4] Similarly, control of territory is the basis of international understandings of state authority since states in Europe fought about land. Thus, Gilpin argues, "The control and division of territory constitute the basic mechanism governing the distribution of scarce resources among the states in an international system."[5]

Forced to anchor their analyses in the control of territory, many scholars make the mistake of suggesting that precolonial Africa had neither states nor state systems. For instance, Robert H. Jackson argues, "Africa was a continental archipelago of loosely defined political systems: a world of societies rather than states and far more recognizable to anthropology than to international relations."[6] However, students of anthropology and history have not attempted to aggregate knowledge of institutions on a comparative basis. Instead, their focus has been on specific issues within particular societies. As a result, a comparative project cannot be discerned. Goody's 1971 remark that, "progress in the comparative study of centralized institutions in Africa has not been great"[7] still applies decades later.

[3] Samuel E. Finer, "State-Building, State Boundaries, and Border Control," *Social Science Information* 13 (August–October, 1974): p. 79.

[4] See, for instance, Max Weber, "Structures of Power," in *From Max Weber: Essays in Sociology*, ed. H. H. Gerth and C. Wright Mills (England: Routledge, 1991), p. 165.

[5] Gilpin, *War and Change in World Politics*, p. 37.

[6] Robert H. Jackson, *Quasi-states: Sovereignty, International Relations, and the Third World* (Cambridge: Cambridge University Press, 1990), p. 67. For a similar view see E. J. Hobsbawm, *The Age of Empire, 1875–1914* (London: Weidenfield and Nicolson, 1987), p. 23.

[7] Jack Goody, *Technology, Tradition, and the State in Africa* (Cambridge: Cambridge University Press, 1971), pp. 16–7.

Assuming that states and systems of states did not exist in Africa simply because the European model was not followed demonstrates, at the minimum, a lack of imagination and, more importantly, a rather narrow conception of how power can be organized. To equate states with firm territorial control is to misread even much of Europe's own history. Precolonial Africa was, in many ways, similar to medieval Europe, where shared sovereignty between the church and various political units was not uncommon.[8] Hard territorial boundaries were also a rather late development in Europe.[9] Similarly, citizenship laws—regulations that tie individuals to a unique geographic entity—were generally not codified in Europe until the nineteenth century.[10] Finer, in his world history of government, is able to analyze medieval states as states, despite their very different conceptions of territorial control, and to compare them to other types of states.[11] There should therefore be no objection to studying precolonial African states as states and including them in a comparative analysis.

In fact, states and state systems can be discerned in precolonial Africa if preconceptions based on Europe's recent history are discarded. African states did broadcast authority, did have firm notions of what consolidation of power meant, and did develop conventions for relations between states. Thus, Robert S. Smith, in the most detailed historical account of warfare and diplomacy in precolonial Africa, noted that, for large parts of West Africa, "international relations in peace and war were carried out in a more or less recognizable fashion, and, to go a little further, in a coherent and rational manner which showed itself capable under favourable conditions of leading to political, economic, and technical improvements in society."[12]

Mapping Power in Precolonial Africa

In precolonial Africa, land was plentiful and populations thin on the ground, especially as compared to Europe, China, and Japan. Precolonial

[8] F. H. Hinsley, *Sovereignty*, 2nd ed. (Cambridge: Cambridge University Press, 1986), p. 60.

[9] John Gerard Ruggie, "Continuity and Transformation in the World Polity: Towards a Neorealist Synthesis," *World Politics* 35 (January 1983): p. 274.

[10] A. Heldrich et al., ed., "Persons," chap. 2 in *Persons and Family*, vol. 4, *International Encyclopedia of Comparative Law* (Tübingen: J. C. B. Mohhr, 1995), pp. 291–2.

[11] S. E. Finer, *The History of Government from Earliest Times*, vol. 3. (Oxford: Oxford University Press, 1997), p. 1266.

[12] Robert S. Smith, *Warfare and Diplomacy in Pre-Colonial West Africa*, 2nd ed. (Madison: University of Wisconsin Press, 1976), pp. 141–2. For an important case study, see Joseph K. Adjaye, *Diplomacy and Diplomats in Nineteenth Century Asante*, 2nd ed. (Trenton, NJ: Africa World Press, 1996).

polities were "surrounded by large tracts of land that were open politically or physically or both."[13] As a result, there were few areas where territorial competition was the central political issue because land was plentiful. Reflecting the reality of population scarcity in Africa, property rights over *people* were extraordinarily well developed in Africa compared to other parts of the world.[14]

In addition to the sheer abundance of land, African farmers also depended almost completely on rain-fed agriculture and therefore invested little in any particular piece of territory. As a result, few specific pieces of land were that valuable or worth a great price to defend. African agriculture was extensive, with low fixed investments in any particular piece of land, because the fundamental tool of intensive farming, the plough, spread throughout Eurasia without ever reaching Africa (except, it should not be a surprise to learn, Ethiopia). Goody describes the results of the failure to develop the plough:

> In the first place it [the plough] increases the area of land a man can cultivate and hence makes possible a substantial rise in productivity, at least in open country. This in turn means a greater surplus for the maintenance of specialist crafts, for the growth of differences in wealth and in styles of life, for developments in urban, that is, non-agricultural, life. In the second place, it stimulates the move to fixed holdings and away from shifting agriculture. Thirdly (and not independently) it increases the value (and decreases the availability) of land.[15]

A full explanation of why the plough was not adopted by African societies is beyond this study. However, given the sheer availability of land, there may have been very little pressure to adopt instruments to improve the productivity of a given piece of land.[16] At the same time, the failure of any significant society to adopt the plough meant that there was no demonstration effect that could have been the impetus for the general adoption of the technology.

African societies differed markedly from the high density Asian polities Wittfogel called "hydraulic societies" where, because of the (literal) sunk costs in irrigation works, particular pieces of land had great value.[17] A

---

[13] Igor Kopytoff, "The Internal African Frontier: The Making of African Political Culture," in *The African Frontier: The Reproduction of Traditional African Societies*, ed. Igor Kopytoff (Bloomington: Indiana University Press, 1987), p. 10.

[14] Igor Kopytoff and Suzanne Miers, "African 'Slavery' as an Institution of Marginality," in *Slavery in Africa*, ed. Suzanne Miers and Igor Kopytoff (Madison: University of Wisconsin Press, 1977), p. 11.

[15] Goody, *Technology, Tradition, and the State in Africa*, p. 25.

[16] Coquery-Vidrovitch, *Africa: Endurance and Change South of the Sahara*, p. 14. The classic statement is Esther Boserup, *The Conditions of Agricultural Growth: The Economics of Agrarian Change under Population Pressure* (New York: Aldine, 1965).

[17] Karl A. Wittfogel, *Oriental Despotism: A Comparative Study of Total Power* (New Haven: Yale University Press, 1957), p. 34

quick look at the extraordinary paddy works in Asia, the accumulated work of generations that devoted their sweat equity to intensive agriculture, makes it clear just how valuable land was in those regions. Correspondingly, in Asia, and in large parts of Europe, states had a profound interest in controlling areas of intensive agriculture because of the possibilities of high revenue flows from taxes with relatively low collection costs. At the extreme, in China, the state was large and endured through the centuries facing only competition at the borders, in part because Chinese leaders constructed a class alliance with landed warrior nobility.[18] In contrast, in Africa, states found the same amount of territory less valuable because low productivity agriculture meant that there was less in the way of people or surplus to tax and collection costs were probably higher.

The Primacy of Exit

The combination of large amounts of open land and rain-fed agriculture meant that, in precolonial Africa, control of territory was often not contested because it was often easier to escape from rulers than to fight them. Africans, on the basis of sensible cost-benefit equations, would, more often than not, rather switch than fight. They could move and farm on other pieces of land relatively easily because it was not necessary to sink significant investment into the land. For instance, Robert W. Harms, in his history of the central Zaire basin, provides an important account of a society constantly expanding outward because traders responded to competition or quarreling by establishing new villages on virgin land.[19] Migration to escape from social or political problems was also common among the Yoruba, the Edo, the Fon, and many others. A. I. Asiwaju notes, for example, that the reign of Oba Ewuare of Benin, in the mid-fifteenth century, was so unpopular that it generated, "waves of protest migrations which ostensibly led to the foundation of many communities of closely related groups."[20] Similarly, Thomas J. Barfield notes, "the powers of the Dinka chief were weak . . . because rather than submit to his authority, dissident groups could move to a new territory if they were dissatisfied."[21] He goes on to note that the Zulu Empire, one of the largest agglomerations of power in precolonial African history, occurred because the land frontier closed in what is now South Africa during the

[18] Vivienne Shue, *The Reach of the State: Sketches of the Chinese Body Politic* (Stanford, CA: Stanford University Press, 1988), p. 94. See also Wong, *China Transformed*, p. 88.

[19] Robert W. Harms, *River of Wealth, River of Sorrow: The Central Zaire Basin in the Era of the Slave and Ivory Trade, 1500–1891* (New Haven: Yale University Press, 1981), p. 111.

[20] A. I. Asiwaju, "Migrations as Revolt: The Example of the Ivory Coast and the Upper Volta Before 1945," *Journal of African History* 17 (1976): p. 578.

[21] Thomas J. Barfield, *The Nomadic Alternative* (Englewood Cliffs, NJ: Prentice Hall, 1993), p. 38.

nineteenth century after the Boer settlers expanded the territory under their control.[22]

States without Maps

The demographic and political realities in precolonial Africa had a profound effect on the contours of the states. In particular, as control of particular pieces of land was not critical to African societies, "there was no indigenous map-making in Africa or . . . its presence is so insignificant as to justify that generalisation."[23] The only society that had a significant map-making tradition was Ethiopia, which is also one of the very few African societies that had a tradition of writing.[24] It was logical therefore that understandings of what it meant to control a particular territory in precolonial Africa differed markedly from the modern era. In particular, precolonial African societies unbundled ownership and control of land. For instance, Ivor Wilks, in writing about the Ashanti theory of sovereignty, noted that "rights of sovereignty were regarded as distinguishable from the exercise of authority." Thus, it was not an uncommon practice in Ashanti law for the land to belong to one person (e.g., the southern provinces to the Asantahene) but the people to another (in the case of the south, to the Fanti or the British Governor).[25] Similarly, Harms writes of the Nunu in what is now Democratic Republic of the Congo: "The political theory of the Nunu, like that of peoples in many parts of Africa, had long distinguished between guardians of the land and guardians of the people. According to this theory, strangers who settled in an unoccupied part of a guardian's territory could continue to be governed by their own headmen provided they recognized the ritual control of the original guardian over the land."[26] Land disputes between the Zulus and the early Dutch settlers were also aggravated because the Zulus believed that they could let the whites settle on land without giving up ownership while the settlers did not distinguish between occupation and ownership. Conflict between the two groups was further exacerbated by the Zulu tradition of claiming that their authority extended everywhere people had

[22] Ibid., p. 47.

[23] Charles G. Hunt, "Some Notes on Indigenous Map-Making in Africa," in *Maps and Africa*, ed. Jeffrey C. Stone (Aberdeen, U.K.: Aberdeen University, 1994), p. 32. See also Jeffrey C. Stone, *A Short History of the Cartography of Africa* (New York: Edwin Mellon Press, 1995), p. 5.

[24] Hunt, "Some Notes on Indigenous Map-Making in Africa," p. 34.

[25] Ivor Wilks, *Asante in the Nineteenth Century: The Structure and Evolution of a Political Order* (Cambridge: Cambridge University Press, 1975), pp. 191–2.

[26] Robert Harms, *Games Against Nature: An Eco-Cultural History of the Nunu of Equatorial Africa* (New Haven: Yale University Press, 1987), p. 220.

pledged obedience to the king, rather than to the kind of clear territorial claims to which the whites were accustomed.[27]

It is striking how common the distinction between possession and control of land was given the great distances between the polities just cited. As was the case in Europe, the nature of material conditions on the ground helped structure a set of political beliefs about the nature of sovereignty.[28] It is only natural that societies, such as those in Europe and Asia, with relatively high population densities and with land that requires significant investment to yield the necessary level of productivity, will tolerate little ambiguity in demarcating control over territory.[29] Similarly, the African acceptance of far more nuanced understanding of control of territory was made possible by the fact that land often was not a scarce resource and that there were few imperatives to developing a zero-sum understanding of demarcating authority. Thus, the development of particular notions of sovereignty is highly dependent on a particular political geography and is not simply the culmination of a particular line of legal thinking.

Patterns of Territorial Control

In many precolonial societies, a significant difference existed between what control of the political center meant and what the partial exercise of power amounted to in the hinterland. Formal political control in precolonial Africa was difficult and had to be earned through the construction of loyalties, the use of coercion, and the creation of an infrastructure. Otherwise, it was too easy for people to leave. Political control could never be taken for granted given that the environment made it so difficult to continually exert authority over any significant distance. Further, the unbundling of ownership and control of land made it hard to gain complete control of a territory. As a result, the areas leaders were certain to control formally—the political cores—were of limited size and were determined by the development of an infrastructure to broadcast power. For instance, the Ashanti empire was able to extend control over relatively large distances and have some of the attributes of a modern nation-state because of an extensive series of roads that converged on the capital, Kumasi. These roads were vital to the exercise of formal authority because they allowed for the quick movement of troops and bound the

[27] C. de B. Webb and J. B. Wright, ed., *A Zulu King Speaks: Statements Made by Cetshwayo KaMpande* (Pietermaritzburg, South Africa: University of Natal Press, 1987), pp. 1, 27.

[28] Spruyt, *The Sovereign State and its Competitors*, p. 69.

[29] See Moore, *Origins of Dictatorship and Democracy*, p. 169.

territory into a relatively coherent economy. Of places beyond the great roads, it was said, "no Asante is familiar with these places because the King's highways do not run there."[30]

Perhaps the most concrete expression of precolonial African views of the requirements to exercise formal control over an area are found in the so-called Mankesssim Constitution adopted by the Fanti Confederation in 1871 in what is now Ghana. The Confederation coalesced after a war with the Ashanti that saw the British largely abandon the Fanti.[31] The collected chiefs noted that the primary goals of the newly formed confederation were to promote friendly relations, to improve the country, and to build "good and substantial roads (article 8, section 3)." In an exercise of (quite literal) constitutional engineering, the Fanti detailed how wide ("fifteen feet broad") the roads should be (article 26). The Fanti understood that without these roads, they would have no way to broadcast their authority and were therefore so concerned with the development of the political infrastructure that they prominently featured it in their constitution. Having gone through elaborate lengths to highlight the need to create roads in order to give meaning to their confederation, the Fanti still noted that it was up to each king and chief to carry out the resolutions approved by the king president (article 13).[32] Even then, the Fanti noted that their rule would be exercised over those who would join it rather than through extension of control via administrative fiat.[33] Thus, both the very real physical requirements for extending formal authority and the utter precariousness of broadcasting power were readily acknowledged by precolonial leaders who understood the daunting geography they confronted.

Without such infrastructure, African states lacked the capability to formally control large amounts of land beyond the center of the polity because they could not project power in other ways. For instance, Wylie notes "The wealth and food supplies necessary for highly elaborate military organization and the population necessary for large armies simply did not exist in Temneland."[34] Warfare tended to be concentrated on seizing booty since it was hard to hold onto territory. As most farmers had nothing to seize, the most valuable treasure was slaves (i.e., the farmers them-

[30] See Wilks, *Asante in the Nineteenth Century*, pp. 1–2.

[31] The history is reviewed in J. E. Casely Hayford, *Gold Coast Native Institutions* (London: Frank Cass and Co., 1970), pp. 183–4.

[32] The Fanti Constitution is reprinted in John Mensah Sabah, *The Fanti National Constitution* (London: Frank Cass and Co., 1968), pp. 201–3.

[33] Fanti Confederation, "Scheme to be Submitted to His Excellency Governor J. Pope Hennessey," in ibid., p. 194.

[34] Kenneth C. Wylie, *Temne Government in Sierra Leone* (New York: Africana Publishing Company, 1977), p. 55.

selves).[35] Due to the slave trade, capturing people who later could be sold to the Europeans or Omanis or other Africans was, in fact, one of the most profitable activities that could be undertaken at particular times in many parts of the continent. Of course, the slave trade only contributed to the notion that true power was not synonymous with the control of land. Many African states continually tried to make forays into the interior to feed the continual demand for slaves but did not try to extend formal control into those areas because it was not profitable.

Central governments were often not concerned about what outlying areas did as long as tribute was paid (sometimes in the form of slaves), and there were no imminent security threats emerging to challenge the center.[36] This particular view of what control meant was made possible by the ability to separate ownership and control of land. Thus, a ruler might view a distant territory as owing some kind of tribute to him (leaders were all men) without any notion that he controlled the actions of the people in the outlying areas on a day-to-day basis. Kopytoff describes the general pattern of precolonial political authority:

> The core, usually the area of earliest political consolidation, continued to be ruled directly by the central authority. Then came an inner area of closely assimilated and politically integrated dependencies. Beyond it was the circle of relatively secure vassal polities. . . . This circle merged with the next circle of tribute-paying polities, straining at the center's political leash. Beyond, the center's control became increasingly symbolic . . . The center could only practice political intimidation and extract sporadic tribute through institutionalized raiding or undisguised pillage.[37]

Thus, even a famous kingdom such as fourteenth-century Mali maintained what was only described as "loose political ties with the far-flung districts of an empire."[38] Or, consider the following description of Borgu's political power in western Sudan:

[35] Goody, *Technology, Tradition, and the State*, p. 36.

[36] Jan Vansina, *Kingdoms of the Savanna* (Madison: University of Wisconsin Press, 1966), p. 82. Similar views regarding the reach of certain African states have been noted by, among others, D. N. Beach, *The Shona and Zimbabwe, 900–1850* (Gweru, Zimbabwe: Mambo Press, 1984), p. 36; Toyin Falola and Dare Oguntomisin, *The Military in Nineteenth Century Yoruba Politics* (Ile-Ife, Nigeria: University of Ife Press, 1984), p. 25; S. P. Reyna, *Wars without End: The Political Economy of a Precolonial African State* (Hanover, N.H.: University Press of New England, 1990), pp. 156–7; and Sundiata A. Djata, *The Bamana Empire by the Niger* (Princeton: Markus Wiener, 1997), p. 23.

[37] Kopytoff, "The Internal African Frontier," p. 29. See also Max Gluckman, *Politics, Law, and Ritual in Tribal Society* (Oxford: Basil Blackwell, 1965), pp. 163–4; J. Vansina, "A Comparison of African Kingdoms," *Africa* 32 (October 1962): p. 330; and Reyna *Wars without End*, p. 67.

[38] Charlotte A. Quinn, *Mandingo Kingdoms of the Senegambia: Traditionalism, Islam, and European Expansion* (Evanston, IL: Northwestern University Press, 1972), p. 35.

Bussa's supremacy was not based on its political strength or extensive do-mains. . . . Whether tribute was paid or not depended on the strength of the Bussa king: a strong ruler had little trouble in enforcing payment of tribute for two reasons: first, if tribute was not forthcoming retaliatory action would have occurred, and second, the benefits of security and protection which accrued from an alliance with a strong ruler constituted an added incentive for pay-ment.[39]

Similarly, Reyna describes precolonial east-central Sudan as a "vast point-illist landscape" with each point being "a polity within a field of empire."[40] Finally, when Ashanti took over Dagomba, it "continued to be governed by its own king and chiefs, under its traditional laws and constitution, on condition that its capital and large towns paid, each year, a handsome tribute to Kumasi."[41]

Correspondingly, it was natural that many precolonial African states were exceptionally dynamic. Political organizations were created, rose, and fell naturally in response to opportunities and challenges.[42] Many outlying territories found that they could escape their rulers' authority relatively easily. For instance, Jan Vansina writes of the central African kingdoms: "provinces could break off from the kingdom whenever cir-cumstances were favorable. This happened in Kongo, in the Kuba king-dom, and in the Lunda empire, where every ruler who was far enough away . . . became independent."[43] Colson claims that, "Breakaway move-ments were common even in West Africa and the few other favoured regions where men made material improvements upon the land. Else-where they formed part of the history of every state."[44]

Because the broadcasting of power was constrained, there was much more cultural diversity even within precolonial empires than in later Eu-ropean empires. African empires in the western and central Soudan, such as Mali and Kanem-Bornu, were similar to the loose-knit empires of the European Middle Ages such as the Holy Roman Empire and the large kingdom of the Angevins that existed on both sides of the English Chan-nel. In all these empires, "the territorial extent of the empire depended not upon the ethnic or cultural unity of the subjects but upon the mili-

[39] Majorie H. Stewart, *Borgu and its Kingdoms: A Reconstruction of a Western Sudanese Polity* (New York: Edwin Mellon Press, 1993), p. 208.

[40] Reyna, *Wars without End*, p. 165.

[41] William Tordoff, "The Ashanti Confederacy," *Journal of African History* 3 (1962): pp. 402–3.

[42] Among the many studies making this point, see S. I. G. Mudenge, *A Political History of Munhumutapa, c. 1400–1902* (Harare, Zimbabwe: Zimbabwe Publishing House, 1988), p. 76.

[43] Vansina, *Kingdoms of the Savanna*, p. 247.

[44] Colson, "African Society at the Time of the Scramble," p. 44.

tary predominance and the dynastic alliances of the small ruling group."[45] Indeed, African invaders tended to be absorbed into the ranks of the conquered, especially as they tended to marry the daughters of commoners.[46] Of course, that type of conquest contained the seeds of its own demise. As in medieval Europe, "appointed officials tended to become hereditary, and hereditary subordinate rulers to become less zealous in carrying out the wishes of the paramount ruler. Control became more nominal, and less real, the more remote the center was. Dispersal of taxing rights invites—indeed, constitutes—fragmentation of sovereignty."[47]

In most parts of Africa, ethnic and other attachments were constantly in flux as polities continually expanded and contracted. Thus, Colson notes the Ibo (in what is now Nigeria) who, starting in 1967, shed a tremendous amount of blood to create their own ethnic state:

> In 1870 the Ibo lived in small autonomous village communities that warred on one another. They recognized no common political leaders, though adherence to a few popular shrines provided a means of exerting widespread influence. . . . The Ibo communities may have felt some common identification as against communities of non-Ibo speakers, but this was probably minimal since they had no common names for themselves nor any tradition of a former unity.[48]

The Ibo, and many other groups, were organized in such a decentralized manner because, in their areas, it was simply too costly to create polities with a larger geographic reach and because no other polity could reach far enough to extend formal authority over them. Ibo identity would change over the next century as cost structures evolved to favor larger territorial units.

Imagining Power

Not surprisingly, African conceptions of how power was broadcast over distance reflected their states' capabilities and their particular material environments. While generalizations are inevitably faulty across such a broad range of polities, it can be said that power was (quite realistically) conceived of as a series of concentric circles radiating out from the core. Wilks, in his excellent study of Ashanti authority, reports two informants

---

[45] Roland Oliver and Anthony Atmore, *The African Middle Ages, 1400–1800* (Cambridge: Cambridge University Press, 1981), p. 3.

[46] Jack Goody, "Decolonisation in Africa: National Politics and Village Politics," *Cambridge Anthropology* 7 (1982): p. 8.

[47] Peter Wickins, *An Economic History of Africa: From the Earliest Times to Partition* (Cape Town: Oxford University Press, 1987), p. 229.

[48] Colson, "African Society at the Time of the Scramble," p. 28.

one hundred and fifty years apart describing Ashanti authority in the same manner: rippling out from a center point. In a rather stunning example of how little topography mattered to precolonial rulers, power was seen as radiating out in a perfect circle despite the fact that the ocean essentially cut off the southern boundary long before it "should" have ended.[49] Similarly, in two of the very rare maps drawn by African leaders in the precolonial or early colonial period, the dispersal of power is portrayed in much the same manner. In the map drawn by Caliph Muhammad Bello for Captain Clapperton in 1824 (Map 2.1) and the more detailed one drawn by Sultan Njoya of Bamum when offering his kingdom to British suzerainty in December 1915 (Map 2.2), power is displayed as radiating out from a center. As Yearwood notes:

> both [maps] were dominated by a centrally placed capital with its main buildings, while the outlying territories were greatly compressed. The Sokoto Caliphate appeared as a set of cities, shown as circles, dominated by the mosques and places of Sokoto; Bamum as a network of roads linking outlying towns to the capital. In Bello's map there was no political border, while in Njoya's it was an inconspicuous feature.[50]

The emphasis on the political center and the relative inattention paid to the hinterland nicely reflects the reality of power in precolonial Africa.

The Determinants of Power

The physiology of the precolonial African state was radically different from what was found in postmedieval Europe, where more attention was devoted to physically controlling (more valuable) territory and, in particular, significant assets were placed in the hinterland to deter and to defeat possible invaders. While African leaders would not want, under normal circumstances, to lose territory to other powers, it would often not be worth the price to actually try to defend outlying areas. The foregone revenue was probably not great since the area was at the periphery of the state. Given that sovereignty was not exclusive over many areas, it was quite possible that some revenue might still be received if the center could manage to mount attacks that might scare the outlying populace into paying tribute, no matter what the new masters did.

The diameters of the circles of authority were determined by how far

[49] Ivor Wilks, "On Mentally Mapping Greater Asante: A Study of Time and Motion," *Journal of African History* 33 (1992): pp. 182–3.

[50] Peter J. Yearwood, "From Lines on Maps to National Boundaries: The Case of Northern Nigeria and Cameroun," in *Maps and Africa*, ed. Jeffrey C. Stone (Aberdeen, U.K.: University of Aberdeen, 1994), pp. 36–7. The original citations are listed on the maps.

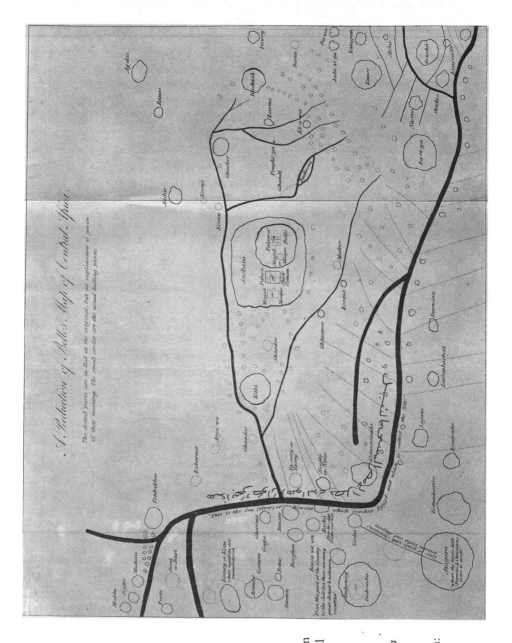

Map 2.1. A Reproduction of Bello's Map of Central Africa. *Source:* Dixon Denham, Hugh Clapperton, and Walter Oudney, *Narrative of Travels and Discoveries in Northern and Central Africa in the Years 1822, 1823, and 1824* (London: John Murray, 1828), insert after p. 370.

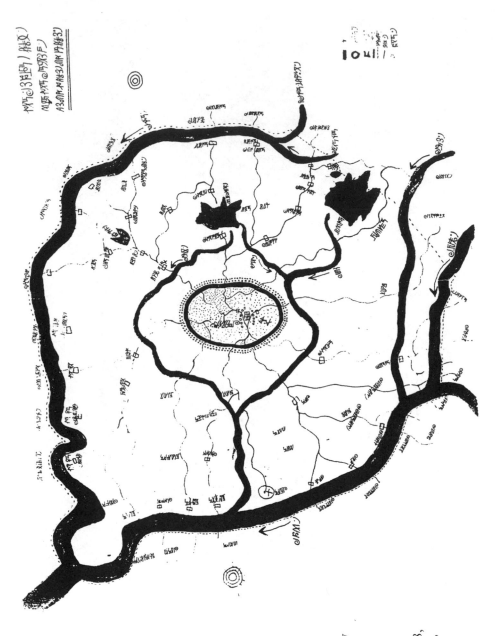

Map 2.2. Map Drawn by
Sultan Njoya of Bamum
when offering his
Kingdom to British
Suzerainty in 1915.
Source: C0649/7/10908,
Colonial Office Archives,
Public Record Office
(Kew).

the center actually could project the different types of authority. Wilks reports that the Ashanti conceived of their empire as radiating out in all directions for twenty days walking or roughly a month for a messenger to depart from the capital Kumasi and return from the frontier. Any farther was deemed too difficult to administer because the lag in response time was too great. While the armies of Ashanti occasionally campaigned beyond the border, the "reach of government . . . was recognized as less than that of the military . . . The mental map of Greater Asante as a month reflected, it may be supposed, a rational recognition of reality: that without any major change in the speed of communications, no lands more distant that a month from Kumase, in and out, could effectively be administered even though they might be subdued for the duration of a campaign."[51] Wilks's estimate of individuals covering about ten miles a day is similar to Hilton's estimate of twelve miles per day in the Kongo Kingdom in what is now Angola and Democratic Republic of the Congo.[52] The actual distance a messenger could walk in a reasonable period of time defined the boundary because the exercise of authority was bound tightly to the ability to project coercion. Olfert Dapper, a seventeenth-century Dutch geographer, provided a contemporary account of the inevitable result of not physically being able to reach an area in a reasonable period of time: "The Count of Soyo is the most powerful vassal of the King of Congo, but he is not the most faithful or the most subject. Because the forest of Findemguolla encompassing his states serves as a strong bulwark and renders him nearly inaccessible to a great army, this count no longer wants to recognize the King of Congo as his sovereign and believes that he should be given the status of an ally."[53]

Across Africa, states were naturally largest in the savannah belt of West Africa because, "only here could horses and camels be used to speed the movement of armies and to permit large-scale trade between the various regions."[54] At the other end of the spectrum, in some areas of Africa, it was so difficult to broadcast power that there were, esentially, no centralized political organizations above village level. Although African historiography has shown a profound bias against studying stateless societies, there were areas, such as Eastern Nigeria, where the broadcasting power did not extend beyond each individual village.[55]

African states were expanding in the nineteenth century immediately

[51] Wilks , "On Mentally Mapping Greater Asante," p. 184.

[52] Anne Hilton, *The Kingdom of the Kongo* (Oxford: Clarendon Press, 1985), p. 83.

[53] Olfert Dapper, "The Kingdom of Congo," in *Central and South African History*, trans. Robert O. Collins (New York: Markus Wiener Publishing, 1990), p. 35.

[54] Colson, "African Society at the Time of the Scramble," p. 35.

[55] David Northrup, *Trade Without Rulers: Pre-Colonial Economic Development in South-Eastern Nigeria* (Oxford: Clarendon Press, 1978), p. 3.

before the European division of the continent. Hargreaves speaks of an "African partition of Africa" in West Africa during the nineteenth century citing, among other developments, the Fulani jihad of Sokoto, the rise of Bornu, and the empires of Samory and Rabeh.[56] Elsewhere in Africa, relatively large states were being created, including the rise of the Zulu empire, the strengthening of the Malagassy state under Radama I, and the cementing of the Omani hegemony on the East African coast under Sayyid Said. As Hrbek notes, there was in many parts of Africa in the nineteenth century, "the growth of a unified and highly centralised state with an absolute monarch unrestricted in his power by any freely elected council."[57]

The expansion of some states in Africa in the nineteenth century was an important development. While local forces were undoubtedly crucial in the rise of these states, "all these processes were going on in the 'contact' zones and were due to some extent to external impact and influence."[58] Many states grew because of their ability to participate in the increasing amount of international trade generated by the growing European presence on the coasts of Africa. Thus, Wilks describes the building of the Akan state: "Those who controlled the production and sale of gold were those able to procure a supply of unfree labor. Those who procured unfree labor were those able to create arable land within the forrest. Those who created the arable [land] were those who founded the numerous early Akan polities."[59] Even more important was the introduction of the gun into parts of Africa in the nineteenth century. The gun, wielded by soldiers on horses, changed some of the calculations of power in Africa because these weapons made it easier to conquer relatively large amounts of low-value territory. One commentator on the rise of Bornu noted the effects of firearms:

> Among the benefits which God (Most High) of His bounty and beneficence, generosity, and constancy conferred upon the Sultan was the acquisition of Turkish musketeers and numerous household slaves who became skilled in firing muskets. Hence the Sultan was able to kill the people of Amaska with muskets, and there was no need for other weapons, so that God gave him a great victory by reason of his superiority in arms.[60]

[56] John D. Hargreaves, "West African States and the European Conquest," in *Colonialism in Africa, 1870–1960*, ed. L. H. Gann and Peter Duigan vol. 1 (Cambridge: Cambridge University Press, 1969), p. 199.

[57] Ivan Hrbek, "Towards a Periodisation of African History," in *Emerging Themes of African History*, ed. T. O. Ranger (Nairobi: East African Publishing House, 1968), p. 48.

[58] Ibid.

[59] Ivor Wilks, *Forests of Gold: Essays on the Akan and the Kingdom of the Asante* (Athens: Ohio University Press, 1993), p. 96.

[60] Quoted in Goody, *Technology, Tradition, and the State*, p. 54.

Guns also reinforced the centralization of power because, unlike the bow and arrow, they could be kept in magazines until they were needed and then collected. The fact that gun manufacturing did not become significant in Africa, in contrast to Japan and Ceylon, which quickly developed indigenous means of manufacturing firearms, furthered centralization because the weapons could only be garnered in trades with Europeans, transactions that usually were controlled by the central state.[61]

Although trade and the introduction of the gun may have allowed African polities during the nineteenth century to expand their circles of rule, different practices and traditions regarding the expansion and consolidation of state power did not emerge. The large states and empires that appeared were not able to develop fundamentally different systems for ruling their hinterlands that would have allowed for the extension of more formal types of control. There may simply not have been enough time, given that the European conquest of Africa followed shortly after the introduction of the gun. At the same time, the basic fact that population densities were so low that the value of land was fundamentally different than in Europe and Asia had not changed.

That the size of some African polities changed in response to new economic opportunities and technological developments suggests that precolonial Africa had dynamic states that can, in fact, be understood using the traditional tools of politics. Rather than simply being "primitive" or so unlike other states that they were unique, precolonial African polities developed as logical responses to their physical environments, most notably the cost of extending power over distance, much like European states developed characteristics in response to the overwhelming characteristic of their political environment: war for territory. Those who consign precolonial polities to the realm of anthropology miss a great deal.

However, those who would romanticize the African past also ignore the rather brutal power calculations that African leaders were making. For instance, Basil Davidson, in his history of the state in Africa, claims that "They [precolonial states] endured because they were accepted. And they were accepted because their rules of operation were found to be sufficiently reasonable in providing explanation, and sufficiently persuasive in extracting obedience. . . . Dissidence and protest might be frequent. The structures of accountability could well enough absorb them."[62] Similarly, Bates claims that in precolonial Africa, "those who held positions of privilege had to insure that the benefits created by the states were widely shared" because otherwise the citizenry would leave.[63] In fact,

---

[61] This discussion depends on ibid., p. 52.
[62] Davidson, *Black Man's Burden*, p. 88.
[63] Bates, *Essays on the Political Economy of Africa*, p. 42.

there is little evidence from this review of power in precolonial Africa that the primary determinant of a state's duration was accountability (Davidson does not provide any either). Rather, the opposite appears to be true: states rose and fell, expanded and contracted, largely in relation to the amount of coercion they were able to broadcast from the center. Those states that expanded in the nineteenth century did so because the technologies of coercion, rather than of accountability, improved. Throughout the precolonial period, African states were exquisitely designed around the precise amounts of authority they were able to broadcast in particular areas, hardly an indication that the norms of reciprocity and accountability held major sway in precolonial Africa.

Buffer Mechanisms

Given the centrality of mechanisms for broadcasting power in precolonial Africa to the design and size of the state, buffer mechanisms are particularly important to examine. If African states could avail themselves to ways of regulating flows of people, money, or goods from neighboring states, they might be able to strengthen their presence in outlying areas without depending on the rather expensive deployment of coercion. In fact, buffer mechanisms were largely absent in Africa. As a result, the ambiguous nature of authority in outlying areas was aggravated because there was no way for states to substitute for the use of coercion when extending their writ of authority.

The absence of buffer mechanisms is most obvious when examining territorial boundaries. Societies without maps were hardly in a position to create hard territorial boundaries. In fact, the notion of the "frontier as boundary," was largely unknown in precolonial Africa.[64] Power tended to dissipate in increasingly distant hinterlands that were under the nominal control of a distant center rather than be marked by sharp geographic disjunctures. Frontiers tended to be thought of as border regions or zones where more than one polity could actively exercise authority and where the contours of power were confused rather than corresponding to the rigid demarcations of the modern world.[65]

Similarly, precolonial African states lacked the ability to control two of the most common and important flows across boundaries: people and money. For instance, the free movement of people was a widely accepted tenant in many precolonial polities. Shack notes, "there is just enough evidence to suggest that African strangers, and indeed strangers of other

[64] A. I. Asiwaju, "The Concept of Frontier in the Setting of States in Pre-Colonial Africa," *Presence Africaine* 127/128 (1983): p. 45.

[65] Ibid., p. 46. See also Aidan W. Southall, *Alur Society: A Study of Processes and Types of Domination* (Nairobi: Oxford University Press, 1970), p. 248.

racial and ethnic origins, once moved with relative ease between indigenous African polities."[66] Of course, relatively large amounts of open land
allowed for the easy acceptance of strangers but the fact remains that no
mechanism or set of norms was ever developed to control inflows of
people in most precolonial polities.

Also, many African polities had no official currency that might reinforce their physical presence in remote areas by demanding that legal
tender be in a particular form. Instead, states adopted the currency that
was most popular throughout the trading region. For instance, by the
end of the seventeenth century, both iron and copper rods were commonly found in West Africa. During the nineteenth century, cowrie shells
became increasingly important, and their use was particularly noticeable
along major trade routes of West Africa. However, even during much of
the nineteenth century, manillas (horseshoe-shaped currencies made of
copper and brass) and metal bars were used in many parts of the region,
especially in the hinterland away from major trading areas.[67]

The uses of cowries and metal rods as currency in West Africa meant
that there was no currency exchange mechanism. Cowries were used, for
instance, to pay for goods from East Africa and were also circulated
throughout the West African internal market. There were multiple
sources of cowries and of other currencies. Since no one state controlled
the money supply, sudden inflations sometimes occurred because new
technologies or new traders could suddenly drastically increase the supply
of one or more of the currencies. For instance, after 1850, West Africa
experienced the great cowrie inflation when the currency rapidly lost
value, in part because of increases in its availability due to importation of
the shells by the European powers.[68] Precolonial states were unable to
protect themselves from this sudden debasement of their own currency.
It would be hard to find a more dramatic example of how difficult it was
for these states to mediate pressures from the international environment.

State Systems without Maps

Just as individual African polities were designed in accordance with their
environments, so precolonial African international relations evolved according to the particular domestic circumstances facing individual states.

[66] William A. Shack, introduction to *Strangers in African Societies*, ed. William A. Shack
and Elliott P. Skinner (Berkeley: University of California Press, 1979), p. 8.

[67] On currency history, see Northrup, *Trade Without Rulers*, pp. 157–63 and Marion
Johnson, "The Cowrie Currencies of West Africa, Part One," *Journal of African History* 11
(1970): pp. 32–7.

[68] Okonkwo A. Nwani, "The Quantity Theory in the Early Monetary System of West
Africa with Particular Emphasis on Nigeria, 1850–1895," *The Journal of Political Economy*
83 (February 1975): p. 190.

Arguably, the most distinctive aspect of precolonial international relations, in contrast to the current international system, was the diversity of
states. African states were not necessarily unitary because the extension of
power was so confused. Cursory examination of what appear to have
been unitary states immediately reveals a much more complex reality
made possible, in part, by the unbundling of ownership and control of
land. In the Sokoto Caliphate, and undoubtedly elsewhere, Adeleye reminds us that even at the height of that state's power, "the area within its
perimeter did not wholly come under its jurisdiction" as there were still
"pockets of enemy states and people."[69] Similarly, as Wilks notes for Ashanti, "It is arguable that the union, the Asanteman, has survived precisely
because different (and even conflicting) concepts of its nature have always
been possible. Did member states, for example, have a right to secede, or
was the union indissoluble?"[70] Finally, the early Yoruba kingdom of Oyo
is described as "a large number of internally autonomous kingdoms
whose rulers were said to derive their crowns from Oyo and were the
vassals of the Alafin."[71]

African international relations reflected the complexity of shared sovereignty and multiple state forms. Thomas Hodgkin provides some very
good examples:

> This aspect of international untidiness, so to speak, may help one to understand
> why the Merinid sultan should on occasion address the ruler of independent
> Mali as though he were a vassal; why Idris Aloma should at the same time
> regard himself, and generally be regarded, as *Khalifa* and appear to accept the
> Caliphate of al-Mansur; why Umar, Shehu of Bornu, should describe himself as
> "the Mutawalli of Bornuh Province" when addressing the Pasha of Tripoli, just
> as almost three centuries earlier Mai Idris, while clearly recognized as the ruler
> of an independent state beyond the frontiers of the Ottoman Empire, can yet
> be described by Murad III as *wali* of the *waliya* of Bornu; why for a long
> period of time it should have been uncertain whether Masina under Shaikh
> Ahmadu fell within the Sokoto Caliphate or was a Caliphate in its own right.[72]

This confusion was similar to that experienced in medieval Europe when
there was a much less clearly defined international system. As Garrett
Mattingly notes, "Kings made treaties with their own vassals and with the

---

[69] R. A. Adeleye, *Power and Diplomacy in Northern Nigeria, 1804–1906* (New York: Humanities Press, 1971), pp. 52–3.

[70] Wilks, *Forests of Gold*, p. 112.

[71] Peter Morton-Williams, "The Yoruba Kingdom of Oyo," in *West African Kingdoms in the Nineteenth Century*, ed. Daryll Forde and P. M. Kaberry (Oxford: Oxford University Press, 1967), p. 37.

[72] Thomas Hodgkin, "Diplomacy and Diplomats in the Western Sudan," in *Foreign Relations of African States*, ed. K. Ingham (London: Butterworths, 1974), p. 22.

vassals of their neighbors. They received embassies from their own subjects and from the subjects of other princes, and sometimes sent agents
who were in fact ambassadors in return. Subject cities negotiated with
one another without reference to their respective sovereigns."[73] The precolonial African state system nicely reflected the domestic realities on the
ground. As power was shifting and difficult to maintain over distance, the
very nature of diplomacy between units was likely to be complicated.
Interstate relations were not seen as completely distinct from the domestic maintenance of power. For instance, there were few instances in precolonial Africa of separate offices to handle foreign affairs.[74] Embassies
tended to be of the "visiting" type because communications were so
poor and because the hierarchy of power was so ill-defined that permanent missions were impossible to establish and probably unnecessary.[75] As
boundaries were confused, often there was simply no clear line to demarcate the end of domestic politics and the beginning of foreign affairs,
although formal diplomacy between distinctly different states was possible and did occur.

Overall, precolonial Africa was a state system without fictions. Instead
of pretending that a state controlled an area that it could not physically
reach, much more nuanced and subtle possibilities of shared sovereignty
were possible. Instead of simply assuming that the formal political center
spoke for the entire polity, there was far less of a distinction between
domestic and foreign affairs as the state negotiated with other states and,
sometimes, its composite parts. Finally, instead of developing a template
that all states had to fit, there was a diversity of forms in precolonial
Africa that was appropriate to the very different physical and economic
settings in different parts of the continent. Rather than simple "primitiv-
ism," these developments reflect an appreciation of how power was actually deployed in precolonial Africa. The form and practice of domestic
and international politics was in harmony with the challenges posed by
the political geography.

Conclusion

Using the analytic scheme developed in chapter one, it is now possible to
understand in a comprehensive manner the extension of authority in precolonial Africa. Cost calculations directed leaders to formally control only
a political core that might be a small percentage of the territory over
which they had at least some claim because the cost of extending formal

[73] Mattingly, *Renaissance Diplomacy*, p. 26.
[74] Smith, *Warfare and Diplomacy in Pre-Colonial West Africa*, pp. 10–11.
[75] Hodgkin, "Diplomacy and Diplomats in the Western Sudan," p. 20.

authority in Africa was very high. This particular cost structure came about for several reasons. First, the physical geography was daunting to leaders, especially given the limited technologies of coercion that they could employ, although states did expand when the technologies of power, especially after the introduction of the gun, improved. Second, formal control was difficult to achieve given the primacy of exit and the unbundling of sovereignty and control. The immediate fixed costs facing any leader who wished to extend authority were thus extremely high as roads were expensive to build and armies could only be deployed so far. As a result, beyond the political core, power tended to diminish over distance.

Second, African states had few ways in which to mediate the pressures from outside their core areas, especially regarding the regulation of flows of people or money. This was hardly surprising given that boundaries were soft: the presence of zones where sovereignty was essentially shared with neighboring polities made it very difficult for strong mechanisms to exist that would have insulated individual units from flows of people and money. At the same time, the physiology of African states meant that there was little need to establish firm buffer mechanisms because many developments affecting people and money in outlying areas were of little concern to the core, given that the central political authorities did not have the ambition of formally ruling over distant areas. Of course, the lack of buffer mechanisms also strengthened the need for states to have differing levels of authority over different areas.

Finally, the state system that precolonial Africans developed also heightened the costs African leaders faced when extending power. Precolonial leaders received no help from the international system. If they only partially controlled an outlying area, some other state was able to fill the remaining vacuum. If no state could extend authority of any type into an area, then a vacuum was tolerated and decentralized villages were left to govern themselves. Further, if a state's hold over an outlying area became more tenuous, it was perfectly legitimate for the hinterland to break away. The bill for extending authority was always due and it could never be avoided.

In terms of the basic model developed in chapter one, all three factors (cost, boundaries, and the state system) under consideration make it relatively difficult to extend the power of the state. States found it hard to extend authority from the center outward. At the same time, the weakness of boundaries made it impossible to delimit an area that could then be claimed exclusively by a state. Finally, the state system was unforgiving and did not allow for the extension of formal authority without the deployment of a corresponding power infrastructure. As a result, considerations revolving around the costs of extending power dominated political

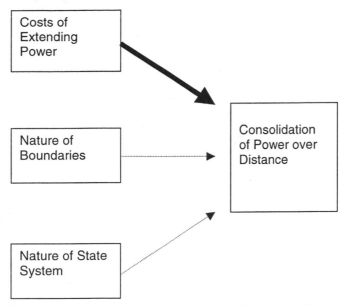

Figure 2.1. Paths to State Consolidation in Precolonial Africa

calculations. Precolonial African states therefore had precisely the opposite physiology of many in Europe: the power assets were concentrated in the center with gradations of authority extending into the hinterland. The European model of placing significant assets in the hinterland to protect against outsiders and to make the boundaries real was neither viable nor relevant.

Given time, it is possible that basic calculations of power, and the African state system itself, might have changed fundamentally in light of the developments prompted by increased international trade and new weaponry in the nineteenth century. The dynamism of the precolonial portion of the nineteenth century suggests that African leaders were beginning to dramatically change their calculations of how it was possible to broadcast power. However, just as these new developments were becoming salient and the new African states were reaching maturity, the European conquest of Africa began in earnest. Africans were suddenly confronted with peoples who had very different conceptions of power but who would have to operate in the same physical environment as the precolonial leaders. What the Europeans did and did not change is the focus of the next chapter.

Three

The Europeans and the African Problem

> The problem continues unsolved. The
> conquering races of the world stand perplexed
> and worried before the difficulties which beset
> their enterprise of reducing that continent
> [Africa] to subjection.
>   Edward W. Blyden, *The African Problem and*
>   *the Method of its Solution*

THE PROFOUND CHANGES wrought by European colonialism in Africa have legitimately been cited as so fundamental as to mark a new era in African politics. Crawford Young, in his monumental review of the African colonial state, argues that many of the pathologies of modern Africa can be traced to the particularities of colonialism in Africa.[1] In addition to creating the immediate predecessors to today's states, the Europeans brought about a host of other changes in Africa that have reverberated to our own time: they created a system of boundaries and frontiers new to Africa; they established novel economic systems based on mines and cash crops; they built infrastructure systems that still determine patterns of trade; and they left their religions, languages, and cultural practices.

However, the significance of the profound changes the Europeans wrought often obscures the fact that they also developed an intricate set of responses to the problem of how to control people and territory in sparsely settled lands while devoting the absolute minimum to administration. What the Afro-Caribbean diplomat Edward W. Blyden called "the African Problem"—the inability of Europe to conquer Africa in the same manner as other regions—continued throughout the brief (by historical standards) period of formal European rule. As a result, analyzing the European extension of power in Africa is particularly difficult because the massive changes imposed by the Europeans direct attention away from the incomplete and highly differentiated manner in which they actually ruled over different parts of the continent.

Given the schizophrenic nature of colonial power in Africa, it is not

[1] Young, *The African Colonial State*, p. 9.

surprising that a remarkable amount of disagreement exists about the nature of the states the Europeans created. On one side, there is Robert H. Jackson's almost benign description of colonialism: "In most cases they [the colonial governments] were little more than elementary bureaucracies with limited personnel and finances and were more comparable to rural country governments in Europe than to modern independent States."[2] In other work, Jackson has argued that colonialism was a highly legalistic, rule-based system:

> It is obvious that Western powers had certain military and economic interests in partitioning the non-Western world into various dependencies. They staked their claims on a wide scale in the latter half of the [nineteenth] century; but they rarely did so outside of a legal and moral framework that, while accommodating the interests of the great powers, also recognized and respected the legitimate concerns and rights of all sovereign states, large and small.[3]

On the another side, Crawford Young repeatedly uses the image of *Bula Matari*, the crusher of rocks, to describe colonial states in Africa, which had despotic tendencies despite the precariousness of their rule. Young writes that the colonial state, "managed in a short time to assert a powerful hold on subject society and smash its resistance."[4] Young finds the motivation for creating this instrument of hegemony in the Berlin West African Conference (hereafter called the "Berlin Conference") of 1884/1885, which demanded effective occupation as the basis for the exercise of sovereign power. He suggests:

> The affirmation at Berlin of the "effective occupation" doctrine made clear that sketching out vague spheres of influences would not suffice for confirmation of proprietary title. . . . The hegemony imperative, driven by the doctrine of effective occupation, immediately required a skeletal grid of regional administration. Its priorities were clear, its tasks minimal: the imposition of basic order and the creation of a revenue flow.[5]

As a result, by World War I, Young finds that, "the basic superstructure of hegemony was in place. The allocation of colonial space among the imperial occupants had been resolved; the territorial grid of alien domination was firmly in place."[6] Thus, it is hardly surprising that Young and

---

[2] Robert H. Jackson, "Sub-Saharan Africa," in *States in a Changing World: A Contemporary Analysis*, ed. Robert H. Jackson and Alan James (Oxford: Clarendon Press, 1993), p. 139.

[3] Robert H. Jackson, "The Weight of Ideas in Decolonization: Normative Change in International Relations," in *Ideas and Foreign Policy*, ed. Judith Goldstein and Robert Keohane (Ithaca: Cornell University Press, 1993), p. 115.

[4] Young, *The African Colonial State*, p. 139.

[5] Ibid., pp. 96, 100.

[6] Ibid., p. 138.

Turner could describe the Congolese state, that bastard child of colonialism, as having a desire to organize the economic and political space of the colony so that no subject could "escape the overarching uniformities imposed by the nature of the state, its vocation of total control of the subject population, and its productionist orientation."[7] They approvingly cite Balandier when noting that "domination—pervasive, systematic, comprehensive characterized all aspects of the 'colonial situation.'"[8]

Mahmood Mamdani has a different vision of colonialism but one that reaches many of the same conclusions as Young regarding the hegemonic reach of the colonial state. He starts by arguing that the overwhelming motivation for European colonialism in Africa was economic: "The end of slavery in the Western hemisphere underlined the practical need for organizing a new regime of compulsions, except this time within newly acquired African possessions." Mamdani suggests that as slavery ended, Europeans needed to colonize Africans at home so that they could grow cotton for "the Satanic Mills."[9] As a result, a central assumption by Mamdani, like Young, is that the European powers were highly motivated. However, he places much more emphasis in his major work on the colonial state on the invention of tradition, an analytic concept first fully deployed in Africa by Terrence Ranger.[10] For Mamdani, the Europeans had a clear cultural model that they worked methodically to impose on Africa in order to rule: "Like all colonial powers, the British worked with a single model of customary authority in precolonial Africa. The model was monarchical, patriarchal, and authoritarian. It presumed a king at the center of every polity, a chief on every piece of administrative ground, and a patriarch in every homestead or kraal."[11] Similar to Young, Mamdani argues that colonialists were able to extend their rule throughout their African possessions: "The more custom was enforced, the more the tribe was restructured and conserved as a more or less self-contained community—autonomous but not independent—as it never had been before. Encased by custom, frozen into so many tribes, each under the fist of its own Native Authority, the subject population was, as it were, containerized."[12]

However, he places far less emphasis on the level of physical force (the

---

[7] Crawford Young and Thomas Turner, *The Rise and Decline of the Zairian State* (Madison: University of Wisconsin Press, 1985), p. 36.

[8] Ibid., p. 24.

[9] Mahmood Mamdani, *Citizen and Subject: Contemporary Africa and the Legacy of Late Colonialism* (Princeton: Princeton University Press, 1996), p. 37.

[10] Terrence Ranger, "The Invention of Tradition in Colonial Africa," in *The Invention of Tradition*, ed. Eric Hobsbawm and Terrence Ranger (Cambridge: Cambridge University Press, 1983).

[11] Mamdani, *Citizen and Subject*, p. 39.

[12] Ibid., p. 51.

crushing of rocks) than Young. Rather, Mamdani argues that, "European rule in Africa came to be defined by a single-minded and overriding emphasis on the customary." He suggests that this focus came about because of the British experience in India which evolved from a belief in a civilizing mission to a "law-and-order obsession with holding the line."[13] This is not to say that the colonialists were content to do little when they ruled Africa. Rather, Mamdani's book is a long analysis of the many actions the Europeans took to create a "decentralized despotism" whereby, "achieving a hegemonic domination was a cultural project: one of harnessing the moral, historical, and community impetus behind local custom to a larger colonial project."[14]

These debates revolve, in fact, around very different assumptions about how colonialism was able to project power. Jackson focuses on the very small size of the colonial governments, while Young is more concerned with the coercion that these small units (there is no debate about the limited presence of Europeans) imposed on African social systems. Mamdani finds that the Europeans were able to exercise power not in the traditional manner of direct rule but through changing notions of what was customary culture to both divide and rule.

It is clearly necessary, given the widely different views of colonialism, to develop a much more systematic view of the extension of European authority. Following the analytic scheme previously developed, this chapter explores the broadcasting of European power by examining the cost structure facing white leaders attempting to broadcast power, the nature of the boundaries established by the Europeans, and the state system that was created by the particular needs of state-builders and which, in turn, greatly affected the consolidation of power. However, unlike the three works discussed above, or almost any other study of European colonialism, this chapter does not simply assume that European rule represented a fundamental break in the way power was exercised on the African continent.

Colonialism before the Scramble

The harshness of European colonization of Africa during the twentieth century often obscures just how late formal control of territory by Europeans, especially in the hinterland, came to the continent. In fact, before 1885, very little territory beyond the coasts was formally controlled. For instance, the Portuguese, during their centuries of contact with Africa after 1500, opted not to conquer large amounts of territory, as the Span-

[13] Ibid., p. 50.
[14] Ibid., p. 286.

ish did in the Americas, but instead tried to influence existing African polities by converting them to Christianity (e.g., the Kongo Kingdom based in São Salvador). Or a coastal capital was created to coordinate a system of trading bases that would obviate the need for formal control of the interior. Thus, the castle at Elmina controlled the entire Portuguese and later Dutch activities in West Africa while Cape Coast and Christenburg were the capitals for the English and Danish enterprises on the Guinea Coast. Eventually, the British would gain control over all three coastal outposts and select Accra as their capital.[15]

Little to nothing was done to formally control the interior. Thus Earl Grey, writing in 1853, wanted to consolidate and increase the influence of Britain on the Gold Coast and, in particular, hoped to build roads, which, he noted, "are in all countries among the most efficient instruments of civilization." However, Parliament was unwilling to increase the vote for that purpose.[16] Grey and the Fanti Confederation clearly had much the same idea about the necessary infrastructure for rule, but Britain was unwilling to pay the fixed costs necessary to exercise control over the hinterland. In fact, British administrators, in what would become Ghana, argued as late as 1870 that there was no reason to maintain the old road network that had been central to the exercise of power in the past.[17]

The Select Committee on West Africa reporting in 1865 provides an excellent window into the specifically British, and more generally European, view of Africa twenty years before the Berlin Conference. The Select Committee had been asked to consider the status of British establishments on the West Coast of Africa. After taking extensive testimony, the committee acknowledged that the British government could not withdraw from West Africa, although there was clearly some sentiment among committee members to do so. The committee did recommend that there be a policy of not extending British presence to new territory or otherwise expanding the responsibility of the government except to promote the administration of existing settlements. Further, the committee hoped that British policy would be to encourage the transfer of administration to Africans.[18] There was no vision of how Britain might actually formally control even the land near its then meager holdings in West Africa.

Thus, in 1865, the Lieutenant-Governor in the Cape Coast informed the secretary of state for the colonies that he had posted a notice defining

<hr>

[15] Christopher, "Urbanization and National Capitals in Africa," p. 410.

[16] Earl Grey, *The Colonial Policy of Lord John Russell's Administration*, vol. 2 (London: Richard Bentley, 1853), p. 280.

[17] Wilks, *Asante in the Nineteenth Century* p. 12.

[18] Select Committee on Africa (Western Coast), *Report* (London: House of Commons, 1865), p. iii.

the limits of British territory as the distance of a cannon shot, or five miles from each castle or fort, in order to bring European laws to the Africans while not interfering with domestic slavery. The secretary of state responded that the Cape Coast government should "avoid any expression" that "bore the appearance of extended jurisdiction over territory at the Gold Coast."[19] Similarly, before 1884, Germany and France were officially opposed to expansion into Africa and Portugal was too weak to realize her colonial ambitions.[20]

Not surprisingly, given their limited ambitions for territorial control, the Europeans had adopted a very African view of space and boundaries. As late as 1750, the "film of fact" that Europeans had for Africa, in comparison to the much more distant Asia and the Americas, was very thin. For instance, "nothing was known of the course of the White Nile before it met with the Blue beyond the reports of Ptolemy sixteen hundred years before, the course of the Congo was unknown except for the last one hundred and fifty miles, and even the direction of the flow of the Niger was uncertain."[21] Colonel Ord, when testifying before the Select Committee in 1865 admitted, when asked what constituted the northern boundary of the Cape Coast protectorate, "We know so little of the interior of the country, that I am unable to say. The natives themselves, no doubt, are fully aware of what constitutes the boundaries between their respective countries [sic]." He went on to admit that as regards the eastern frontier, "There is no definite boundary."[22]

There were many reasons for the late and limited European interest in Africa. Lack of commercial opportunities was certainly important. Hallett concludes that, "Europe possessed no strong incentive to explore what was, after all, by far the poorest of the great continents."[23] Even in the early 1880s, on the eve of the scramble for Africa, the British government still expressed little interest in African colonies, demanding that they pay for themselves, an unlikely prospect given the high fixed cost of establishing administrative structures. In the words of the permanent under secretary of the Colonial Office, Sir Frederick Rogers, African colonies were "expensive and troublesome."[24] In addition, Europeans tended to die in large numbers when they tried to live on the continent. That West Africa was "the white man's grave" convinced James Africanus

---

[19] Africanus B. Horton, *Letters on the Political Conditions of the Gold Coast*, 2nd ed. (London: Frank Cass and Co., 1970), p. 155.

[20] Michael Crowder, *West Africa under Colonial Rule* (Evanston, IL: Northwestern University Press, 1968), p. 17.

[21] Robin Hallett, "The European Approach to the Interior of Africa in the Eighteenth Century," *Journal of African History* 4 (1963): p. 191.

[22] Quoted in Select Committee on Africa, *Report*, p. 41.

[23] Hallett, "The European Approach to the Interior of Africa," p. 196.

[24] Crowder, *West Africa under Colonial Rule*, p. 48.

Horton that the permanent occupation of West Africa "is impossible of realization; it is a mistake and a delusion."[25]

South Africa, after the discovery of the Witswatersrand, was an exception to the general African pattern. Starting in the mid-nineteenth century, the tremendous mineral discoveries around the Rand prompted massive white immigration and the creation of what was, in places, an extraordinarily well-developed state apparatus. However, despite the effort by Rhodes and others to find the "second Rand" in other parts of Southern Africa (often called "the white man's sanitarium"), a significant European presence did not develop there until very late in the colonial period. Great Britain only reluctantly took control of Southern Rhodesia in 1923 after the failure of the British South Africa Company to find another mineral extravagance. In fact, half of the Rhodesian white population immigrated after 1945. Similarly, Portuguese rule in Mozambique and Angola, while stretching back centuries, was sporadic, and Lisbon was unable to move much beyond its coastal acquisitions. Colonies were allowed to disappear and the large white settlements that characterized both territories right before independence in the 1970s were products of the *Estado Novo* created by Antonio Salazar in 1928.[26]

For most of the nineteenth century, as Hargreaves notes, "The object of 'free-trade imperialism' was to extend the area open to European activity, rather than to establish national reservations."[27] European practices were largely congruent with existing precolonial politics that did not stress the control of territory. As a result, in the mid-nineteenth century, the great West African leader Al Haj 'Umar said, "the whites are only traders."[28] In many ways, before 1885, the Europeans were just another African group that played the political game according to long-established rules. Especially beyond the coasts, there is little evidence of any kind of significant colonial project that would foreshadow European domination of Africa in later years.

A State System for Conquest on the Cheap

The scramble for Africa that broke out in the last decades of the nineteenth century is not easily explained. A necessary development was the advent of new technologies that finally allowed Europeans to conquer

[25] James Africanus Horton, *West African Countries and Peoples* (Edinburgh: Edinburgh University Press, 1969), p. 69.

[26] Young, *The African Colonial State*, p. 152.

[27] J. D. Hargreaves, "The Making of the Boundaries: Focus on West Africa," in *Partitioned Africans: Ethnic Relations across Africa's International Boundaries, 1884–1984*, ed. A. I. Asiwaju (New York: St. Martin's Press, 1985), p. 19.

[28] Quoted in ibid.

the continent nearest to them. By the 1850s, quinine prophylaxis reduced deaths from malaria by four-fifths and made occupation possible.
More importantly, by the mid-1880s, French forces had adopted the
Maxim gun, which fired eleven bullets per second. Muskets used early in
the 1800s took a minute to load, had a range of 80 meters, and misfired
30 percent of the time.[29] Given these advances as context, a variety of
factors motivated the scramble: European rivalries, the disappearance of
open land to conquer elsewhere in the world, significant efforts by "the
man on the spot" to extend colonial boundaries irrespective of the wishes
of the metropole, and, last but not least, a sudden hysteria across Europe
about being be left out of the division of Africa, even if there was very
little certainty about the nature of the spoils to be garnered.

The precise factor that was most important in the European conquest
of Africa varied from region to region, yielding a rich historical debate
that will inevitably be inconclusive in its search for a general explanation.[30]
Hobson's and Lenin's view of colonialism inspired by metropolitan greed
has a resonance in South Africa, where there was much mineral wealth to
be had, but makes little sense for the rest of Africa. As Iliffe noted,

> Africa was not central to European economies: during the 1870s it accounted
> for little more than 5 per cent of Britain's trade, most of it with Egypt and
> South Africa. Commercial interests in tropical Africa were vital to annexations
> on the west coast, but elsewhere merchants, such as Germans in Zanzibar,
> often opposed colonial conquest lest it disrupt existing trade. . . . Rhodes's
> British South Africa Company never paid a dividend during the thirty-three
> years it administered Rhodesia.[31]

As is now well known, for Great Britain, the vast majority of investments
after 1870 did not go to Africa or Asia, but to other parts of the commonwealth and to South America.[32] There is, for example, very little evidence that land was conquered for cotton, the commodity Mamdani
highlights. Indeed, when the French tried to foster cotton in areas they
had conquered (note the sequencing), they failed, in part because they
were not that committed: "Had the opposing forces within the colonial
state agreed on a consistent strategy of colonial development, had it had
better access to financial and ideological resources, and had the senior

[29] Iliffe, *Africans*, p. 192.
[30] The debate is a long and interesting one. The major statements include D. K. Fieldhouse,
Economics and Empire, 1830–1914 (London: Weidenfeld and Nicoloson, 1973); J. A. Hobson, *Imperialism: A Study* (New York: James Pott and Company, 1902); Ronald Robinson
and John Gallagher, *Africans and the Victorians: The Official Mind of Imperialism* (London:
Macmillan Press, 1963); and V. I. Lenin, *Imperialism the Highest Stage of Capitalism* in *The
Lenin Anthology*, ed. Robert C. Tucker (New York: W. W. Norton, 1975).
[31] Iliffe, *Africans*, p. 192.
[32] D. K. Fieldhouse, "'Imperialism:' An Historiographical Revision," *The Economic History Review* 14 (1961): p. 199.

colonial administration been less ambivalent about the use of compulsion, perhaps the outcome would have been different."[33] Lewis concludes, generally for tropical administration: "The prevailing posture of colonial governments continued to be one of neglect, even after the transport revolutions had opened up new possibilities."[34]

The True Colonial Achievement

What is most remarkable about the scramble for Africa is not that it happened, but that it occurred so late, so fast, and without significant fighting between the colonialists. In the twenty-five years beginning in 1880, Africa—still mysterious in the mid-1870s, and then considered *terra incognita*—was colonized, and ten million square miles and one hundred and ten million people (including North Africa) were brought under European rule.[35] Maps 3.1, 3.2, and 3.3 demonstrate how quickly the Europeans moved from 1880 to 1914, when colonial occupation was largely finished. It was not obvious, *a priori*, that Europe could have divided up so a large land mass so quickly without conflict given the tensions on the European continent at the time and the rather remarkable tendency for Europeans to go to war.

Further, adding to the complexity of the European task of dividing Africa was the nature of the changes in frontiers formal colonialism imposed. The Europeans could not continue to play by African rules given that the norm of unambiguous sovereignty was so deeply imbedded in their operational code, especially the precept that each square foot of land could be controlled by one and only one power. During the conquest, they rejected the fuzzy borders that had been adopted through the long period of partial European occupation of the coast. Lugard wrote, "something had to be done to prevent European rivalries developing into war. . . . Our rivals were constantly enroaching on our shadowy boundaries."[36] Tellingly, the scramble initiated a huge effort to map Africa. As the colonial project progressed, geographers were soon asking, "How can we get maps of Africa?"[37]

[33] Richard L. Roberts, *Two Worlds of Cotton: Colonialism and the Regional Economy in the French Soudan, 1800–1946* (Stanford, CA: Stanford University Press, 1996), p. 10. See generally Anne Phillips, *The Enigma of Colonialism: British Policy in West Africa* (London: James Currey, 1989), p. 156.

[34] W. Arthur Lewis, *Growth and Fluctuations* (London: George Allen and Unwin, 1978), p. 212.

[35] Thomas Pakenham, *The Scramble for Africa* (New York: Avon Books, 1991), p. i.

[36] Lord Lugard, *The Dual Mandate in British Tropical Africa*, 5th ed. (London: Frank Cass and Co., 1965), p. 14.

[37] See the article with that title by J. H. Holdich, *The Geographic Journal* 18 (1901): especially p. 591.

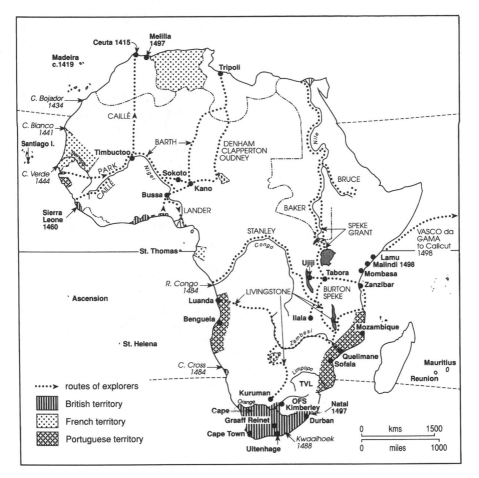

Map 3.1. European Penetration to 1880. Source for Maps 3.1, 3.2, and 3.3 is Ieuan L.L. Griffiths, *The Atlas of African Affairs*, 2nd ed. (London: Routledge, 1994). Used with permission of the publisher.

Neither Administrators nor Conquerors

While the Europeans, rather suddenly in the mid-1880s, had decided to conquer Africa, they were extremely ambivalent about ruling Africa. In particular, Britain, France, and the other powers were unwilling, given the high cost of administration and the low probability of reward, to develop extensive administrative networks. As was the case with the Ashanti, European armies often operated beyond the space that could be administered by their state. H. F. Morris notes for Great Britain (and

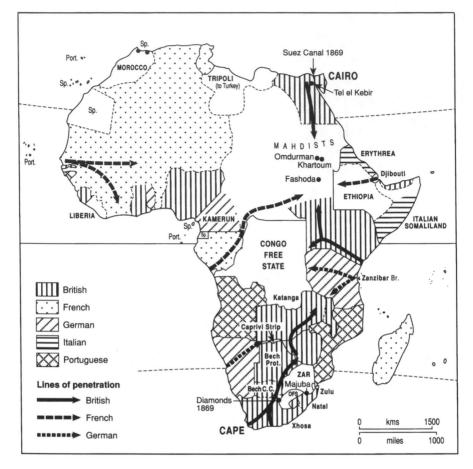

Map 3.2. The Scramble

undoubtedly the other European countries), "annexation would have en-
tailed the establishment of elaborate administrative control over these
great areas, and this Britain was in no position to undertake, even had she
at that time the wish to do so." He notes that Britain was unwilling to
"incur more than a minimum financial commitment," because the geographic limits of the African territories were "nebulous" and because it
was difficult to determine who the indigenous rulers were.[38] Reflecting
the reluctance to go into Africa and assume control, Lord Salisbury

---

[38] H. F. Morris, "Protection or Annexation? Some Constitutional Anomalies of Colonial
Rule," in *Indirect Rule and the Search for Justice: Essays in East African Legal History*, ed.
H. F. Morris and James Read (Oxford: Clarendon Press, 1972), pp. 42–3.

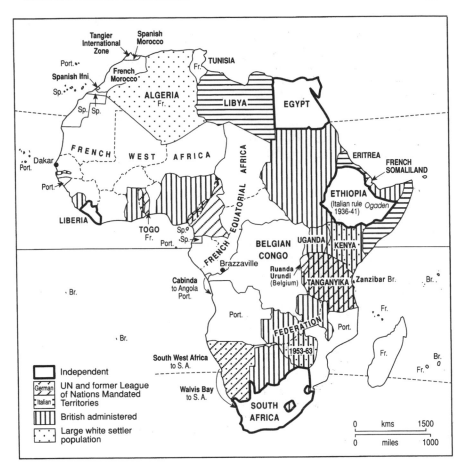

Map 3.3. Colonial Africa

would bemoan the "inconvenience of protectorates," which was caused by the scramble for formal control of Africa.[39]

The Europeans were also not interested in war—the other method of unambiguously conquering territory—because costs would be high and benefits were similarly unclear. The rhetoric of the time spoke of "neutralizing Africa" so that the principle of "no European wars beyond the line" could be respected.[40] As *The Economist* reported in 1884, the actual

[39] As quoted by Margery Perham, *Lugard: The Years of Adventure, 1858–1898* (London: Collins, 1956), p. 88.

[40] Ronald Robinson, "The Conference in Berlin and the Future in Africa, 1884–1885," in *Bismarck, Europe, and Africa: The Berlin Africa Conference 1884–1885 and the Onset of*

boundaries in Africa were less important to the colonialists than avoiding conflict amongst themselves in a part of the world that was of questionable value and far from home:

> Nothing could be worse for West Africa or for Europe than to leave to local officials opportunities of quarrel, which they are sure to use. No one wants informal war all along the Congo, with Portugal pleading her weakness as an excuse for claiming everything, and France talking about her susceptibilities, and Germany sending out Professors with flags which nobody may touch, and England stubbornly determined that the wishes of the blacks, who are usually on her side, shall be sufficiently regarded.[41]

Similarly, *The Observer* argued, "it is scarcely more than the truth to say that the most important thing in colonial matters is to have a clear and unambiguous policy."[42]

The refusal to either administer territory or fight over it was especially important in Africa because the continent's political geography did not allow any other principle around which to organize territorial control. The practice of precolonial African politics, especially the lack of territorial boundaries, the ease of exit, and the existence of traditions of shared sovereignty, provided relatively little information to would-be boundary creators.

Also, topography alone could not provide guidelines for creating a system of borders in Africa. First, Africa does not have the kind of mountain ranges that have served as political boundaries in some places, and in any case, mountains need to be exceptionally high in order to affect political organization.[43] More generally, topography seldom, if ever, can provide the foundation for a system of political boundaries. The assumption that there are "natural frontiers" that can somehow be delimited on the basis of topography, and that would therefore be less arbitrary than borders drawn by people, is much more problematic than is normally assumed. As Jan Broek deftly noted, "No doubt certain physiographic features may be more useful than others as boundaries, but it is man who determines which of these will be used. This also explains the remarkable fact that

---

Partition, ed. Stig Förster, Wolfgang J. Mommsen and Ronald Robinson (London: Oxford University Press, 1988), p. 23.

[41] *The Economist*, 15 November 1884, reprinted in Elfi Bendikat, ed., *Imperialistische Interessenpolitik und Konfliktregelung 1884–5* (Berlin: Wissenschaftlicher Autoren-Verlag, 1985), p. 156.

[42] *The Observer*, 19 October 1884 in ibid., p. 137.

[43] The political implications of Africa's topography are explored by Derwent Whittlessey in *The Earth and the State: A Study of Political Geography* (New York: Henry Holt, 1939), p. 304, and by S. Whittemore Boggs in *International Boundaries: A Study of Boundary Functions and Problems* (New York: Columbia University Press, 1940), pp. 155–75.

nations usually envisage their natural frontiers as lying beyond their actual borders."[44]

The Berlin Conference

The Europeans were therefore faced with the difficult problem of wanting to demarcate a vast but not clearly differentiated territory, but having no desire to either administer it formally or fight amongst themselves over it. How then was the scramble for Africa to proceed? Instead of acting as combatants in an international system typically described as anarchical, the colonial powers devised a way to collude for their common good. The specific mechanism used to divide up Africa peacefully was the Berlin Conference of 1884/5.

The conference helped resolve a profound conflict between the European powers over how the extension of power was to proceed in Africa. To simplify, on one side of the debate was Germany. Its view was that "future powers occupying territory there [Africa] should have no legal claim to it unless they exercised strong and effective political control."[45] As the newest colonizer, Germany had an interest in trying to embarrass the older colonizers and attempting to invalidate their claims. The latecomer to colonialism was unlikely to gain wide swaths of territory and therefore could conveniently argue that each colonial possession had to be effectively controlled or be given up. Great Britain, on the other hand, wanted, in light of her relatively large colonial possessions, to minimize the responsibilities of occupying powers because her existing protectorates might be called into question if there were new rules adopted that set up costly responsibilities for the occupying powers.[46]

In the end, contrary to what Young implies, the British view prevailed. The Berlin Conference went to considerable lengths to stress the minimalist nature of the obligations Europeans assumed when they claimed formal control of territory in Africa. The two relevant chapters of the conference's final protocol deserve to be quoted at some length because they are quite telling about the extent to which the new international system was designed to take into account the disinclination to rule what the Europeans had conquered:

[44] Jan O. M. Broek, "The Problem of 'Natural Frontiers,'" in *Frontiers of the Future*, ed. Jan O. M Broek (Los Angeles: California University Committee on International Relations, 1941), p.11.

[45] S. E. Crowe, *The Berlin West African Conference, 1884-1885* (London: Longmans, 1942), p. 177.

[46] Ibid.

Article 34: Any Power which henceforth takes possession of a tract of land on the coasts of the African continent outside of its present possessions, or which, being hitherto without such possessions, shall acquire them, as well as the Power which possesses a Protectorate there, shall accompany the respective act with a notification thereof addressed to the other signatory powers of the act, in order to enable them, if need be, to make good any claims of their own.

Article 35: The signatory powers of the present act recognise the obligation to ensure the establishment of authority in regions occupied by them on the coasts of the African continent, sufficient to protect existing rights, and, as the case may be, freedom of trade and of transit under the conditions agreed upon.[47]

All that a European country had to do was establish some kind of base territory on the coast, and then it was free to expand inward without having to establish, except in an ill-defined "reasonable time," an administrative presence in order to fulfill the obligations of effective occupation.

There appears to have been no belief on the part of the participants at the time of the Berlin Conference, or after, that the rules of occupation demanded the creation of European hegemony on the ground. For instance, a Belgian amendment that "effective occupation" should include provisions "to cause peace to be administered" was struck out from the final Berlin proclamation.[48] Rather, Berlin enabled the Europeans to conquer Africa while doing as little as possible to control it. The rules were so vague that they would be difficult, if not impossible, to enforce.[49] Indeed, "occupation" did not actually refer to seizure of land but was a more generic term for the acquisition of sovereignty. Most territory in Africa was not actually physically conquered but ceded, more or less legitimately, by African rulers.[50] Thus, many misunderstand the fundamental purpose of the Berlin Conference.

The conference never dealt explicitly with the interior of Africa. Quickly, the "hinterland theory" was promulgated. Under this theory, any power occupying coastal territory was entitled to claim political influence over an indefinite amount of inland area. In an irregularly sized continent, this was bound to cause problems, and a certain level of ridiculousness was reached when France tried to restrict the borders of

[47] "General Act of the Berlin Conference," in *The Scramble for Africa*, ed. R. J. Gavin and J. A. Betley (Ibadan, Nigeria: Ibadan University Press, 1973), pp. 299–300.

[48] The relevant diplomatic history is provided by Crowe, *The Berlin West African Conference*, pp.176, 191.

[49] Jörg Fisch, "Africa as *terra nullius*: The Berlin Conference and International Law," in *Bismarck, Europe, and Africa: The Berlin Africa Conference 1884–1885 and the Onset of Partition*, Stig Förster, Wolfgang J. Mommsen and Ronald Robinson (London: Oxford University Press, 1988), p. 351.

[50] Malcolm Shaw, *Title to Territory in Africa* (Oxford: Clarendon Press, 1986), pp. 34, 38.

Nigeria on the basis of a line that formed the hinterland of Algeria.[51] In the end, the hinterland theory was rejected because it was unworkable.[52] However, the fact that it was even seriously considered suggests that the need to prove effective occupation was not central to gaining control over the vast majority of Africa, beyond the coasts. Elizabeth Hopkins was left to conclude that, "The principle of effective occupation, so central to the claim of imperial legitimacy on coasts following the Berlin Conference, would have little bearing on the partition of Africa inland."[53]

Administration on the Cheap

The Berlin Conference was exceptionally successful in establishing the rules for the conquest of Africa without requiring extremely expensive formal systems of administration. First, the conference's rules allowed any European power to preclude others from contesting a piece of territory that it had claimed as under its sphere of influence.[54] For instance, the British assumed a "paper protectorate" through the Royal Niger Company after 1886 in the Oil Rivers Protectorate in what would later become Nigeria. In the words of the new vice-consul, "our policy may for the present chiefly assume a negative character. So long as we keep other European nations out, we need not be in a hurry to go in."[55] These are not the words of an official with a hegemonic project. Or, as Morris argues,

> The establishment of protectorates was for Britain in the 1880s and 1890s an ideal solution to the problem of the international scramble for African possessions. She would thus exclude her rivals from gaining control over the area concerned, while retaining a free hand as to what degree of internal control she would then or later decide to exercise, and, indeed, as to whether she might not later wish to withdraw completely.[56]

[51] Lugard, *The Dual Mandate*, p. 12.
[52] G. N. Uzoigwe, "Spheres of Influence and the Doctrine of the Hinterland in the Partition of Africa," *Journal of African Studies* 3 (1976): pp. 196–7.
[53] Elizabeth Hopkins, "Partition in Practice: African Politics and European Rivalry in Bufumbira," in *Bismarck, Europe, and Africa: The Berlin Africa Conference 1884–1885 and the Onset of Partition*, ed. Stig Förster, Wolfgang J. Mommsen, and Ronald Robinson (London: Oxford University Press, 1988), p. 415.
[54] M. F. Lindley, *The Acquisition and Government of Backward Territory in International Law* (London: Longmans, Green, 1926), p. 210.
[55] Quoted in Crowder, *West Africa under Colonial Rule*, p. 117. See also H. L. Wesseling, *Divide and Rule: The Partition of Africa, 1880–1914* (Westport, CT: Praeger, 1996), p. 193.
[56] Morris, "Protection or Annexation?" p. 43. See also William Edward Hall, *A Treatise on the Foreign Powers and Jurisdiction of the British Crown* (Oxford: Oxford University Press, 1894), p. 224.

Second, by requiring the exchange of information in an environment where knowledge of boundaries was otherwise lacking, the conference enabled European countries to avoid conflict over territories that had already been claimed. M. F. Lindley notes the importance of this process:

> It was largely owning to their use [the arrangements recognizing the protectorates of other states] that despite the keen competition for territory in Africa and Oceania, the primary division amongst them of those parts of the world was effected by peaceful methods. Difficulties were anticipated and avoided by the exercise of an accommodating spirit on both sides; and force, which loomed so largely in the colonial settlements of the eighteenth century, gave place to agreement.[57]

At the same time, the Europeans found it easy to conquer African polities, although there would be some limited armed resistance. For instance, the imperialist Richard Meinertzhagen was able to conquer half a million Africans with three white men, twenty black soldiers, and fifty black police.[58] In his review of African resistance to European colonialism, Crowder notes, "Perhaps the most striking feature of the invading armies was their small size in comparison with the African armies which opposed them."[59] The cost to Britain of conquering seventy million African subjects was about fifteen pence each, most of that spent not on armies but on railroads that followed the soldiers.[60] There would be much unarmed resistance to colonialism but, as will be discussed, not of the type or of the magnitude to physically challenge European rule.

The Europeans took advantage of the weak indigenous threats to their rule and the peaceful international environment established by Berlin to gain what would, under most circumstances, have been a highly questionable, and contestable, title to territory. For instance, the conference allowed Europeans to legitimate the practice of signing treaties with African chiefs so as gain control of territory in a legalistic manner instead of conquering it, even though few traditional African leaders actually had control of their land as understood by the Europeans. Lugard describes the treaty-making:

---

[57] Lindley, *The Acquisition and Government of Backward Territory*, pp. 210–1. See also Friedrich Kratochwil, "Of Systems, Boundaries and Territoriality: An Inquiry into the Formation of the State System," *World Politics* 39 (October 1986): p. 39.

[58] Crowder, *West Africa under Colonial Rule*, p. 422.

[59] Michael Crowder, "West African Resistance," in *West African Resistance: The Military Response to Colonial Occupation*, 2nd ed., ed. Michael Crowder (London: Hutchinson University Library for Africa, 1978), p. 6.

[60] Bruce Berman and John Lonsdale, *State and Class*, bk. 1 of *Unhappy Valley: Conflict in Kenya and Africa* (London: James Currey, 1992), p. 18.

Treaties were produced by the cartload in all the approved forms of legal verbiage—impossible of translation by ill-educated interpreters. It mattered not that tribal chiefs had no power to dispose of communal rights, or that those few powerful potentates who might perhaps claim such authority looked on the white man's ambassador with contempt. . . . The Sultan of Sokoto, for instance, regarded the subsidy promised to him by the chartered company as a tribute from a vassal.[61]

Where local treaties were not adequate for territorial division, the Europeans relied on arbitrary lines based on latitude and longitude.[62] As a result, about 44 percent of African boundaries are straight lines that either correspond to an astrologic measurement or are parallel to some other set of lines.[63]

Chartered companies, in a kind of privatized imperialism, also were often used by the metropolitan powers to rule over large parts of Africa. Lugard admitted that these companies were, at best, an imperfect form of government. However, "they came forward at a moment when the Government, compelled by the action of other Powers to take some decision, not unnaturally shirked the responsibility of directly administering great regions, at a cost of which no estimate could be made."[64] In particular, the major colonial powers, Britain and France, were sometimes not involved in direct conquest and often ceded their territories to the companies. Company rule continued later in Africa (as late as 1923 for southern Rhodesia) than was the case almost anywhere else in the world.[65] The result of ruling through these traditional and commercial agents, Lugard pithily noted, was that Europeans could, "persuade themselves that the omelette had been made without breaking any eggs."[66] Or as one colonial official in West Africa wrote in 1890: "the old dread of increasing our responsibilities by taking over more territory has, I venture to think, been proved by experience to be somewhat of a bugbear."[67]

An examination of the final colonial map suggests just how little power capabilities had to do with the extension of authority in Africa. Britain,

[61] Lugard, *The Dual Mandate*, p. 15.

[62] J. D. Hargreaves, " West African Boundaries and Partition," p. 319.

[63] K. M. Barbour, "A Geographical Analysis of Boundaries in Inter-Tropical Africa," in *Essays on African Population*, ed. K. M. Barbour and R. M. Prothero (London: Routledge and Kegan Paul, 1961), p. 305.

[64] Lugard, *The Dual Mandate*, p. 23.

[65] Phyllis M. Martin, "The Violence of Empire," in *History of Central Africa*, ed. David Birmingham and Phyllis M. Martin, vol. 2 (London: Longman, 1983), p. 8.

[66] Lugard, *The Dual Mandate*, p. 17.

[67] "A. W. L. Hemming: Minute, West African Expansion, 10 November 1890," in *British Policy towards West Africa: Select Documents, 1875–1914*, ed. C. W. Newbury (Oxford: Clarendon Press, 1971), p. 206.

the power most capable of extending its rule, largely limited its conquests in West Africa to coastal territories. In southern Africa, Britain did gain control of lands in the interior, but these were primarily conquered for it by Rhodes's company and would not fully become part of the empire until the 1920s. The French did control significant interior portions of West Africa, but these trophies reflected less its army's abilities than, rather bizarrely, the desire of the French *navy* to redeem itself after past humiliations.[68] It was the European powers that had not previously demonstrated colonial ambitions—Portugal (the "sick man of Europe"), Bismarck's Germany, the *King* of the Belgians—that formally claimed large amounts of uncontested territory and whose claims were subsequently recognized, despite the fact that they had the most limited abilities to project power.

The disjuncture between power capabilities and extent of empire was possible because, under the Berlin rules, formal European rule could mean almost anything the European capitals decided. Thus,

> the term "protectorate" gradually changed its meaning from that of a pact with the ruler of a State, which maintained its internal but not its external sovereignty, to a declaration of the territorial status of a region included in the Empire, in which not only the external, but in varying degrees the internal sovereignty also, had passed to the controlling Power, in many cases (since unexplored regions were included) without even the "treaty" consent of the people.[69]

The British, at least, did maintain the notion of protectorates throughout the colonial period. However, the Portuguese and French soon were treating their African colonies as integral parts of their mother country through such concepts as the Overseas Provinces of Portugal and Overseas France.[70] That these (rather preposterous) pretences could be so readily accepted, given how detached Lisbon and Paris were from many of the decisions their colonial governors were taking, much less what was happening on the ground, demonstrates the profound effect that the particular international regime constructed for conquering Africa had on imagined relations between Europe and the African periphery.

The Limited Ambitions of the Colonial State

The Berlin Conference, whatever its long-term repercussions, had little immediate effect on politics in most of Africa. As Wesseling duly notes,

[68] Wesseling, *Divide and Rule*, pp. 177–8.
[69] Lugard, *The Dual Mandate*, p. 35.
[70] Crowder, *West Africa under Colonial Rule*, p. 6.

"The partition of Africa was recorded by the Europeans on their maps, but the matter rested there for the time being. . . . In Europe conquests preceded the drawing of maps; in Africa the map was drawn, and then it was decided what was going to happen. These maps did not therefore reflect reality but helped to create it."[71] Or as Blyden mockingly noted in 1890,

> Notwithstanding the reports we receive on every breeze that blows from the East, of vast "spheres of influence" and large European possessions, the points actually occupied by white men in the boundless equatorial regions of that immense continent may be accurately represented on the map only by microscopic dots.[72]

It would be quite some time before the Europeans would even take up, in a serious manner, the task of ruling over large parts of Africa. As Kirk-Greene reminds us, "Occupation was by no means yet synonymous with administration. Any serious move towards the next phase of the new colonial presence, that of consolidation of civilian government and the introduction of economic development plans, was overtaken by the First World War."[73]

Of course, if the European powers had fought significant wars in Africa, either against each other or Africans, part of the inevitable detritus of those conflicts would have been the establishment of some kind of security establishment with the accompanying infrastructure of roads, railroads, and extended administrative systems that armies need to fight. Without such conflict, the infrastructure of rule was slow in coming. As a result, for many rural areas in Africa, formal colonial administration can be counted as only lasting the sixty years starting from the turn of the century. Or as Coquery-Vidrovitch notes:

> At the turn of the century, peasants could still refuse to submit either to African despotism or to White domination. White soldiers and administrators were too few in numbers to be able to impose colonial law in the bush; for example, in 1900, after the failure of attempts at White colonization, Angola contained only some three thousand Portuguese . . . although trade with Europe had been carried on since the sixteenth century, the Shona and Ovambo rural communities had remained in isolation until after 1870.[74]

[71] Wesseling, *Divide and Rule*, pp. 363–4.

[72] Edward W. Blyden, *The African Problem and the Method of its Solution* (Washington, D.C.: Gibson Brothers, 1890), p. 5.

[73] A. H. M. Kirk-Greene, "The Thin White Line: The Size of the British Colonial Service in Africa," *African Affairs* 79 (1980): p. 26.

[74] Coquery-Vidrovitch, *Africa: Endurance and Change South of the Sahara*, p. 185.

In the more distant hinterland, Europeans did not manage to exercise formal authority for several decades after technically gaining control of the territory. Suret-Canale noted that before 1945, "the significant changes affected only the main towns and the big commercial ports. In the bush nothing changed."[75] Harms, in his study of the Nunu, notes that, "life in the swamps did not change drastically until 1926 when the Belgian colonizers consolidated the scattered homestead."[76] The Maka in southeastern Cameroon were not conquered until 1910.[77] Similarly, in 1905, one observer noted, "The Congo was never conquered; vast areas of our colony have never effectively been taken over."[78] For Chad, always the extreme example, DeCalo concludes that "sixty years of colonial rule did not effect any major changes."[79]

Even at the height of colonial rule, governments, reflecting the power gradients made possible by Berlin, penetrated the rural areas in only a partial and incomplete manner. In 1939, the average British district commissioner was responsible, with his staff of Africans, for an area roughly the size of Wales. Ruling over the roughly 43 million people in British tropical Africa in 1939 were a grand total of 1,223 administrators and 938 police.[80] Similarly, there were 3,660 officials to govern 15 million Africans in French West Africa, 887 to govern 3.2 million in French Equatorial Africa, and 2,384 to govern 9.4 million in the Belgian Congo in 1938.[81]

A limited administrative presence was also possible because, even after 1917, the Europeans did little in most parts of the continent to change the biological facts on the ground. The signal aspect of colonialism in Africa was how few European settlers there were. For instance in 1936, near the zenith of the first colonial occupation of Africa, and just before the Second World War would divert European attention and resources elsewhere, the white population in South Africa totaled 2 million and whites accounted for roughly 25 percent of the population. However, in no other settler society could such a critical mass of whites be established. Thus, the ratio of whites to Africans in Kenya was one to two hundred,

[75] Jean Suret-Canale, *French Colonialism in Tropical Africa, 1900–1945* (London: C. Hurst, 1971), p. 155.

[76] Harms, *Games against Nature*, p. 5.

[77] Peter Geschiere, *Village Communities and the State: Changing Relations among the Maka of South-Eastern Cameroon since the Colonial Conquest* (London: Kegan Paul, 1982), p. 133.

[78] Quoted in Coquery-Vidrovitch, *Africa*, p.172.

[79] Samuel DeCalo, "Regionalism, Political Decay, and Civil Strife in Chad," *Journal of Modern African Studies* 18 (March 1980): p. 31.

[80] Kirk-Green, "The Thin White Line," pp. 39–40.

[81] Robert Delavignette, *Freedom and Authority in French West Africa* (London: Oxford University Press, 1950), p. 18.

in Southern Rhodesia (now Zimbabwe), one to twenty, and in South West Africa (now Namibia), one to ten. In the vast majority of colonies without settler populations, the white presence was minimal at most. There were, for instance, only 1.86 French settlers for every thousand Africans in French West Africa in 1938.[82] Similarly, in the colonies where assimilation was possible, it was only done slowly. Thus, by 1950, there were only thirty thousand *assimilados* out of Angola's four million Africans and only five thousand assimilated Africans out of Mozambique's population of six million.[83] Hancock concludes that "South Africa was the only African territory south of the Sahara where the thinly held frontier of European settlement might be said to have evolved into a deeply-rooted European society."[84]

Having few Europeans to protect, the colonial state was notably slow in expanding the spatial reach of the security forces, arguably the essence of any state. As Killingray reminds us, "Colonial Africa, like eighteenth- and nineteenth-century England had only rudimentary policing. Towns were policed by the government, particularly those areas where Europeans and the African educated elite lived . . . Outside the towns and away from the main lines of communication, policing was very much a hit and miss affair where 'much [was] left to hazard.' "[85]

Nothing so epitomizes the limited ambitions of many colonial states, and the failure to establish empirical statehood, as the small size of the security forces that existed in the colonies through the terminal colonial period. In the British-ruled colonies, even during the terminal colonial period, when security forces might have been expected to have burgeoned due to the nationalist upheavals, the number of men in arms was seldom over one per thousand civilians compared to one in a hundred for Britain and other developed countries. As late as 1957, the official report of Northern Rhodesia (now Zambia) stated: "It will be many years before the police force is strong enough to be able to accept the responsibility for enforcing law and order throughout the Territory. There must therefore for some considerable time be a sharing of responsibility between the police and other organizations for the maintenance of law and order."[86] For both France and Britain, Gutteridge concludes that the low

[82] Ibid., p. 17.

[83] James Duffy, "Portuguese Africa, 1930 to 1960," in *Colonialism in Africa, 1870–1960*, ed. L. H. Gann and Peter Duignan, vol. 2 (Cambridge: Cambridge University Press, 1970), p. 179.

[84] W. K. Hancock, *Survey of British Commonwealth Affairs*, vol. 2, pt. 2 (Oxford: Oxford University Press, 1942), p. 1.

[85] The quotation is from William Wickham's description of English policing in the eighteenth century. David Killingray, "The Maintenance of Law and Order in British Colonial Africa," *African Affairs* 85 (1986): pp. 414–5.

[86] Ibid., p. 423.

number of men in arms suggests a "willingness to operate locally on a very narrow margin of safety in relation to any security crisis. . . . The European powers in Africa raised local colonial military forces to fit their world-wide strategic needs; and their criteria, therefore, rested inevitably on imperial rather than on local policy."[87]

Finally, to complete the picture of the weak capabilities and modest ambitions of colonial states, it is important to note the detachment of African colonies from the metropoles that might, under different conditions, have supplied them with the resources to broadcast authority. Reflecting the hubris that propelled them to conquer Africa, the Europeans were initially enormously optimistic about their ability to project power in Africa. King Leopold wrote, "The sea bathes our coast, the world lies before us. Steam and electricity have annihilated distance. All the non-appropriated lands on the surface of the globe (mostly in Africa) can become the field of our operations and our success."[88] However, in reality, African colonial operations were still very distant from the metropole. From the very beginning, the colonial state, and its component parts, had a substantial degree of autonomy. For instance, even in the supposedly highly centralized French system, "Distances and a claim to local expertise made the governor-general almost independent of Paris, whereas the governor was little controlled by his superior in Dakar or Brazzaville. . . . Often [the governor-general] carried out policies diametrically opposed to the regulations coming from Paris."[89] Indeed, the governor-general complained in 1934 of his subordinates' "manifest intention to leave the governor-general in ignorance."[90] In the Belgian territories, "the men on the spot in the Congo were left largely to their own devices."[91] Similarly, in the Portuguese empire, governors in the late-nineteenth century complained "of an ignorant, remote and inflexible Lisbon establishment." It was not until the mid-twentieth century that real changes were made. Thus, the ministry of colonies in Lisbon grew from a staff of seventy-seven in the mid-1890s to more than forty thousand in the late 1960s.[92]

[87] William F. Gutteridge, "Military and Police Forces in Colonial Africa," in *Colonialism in Africa, 1870–1960*, ed. L. H. Gann and Peter Duignan, vol. 2 (Cambridge: Cambridge University Press, 1970), p. 316.
[88] Quoted in Roland Oliver and Anthony Atmore, *Africa since 1800*, 4th ed. (Cambridge: Cambridge University Press, 1984), p. 103.
[89] William B. Cohen, "The French Governors," in *African Proconsuls: European Governors in Africa*, ed. L. H. Gann and Peter Duignan (New York: Free Press, 1978), p. 23.
[90] Ibid., p. 25.
[91] L. H. Gann, "Belgian Administration in the Congo: An Overview," in *African Proconsuls: European Governors in Africa*, ed. L. H. Gann and Peter Duignan (New York: Free Press, 1978), p. 370.
[92] Douglas L. Wheeler, "Portuguese Colonial Governors in Africa, 1870–1974," in *African Proconsuls: European Governors in Africa*, ed. L. H. Gann and Peter Duignan (New York: Free Press, 1978), p. 425.

Developing the Contours of the Colonial State

The practitioners of British and French colonialism were well aware, often to the point of obsession, of just how meekly they had penetrated the vast parts of Africa they had suddenly committed themselves to ruling. Lord Hailey, the great student of British colonialism, noted, for instance, "Every government in Africa has been faced by the initial difficulty of administering an extensive area with a small European staff, frequently ignorant of the local native custom and language."[93] Similarly Delavignette, in many ways the most insightful of the French practitioners, said of the territory that the French had taken over, "The geographical dimensions were large but the density of population was very low. It was in this contrast between the vastness of the territory and the modest size of the population that the administration had to function."[94]

A great deal of ink has been spilled in comparing the British theory of indirect rule through traditional authorities to other types of European colonialism in Africa that depended more on the rule through white officers on the ground ("direct rule"). In theory, European colonialism in Africa could be arrayed across a spectrum from the Portuguese with the most direct system of rule to the famous system of indirect rule theorized by Lugard and practiced at least in northern Nigeria. The French and Belgians were somewhere in between, with the former being more in the direct rule camp and the latter tending more toward the British model.[95]

Reality, as it often has a tendency to do in Africa, always interfered with the theory. For instance, in some British areas, indirect rule meant the appointment of councils of elders whose writ did not extend much beyond a village, while in other areas, it meant the recognition of an already powerful ruler who had authority over hundreds of thousands of people. Sir Philip Mitchell, governor of Buganda from 1935 to 1940, denied that territory was under indirect rule while his successor, Sir Charles Dundas, thought that British relations with the Kabaka were the very model of indirect rule.[96] Similarly, Crowder argues that a central feature of indirect rule was its noninterference with the boundaries of traditional polities, while the French routinely rearranged the land that

[93] Hailey, *An African Survey* (London: Oxford University Press, 1938), pp. 527–8.

[94] Robert Delavignette, "The Territorial Administrator in French Black Africa," in *Robert Delavignette on the French Empire*, ed. Camille Garnier (Chicago: University of Chicago Press, 1977), p. 21.

[95] The typology is developed at some length by Michael Crowder, "The White Chiefs of Tropical Africa," in *Colonialism in Africa, 1870–1960*, ed. L. H. Gann and Peter Duignan, vol. 2 (Cambridge: Cambridge University Press, 1970), pp. 329–36.

[96] D. Anthony Low and R. Cranford Pratt, *Buganda and British Overrule* (Oxford: Oxford University Press, 1960), pp. 163–76.

chiefs governed.[97] However, Barrows reports that in Sierra Leone the British dramatically rearranged the areas individual Mende chiefs controlled.[98] Indirect rule was not a success in Eastern or Western Nigeria, the Gold Coast, Northern Rhodesia (now Zambia), and was not even attempted in Kenya. Indeed, Kirk-Greene finds that even in parts of Northern Nigeria, the *locus classicus* of the theory, colonial precepts were not always followed.[99] It is not a surprise that Djata reports that the French tried both direct and indirect rule in the Middle Niger Valley.[100] The notion of a single-minded colonial approach to ruling Africa is therefore unsupported by the evidence.

Of course, such confusion was probably inevitable, given that so much of "colonial science" was made up in the face of particular exigencies and often by the man on the spot rather than in the colonial capital, much less in Europe. It is important always to remember Hailey summing up French and British colonial theory: "Neither system owes its origin to any preconceived theory of rule."[101] The hallmark of colonial theories was their extreme flexibility at the expense of theory. For instance, the central tenent of the French colonial theory of association was flexibility to meet the particular geographic and ethnic characteristics of the state.[102] In his brilliant lecture on colonial administration, subtitled "*Et Maintenant, Lord Lugard,*" Hubert Jules Deschamps, former governor of the Ivory Coast, noted, "one can scarcely detect the French administrative policy previous to 1945; it differed from yours [Britain's] . . . only in its more familiar style and less clearly defined goals."[103] Such confusion was hardly surprising, given the profound ambivalence with which the Europeans colonized Africa in the first place.

Examining the advent of indirect rule in Northern Nigeria—the supposed model for the rest of British colonial Africa—gives some idea of

[97] Michael Crowder, "Indirect Rule—French and British Style," in *Historical Problems of Imperial Africa*, ed. Robert O. Collins et al. (Princeton: Markus Wiener Publishers, 1994), p. 181.

[98] Walt Barrows, *Grassroots Politics in an African State* (New York: Africana Publishing Company, 1976), p. 79.

[99] Anthony Kirk-Greene, "'Le Roi est mort! Vive le roi!': The Comparative Legacy of Chiefs after the Transfer of Power in British and French West Africa," in *State and Society in Francophone Africa since Independence*, ed. Anthony Kirk-Greene and Daniel Bach (New York: St. Martin's Press, 1995), pp. 19–20.

[100] Sundiata A. Djata, *The Bamana Empire by the Niger : Kingdom, Jihad, and Colonization, 1712–1920* (Princeton: Markus Wiener, 1996), p. 185.

[101] Hailey, *African Survey*, p. 527.

[102] Raymond F. Betts, *Assimilation and Association in French Colonial Theory, 1890–1914* (New York: Columbia University Press, 1961), p. 106.

[103] Hubert Jules Deschamps, "Association and Indirect Rule," in *Historical Problems of Imperial Africa*, ed. Robert O. Collins et al. (Princeton: Markus Wiener Publishers, 1994), p. 172.

how the new conquerors reacted to the central political problem of extending their power. Sir (later Lord) Frederick Lugard—the codifier of indirect rule and without a doubt the most important practitioner of colonialism in Africa—spoke at the dawn of colonial rule during the installation of the Sultan of Sokoto in 1903. He portrayed the British as much as anything as succeeding the old rulers:

> The old treaties are dead, you have killed them. Now these are the words which I, the High Commissioner, have to say for the future. The Fulani in old times under Don Fodio conquered this country. They took the right to rule over it, to levy taxes, to depose kings and to create kings. They in turn have by defeat lost their rule which has come into the hands of the British. All these things which I have said the Fulani by conquest took the right do now pass to the British.[104]

However, rather than hewing closely to an established theory, Lugard justified retaining the old African system of rule as a very practical response to the problems he faced. He argued that "so vast a country, inhabited by many millions, must always be inadequate for complete British administration in the proper sense of the word . . . it was, therefore, imperative to utilise and improve the existing machinery."[105] Lugard himself had no fixed notion as to the extent to which power would be wielded by the Emirs,[106] and much was clearly made up as he went along.

In some ways, the British managed to duplicate many aspects of precolonial rule, including the incomplete domination of the subject population that was inevitable when foreigners tried to rule through local structures. The Africans recognized that the system of indirect rule was, in many ways, a familiar one rather than an invention originating in a grand cultural project Mamdani suggests the British had for their colonial subjects. A. I. Asiwaju summarized what might be called the Ibadan school of historical studies of indirect rule:

> while the white rulers thought of this colonial device [indirect rule] as something they fashioned for their own purpose, the various indigenous African societies thought of it as something that could be adapted and reduced into workable local procedures to serve interests and alliances that both preceded and outlived formal colonial rule in the respective localities. In the particular case of the Yoruba, British Indirect Rule was a most welcome opportunity for

[104] Frederick Lugard, "The Speech at Sokoto," in *The Principles of Native Administration in Nigeria*, ed. A. H. M. Kirk-Greene (London: Oxford University Press, 1965), p. 43.

[105] Frederick Lugard, "Memo no. IX: Native Administration," in *Political Memoranda*, ed. Frederick Lugard (London: Frank Cass and Co., 1970), p. 298.

[106] Mary Bull, "Indirect Rule in Northern Nigeria, 1906–1911," in *Essays in Imperial Government*, ed. Kenneth Robinson and Frederick Madden (Oxford: Basil Blackwell, 1963), p. 50.

specific groups and subgroups to improve their political status vis-à-vis their neighbors; it became a veritable instrument for the continuation of the pre-colonial struggles to impose and resist domination.[107]

The Africans were unimpressed with the extent of the administrative reforms made by the white man. As Alhaji Sir Ahmadu Bello, the Sardauna of Sokoto, noted in his memoirs, "They [the British] made no drastic changes, and what was done came into effect only after consultation. Everything went on more or less as it had done, for what could one Resident, an assistant and a few soldiers in Sokoto do to change so vast an area as Sokoto Emirate?"[108]

The Sinews of Power

However, despite all the caveats, the different theories of colonial rule have had a profound impact on how scholars have viewed the different colonizers. From the perspective of this study, the difference between direct and indirect rule is particularly interesting because the theories suggest very different ways by which the colonial state broadcast power. Unfortunately, while there has been much debate over how much the colonial empires differed from one another, little systematic evidence has been brought to bear. In keeping with the observations of Earl Grey and the Fante who noted the importance of road building in the nineteenth century, I use road density (kilometers of roads per square kilometer) as a way of measuring the colonial ability to broadcast power. When roads finally were built, they, more than railroads or waterways, brought the most profound changes to African society. As the United Nations noted in an early review of African road systems, "Although waterways and railways constitute the main transport routes, roads form a connecting link between them and also with the seaports . . . [roads] serve as the ultimate tentacles which, as further pushed forward, create links between farms and markets and provide access to unexplored areas. It is thus no surprise that roads figured prominently in *Mister Johnson*, a great colonial novel by Joyce Carey,[109] and *The Famished Road*, a classic novel written in the post-independence period by Ben Okri. Okri starts *The Famished Road* in a particularly haunting manner: "In the beginning there was a river. The

---

[107] A. I. Asiwaju, "Indigenization of European Colonialism in Africa: Processes in Yorubaland and Dahomey since 1860," in *Bismarck, Europe, and Africa: The Berlin Africa Conference 1884–1885 and the Onset of Partition*, ed. Stig Förster, Wolfgang J. Mommsen, and Ronald Robinson (London: Oxford University Press, 1988), p. 443.

[108] Alhaji Sir Ahmadu Bello, *My Life* (Cambridge: Cambridge University Press, 1962), p. 19.

[109] Joyce Carey, *Mister Johnson* (London: Michael Joseph, 1961).

river became a road and the road branched out to the whole world. And because the road was once a river it was always hungry."[110]

Unfortunately, surprisingly little attention has been given to roads as a measure of the ability to exert authority. While center-periphery relations were a major topic for modernization theorists, these scholars were more interested in measures that examined changes in identity or overall modernity rather than the extension of the state apparatus.[111] Novelists seem more attuned to how power is really broadcast than those who study political science.

Table 3.1 portrays road density in African colonies in 1935, in 1950, and in 1963. By necessity, data are somewhat sparse but Hailey has a fairly comprehensive collection for the early years. Of course in Africa, a road, very much like beauty, is in the eyes of the beholder. Certainly, what counts as a road in Africa would not necessarily be the same as in Europe. Roads, for the purpose of this study, are defined as anything that could reasonably be said to be able to carry motor traffic at least part of the year (i.e., the dry season).

The overall figures suggest just how unimpressive the colonial extension of power was throughout Africa in the twentieth century. The South African figures are convenient to use as markers because, while that country had large areas that are inhospitable to people and it also had a series of governments that were not intent on serving the African majority, the South African state, having gained independence in 1910, was vitally interested in extending its reach throughout its territory. At the height of the first wave of colonialism in the late 1930s, the figures for all of the colonial possessions already look bleak compared to South Africa. In the following twenty-five years, while there is a significant effort to build some roads in Africa, it is obvious that the colonial reach is nowhere near as impressive as occurs in South Africa. The failure to extend power is hardly surprising given the lack of political or economic incentives to develop true state hegemony.

As expected, there were variations within colonial empires, although the French do not disaggregate their colonial regions to allow for a sensitive analysis. When comparing the different colonial empires, it becomes apparent that the French, despite whatever notions of direct rule they had in theory, were in general less successful in extending their administrative net than the British and, perhaps more surprisingly, probably about as good as the Portuguese in their major colonies. The Belgian effort to extend roads in the Congo, however, is statistically more impressive than what France achieved. Whatever their rhetoric,

---

[110] Ben Okri, *The Famished Road* (Cape Town, South Africa: David Philip, 1992), p. 3.
[111] Barrows, *Grassroots Politics in Sierra Leone*, p. 3.

TABLE 3.1
Road Density in Colonial Africa (Km of Road/Square Km of Land)

Colony	1935	1950	1963
Basotoland	.02	N.A.	.06
Bechuanaland	.001	N.A.	.01
Gambia	.004	.09	.12
Gold Coast	.04	.05	.13
Kenya	.03	.05	.08
Nigeria[a]	.02	.04	.08
Northern Rhodesia	.02	.02	.05
Nyasaland	.06	.07	.11
Sierra Leone	.03	.04	.09
Southern Rhodesia	.04	.06	.19[a]
Swaziland	.11	N.A.	.13
Tanganyika	.02	.04	.04
Uganda	.03	.06	.08
British Empire Average	.02	.04	.09
French Equatorial Africa[b]	.007	.007	.03
French West Africa[c]	.01	.02	.05
French Empire Average	.009	.014	.04
Belgian Congo	.02	.04	.07
Ruanda-Urundi	.10	N.A.	.21[d]
Angola	.02	.03	N.A.
Mozambique	.03	N.A.	N.A.
South Africa	.11	.23	.27[d]

Sources: Road data from Lord Hailey, *An African Survey* (London: Oxford University Press, 1938), pp. 1549–65; International Road Federation, *World Road Statistics 1950* (London: IRF, 1950); United Nations Economic Commission for Africa, *A Survey of Economic Conditions in Africa, 1960–1964* (Addis Ababa: UNECA, 1968), pp. 118–9; Economic Commission for Africa, *A Survey of Economic Conditions in Africa, 1967* (New York: United Nations, 1969), p. 121. Land area from International Road Federation, *World Road Statistics, 1966–1970* (Geneva: IRF, 1971), pp. 11–6 and World Bank, *World Development Report, 1998* (New York: Oxford University Press, 1998), pp. 190–1, 232.

a) Includes British Cameroons

b) Includes Cameroon, Chad, Gabon, Moyen-Congo, Ubangi-Shari (now Central African Republic), but not British Cameroons.

c) Includes Dahomey, Guinea, Ivory Coast, Mali, Mauritania, Niger, Senegal, Upper Volta.

d) Data from 1965

the French started late in their effort to penetrate the African hinterland and critically, never developed the infrastructure to rule directly. As Hailey notes, "In French West Africa roads hardly existed outside certain urban areas in 1914."[112] Subsequently, the French never caught up to the even, slow pace of the British.

The common colonial failure to extend the infrastructure of power probably outweighs whatever differences in colonial practice suggested by the different theories when it comes to the spatial reach of the state. As a prominent French author noted, "In West Africa the differences [between British and French rule] were far less deep than was sometimes imagined. The economic system was the same: the economy was controlled by the same trading monopolies (the Compagnie de l'Ouest Africain, the United Africa Company, and others) and agriculture was left to the 'local peasants.' "[113]

A clear reflection of the inadequacy of the extension of power, via roads or other mechanisms, can be found in the obsession that colonial rulers had with traveling. Because they did not have systems that allowed for a permanent government with a physical presence throughout their territories, colonial officials spent a great deal of time traveling around their territories to bring the state, as it were, to the people. Thus, understanding his limited capabilities, Lugard's scheme for dividing the amalgamated Nigeria into administrative units was based on finding the maximum area an administrator could traverse and "maintain touch with" the population, physical control clearly not being a priority or even an issue.[114] Similarly, Delavignette notes that for the French colonial service, "the art of going on tour" is the "essential principal of ruling. The tour, which could be done by foot, car or horseback, was done to learn what was happening."[115] Van Vollenhoven's comment that "Only one's presence, personal contact, counts. The circular is zero" would be repeated by French colonial administrators until the end of their rule in Africa.[116] The resonance with the Ashanti notion of the perimeters of the state being defined by how far a messenger could walk in a month is palpable.

---

[112] Hailey, *African Survey*, p. 1561.

[113] Suret-Canale, *French Colonialism in Tropical Africa*, p. 348.

[114] Frederick Lugard, "Memorandum on the Administration of Nigeria submitted to the Secretary of State, May 1905," in *Lugard and the Amalgamation of Nigeria*, ed. A. H. M. Kirk-Greene (London: Frank Cass and Co., 1968), p. 211.

[115] Delavignette, *Freedom and Authority in French West Africa*, p. 42.

[116] William B. Cohen, *Rulers of Empire: The French Colonial Service in Africa* (Stanford, CA: Hoover Institution Press, 1971), pp. 63–5.

Exit

Given the European failure to extend power, it is hardly a surprise that migration, the traditional African response to political distress, continued throughout the colonial period. Young, Mamdani, and others who argue for the strength of the colonial state ignore just how great the continuity with precolonial politics was, at least in regard to the major avenue open to Africans disaffected with those who ruled them. While the period of violent protest against colonial rule was brief and snuffed out quickly by superior European firepower in the early part of the twentieth century, Africans continued to subvert the state for many years by simply leaving. During the early colonial period, the presence of open land and weak administrative structures outside the cities made it only natural that many Africans responded to abuses by simply escaping to an area that was not under the direct control of the European power. Thus, Allen F. Isaacman notes that withdrawal was a common response to Portuguese rule in Mozambique. He reports that at times, "entire chieftaincies migrated across national boundaries to avoid Portuguese rule."[117] Similarly, because British colonialism was relatively less oppressive than French rule in West Africa, "massive protest emigrations involving whole villages and townships from the French to the British side of the Nigeria-Dahomey border were common and regular occurrences in Western Yorubaland in the period 1914–1945."[118] Asiwaju goes on to note that,

> Protest migrations were a universal phenomenon in almost all French West African colonies. For example, protest migrations . . . were staged by the Bariba, especially during the rising in French Borgu in 1916, and by the Wolofs from French Senegal to British Gambia. Similar migrations occurred among various ethnic groups moving from French Guinea to both Portuguese Guinea and British Sierra Leone.[119]

In fact, the early colonial period seems to have been the high point of migration in many areas. The abuses of colonial authorities provided incentives for many Africans to migrate but potential barriers, such as borders, were too weak to be real deterrents to people seeking the exit option. There was also a substantial amount of forced migration.[120]

The new migrants apparently had relatively little problem finding land

[117] Allen F. Isaacman, *The Tradition of Resistance in Mozambique: The Zambesi Valley, 1850–1921* (Berkeley: University of California Press, 1976), p. 108.

[118] A. I. Asiwaju, *Western Yorubaland under European Rule, 1889–1945* (London: Longman, 1976), p. 141.

[119] Ibid.

[120] K. C. Zachariah and Julien Condé, *Migration in West Africa: Demographic Aspects* (New York: Oxford University Press, 1981), p. 31.

on which to settle. Asiwaju writes, for instance, that the migrants into British Yorubaland were able to settle on the frontier and establish permanent settlements.[121] In fact, relatively recently in historical time, in many parts of Africa it was easy to move beyond established political authority because, even in states that had established strong central administrative structures, the geographical reach of the centralized political power was extremely limited. For instance, Charles van Onselen describes a "New Nineveh" in the South Africa of the 1890s where a small population could exist separately from the political community on the Witswatersrand by moving a relatively short distance into the hills.[122]

Colonialism's End

The natural progression of colonial rule might well have been to build from the center—where formal control was required by international convention and sheer practicality—outward, so that eventually the entirety of each colony was physically administered by the state. This did not happen for several reasons. First, the colonialists still confronted the traditional African problems: the costs of extending rule turned out to be exceptionally high given limited benefits. Second, events in Europe began to distract the colonial powers in the 1930s until finally the war essentially stopped extension of all administrative systems. As a result, the practice of colonialism before World War II never exceeded the very limited vision formed in the first decade of the twentieth century when Africa was formally conquered. As usual, Frederick Cooper describes the situation deftly,

> The more ambitious projects of colonial conquerors soon proved unrealizable. From roughly the time of World War I to the mid-1930s, France and Great Britain scaled down their ambitions to remake and systematically exploit the African continent, and asserted that their goal was to preserve African societies and culture while permitting only slow changes from within. The much celebrated policy of "indirect rule" . . . represented an attempt to make retreat sound like policy.[123]

Joyce Carey, who published *Mister Johnson* in 1939, describes well the muted ambition of the colonial officials: "No long views—the age for long views ended twenty years ago—and above all, not too much zeal."[124]

[121] Asiwaju, *Western Yorubaland under European Rule*, p. 147.

[122] Charles van Onselen, *New Nineveh*, vol. 2 of *Studies in the Social and Economic History of the Witswatersrand, 1886–1914* (London: Longman, 1982), p. 177.

[123] Frederick Cooper, *Decolonization and African Society: The Labor Question in French and British Africa* (Cambridge: Cambridge University Press, 1996), p. 11.

[124] Carey, *Mister Johnson*, p. 209.

Accordingly, the French were not willing to undertake the costs associated with the politics of assimilation and they abandoned some, but not all, of their goals of making Africans into Frenchmen.[125] Colonial Minister Albert Sarraut in 1932, having already argued that France was not benefiting from its involvement in Africa four decades after Berlin, suggested that France should concentrate on "islands of prosperity" that could be developed for export, primarily along the coast, and that "We can now sketch a map of useful Africa."[126] At about the same time, S. Herbert Frankel, in a critical economic treatise, was calling Africa "a continent of outposts."[127] The Portuguese also only had limited ambitions to penetrate African society. The purpose of the *regime do indigenato* was "fundamentally neither to encourage nor suppress: it was to maintain. The African world in Angola and Moçambique was to exist in a kind of limbo while the Portuguese got on with their job of making a success of white colonial development."[128]

After World War II, it was simply too late to change the power gradients that were the natural result of Berlin. First, the European powers were reconstructing themselves, and therefore hardly had the resources to make a major effort to broadcast power in Africa.[129] The data on road construction displayed in table 3.1 does indicate a significant increase in construction from 1950 to the end of colonialism, but the base was so pathetically low that total road density aggregates are still extremely unimpressive by 1963. Second, although few understood it immediately after World War II, the tidal wave of African nationalism would soon begin, leaving in its wake dozens of independent countries by the early 1960s. Whatever the original colonial administrative project for the 1950s, it quickly became the decade when attention was devoted to, first, forestalling efforts at independence, and then making hurried attempts to prepare colonies for the transfer of power.[130]

Nonhegemonic Rule

To stress the limited and incomplete nature of colonial rule is not to deny its brutality. Indeed, a central feature of colonial rule was violence. In this

---

[125] Crowder, "Indirect Rule—French and British Styles," p. 185.

[126] Cooper, *Decolonization and African Society*, p. 33

[127] S. Herbert Frankel, *Capital Investment in Africa: Its Course and Effects* (London: Oxford University Press, 1938), p. 30.

[128] Duffy, "Portuguese Africa, 1930 to 1960," p. 181.

[129] See, for instance, "The Colonial Empire and the Economic Crisis," circulated in July 1948 to British colonial governors and reprinted in Richard Rathbone, ed., *British Documents on the End of Empire: Ghana*, series B, vol. 1 (London: Her Majesty's Stationary Office, 1992), pp. 90–98.

[130] See, for instance, C. Jeffries, "The Africanisation of the West African Governments," written in March 1943 and reprinted in Rathbone, *British Documents on the End of Empire*, p. 20.

regard, as both Young and Mamdani document at great length, the African colonial state can hardly be likened to an English county government. However, pervasive violence and control should not be confused. The extent of violence was, in many ways, not an indication of control but the result of the very limited presence of administrative structures in many areas outside the major cities. When the colonialists wanted to get something done, they had to use force rather than the regular sinews of government. Phyllis M. Martin, following from Leroy Vail, calls European rule in central Africa, at least before 1920, the "rule of the feeble."[131] The root source of much of the violence that permeated colonial Africa would seem to be in the incomplete nature of European administrative structures on the ground in the African hinterland. After studying cases from the Cameroon, Burnham concludes "the situation could only be altered by a truly radical change, one which succeeded both in completely destroying the permissive social ecology which facilitates population movements as well as one which generated new structures of local-level political control."[132] Burnham suggests that the French did not succeed in making such changes, although they tried to create "natural" villages for the groups who were so mobile.[133]

Nor is it essential to this argument to deny that Europeans often manipulated traditional rule. However, as with the continual resort to violence, the decentralized despotism that Europeans sometimes tried to create was more a sign of weakness than of strength. As Lugard recognized, it was the failure to physically extend the power of the central state apparatus to the rural areas that caused the colonialists to devote attention to manipulating local structures for their own purposes rather than a grand project. However, befitting its status as a second (or third) best strategy, the use of decentralized power did not create hegemony. First, there was no point to creating "hegemony" given the extremely limited colonial interest in most African colonies. For the most part, Europeans only wanted order preserved and their limited economic interests protected. When European rule was challenged during the terminal colonial period, the colonialists would leave rather than fight. In doing so, of course, they were acting like typical African rulers in the precolonial period.

Second, European interest in Africa produced a confused and unsystematic rule that did not in crucial aspects resemble the kind of committed cultural project that Mamdani suggests. If the British could not agree amongst themselves if there was indirect rule in Uganda, how could they be expected to subvert traditional practices in a single-minded

[131] Martin, "The Violence of Empire," p. 8.
[132] Philip Burnham, "'Regroupement' and Mobile Societies: Two Cameroon Cases," *Journal of African History* 16 (1975): p. 593.
[133] Ibid., p. 585.

and competent manner? Such confusion, rather than a systematic determination to rule Africa in a particular way, was the fundamental feature of European colonialism. Robert Heussler concluded for British policy (and undoubtedly for the other Europeans): "There was no overall theme that London stuck to decade by decade, exhorting all of the territories in a uniform way. Often, moreover, it seemed that the influence of colonies on the mother country was more substantial than hers on them."[134] Similarly, the official historian of the colonial office asked what the guiding principles of native administration were during the interwar years and could not find any.[135]

Finally, as David Apter understood before most, the use of traditional authorities over the long-term to administer foreign authority was dysfunctional and led to the destruction of some of the local elites who lost the very basis of their power.[136] The Europeans wanted to use the "existing machinery" but they were not willing to allow the machinery to continually adapt, as it did in the precolonial period, to new political challenges and opportunities. Lugard was aware of what a deleterious effect the system of indirect rule would have on local African authorities: "The advent of Europeans cannot fail to have a disintegrating effect on tribal authority and institutions, and on the conditions of native life. This is due in part to the unavoidable restrictions imposed on the exercise of their power by the native chiefs."[137]

Nowhere is this deadly embrace more evident than in the colonial approach to the extension of traditional authority. In his famous ninth political memorandum, Lugard demanded that colonial officials ignore traditional African practices regarding the mapping of power: "The area over which each Paramount Chief has control will be marked on the map, and no alteration will be made in it except on the Lieutenant-Governor's recommendation, and with the Governor's approval."[138] He had justified this reform in *The Dual Mandate:* "Small and isolated communities, living within the jurisdiction of a chief, but owing allegiance to the chief of their place of origin—a common source of trouble in Africa—should gradually be absorbed into the territorial jurisdiction."[139] It would have been impossible to implement such policies and have African

---

[134] Robert Heussler, "British Rule in Africa," in *France and Britain in Africa*, ed. Prosser Gifford and Wm. Roger Louis (New Haven: Yale University Press, 1971), p. 592.

[135] R. D. Pearce, *The Turning Point in Africa: British Colonial Policy, 1938–48* (London: Frank Cass and Co., 1982), p. 4.

[136] David E. Apter, *Ghana in Transition* (Princeton: Princeton University Press, 1963), p. 151.

[137] Lugard, *The Dual Mandate*, p. 215.

[138] Lugard, "Memo no. IX: Native Administration," p. 312.

[139] Lugard, *The Dual Mandate*, p. 213.

leaders retain their traditional legitimacy because that legitimacy, as explained in chapter two, was derived from their having won control of particular areas or peoples rather than having been assigned them by the whites. Thus, Lord Hailey could write of the African officials the British governed through, "Everywhere the supervision exercised over them must bring home the lesson that the sanction for their authority is no longer the goodwill of their own people, but the recognition accorded to them by the administration."[140]

As a result, there was an extremely mixed record of establishing local authorities. As Peter Geschiere notes in an extraordinary analysis, even in adjoining areas of the same colony, the British and French sometimes succeeded and sometimes failed to establish local agents, depending critically on the adeptness of the white rulers and whether local circumstances favored the new institutions. In other areas of Cameroon, the people continued to have loyalty to authorities whose rule predated the arrival of the whites.[141] Especially given the European ambivalence about ruling Africa and the modest resources they devoted to that task, it is not surprising there were a wide variety of outcomes when the white conquerors tried to co-opt local institutions. Pierre Alexandre describes the outcomes well:

> the diversity of local situations was very great. In one region the customary hierarchy and the imported hierarchy could be reconciled tolerably well . . . In another the customary hierarchy persisted, sometimes underground and sometimes unofficially tolerated, side by side with the white man's chieftaincies or pseudo-chieftaincies . . . Elsewhere the imported hierarchy planted on an anarchical population managed to take root . . . Elsewhere again it proved quite impossible to impose the system.[142]

Terrence Ranger also came to realize that he, or his readers, may have been too dogmatic about the impact of colonialism on local authorities and should have been more appreciative of the diversity of local outcomes in Africa. Ranger would later argue against finding a "single great tradition coming to an end under colonialism" but rather for discovering, "a pluralism both before, during and after colonialism."[143]

---

[140] Hailey, *Africa Survey, 1938*, pp. 539–40.

[141] Peter Geschiere, "Chiefs and Colonial Rule in Cameroon: Inventing Chieftaincy, French and British Style," *Africa* 63 (1993): pp. 166–7.

[142] Pierre Alexandre, "Chiefs, *Commandants*, and Clerks: Their Relationship from Conquest to Decolonisation in French West Africa," in *West African Chiefs: Their Changing Status under Colonial Rule and Independence*, ed. Michael Crowder and Obaro Ikime (New York: Africana Publishing, 1970), p. 39.

[143] Terrence Ranger, "The Invention of Tradition Revisited: The Case of Colonial Africa," in *Legitimacy and the State in Twentieth-Century Africa: Essays in Honour of A. H.*

Conclusion

Rather than centralized or decentralized despotism, the Europeans provided a set of answers to the African problem that allowed them to avoid the costs inherent to hegemony. The cost of extending power beyond the cities and specific highly valuable economic assets such as mines and plantations was still exorbitantly high. The Europeans, whatever their formal theory of rule, were generally unsuccessful in changing cost structures to allow for a systematic expansion of authority into the rural areas. Rather, in a critical example of how the nature of the state system affects the consolidation of authority, the Berlin Conference allowed for a power gradient, whereby formal control was exercised in the cities while authority was highly variable in the rural areas.

Unlike precolonial African leaders, the European proconsuls had created a friendly enough state system so that they could claim formal control over land and people, although their power infrastructures were extremely limited. For the first time in Africa's history, territorial boundaries acquired salience. The common assertion that Africa's boundaries are meaningless because they are arbitrary is wrong. Rather, the boundaries were, in many ways, the most consequential part of the colonial state. The establishment of a territorial grid that was respected by other powers allowed European rulers to be free of competition from other imperial states and enabled them to establish internal administrative structures at a pace that was convenient, given the resources they were willing to deploy. Only the strength of the boundaries allowed the colonialists to have such a mixed record in establishing local authorities. If the boundaries could have been challenged, rule over the hinterland would have had to have been stronger. Osterhammel is correct in arguing that the Europeans established territorial-states, rather than nation-states, in Africa.[144]

Thus, the first critical buffer mechanism that the Europeans created was the physical boundary itself, because the new boundaries successfully mediated pressures from the international system and allowed Europeans to rule on the cheap. As chapters seven and eight show, the creation of a boundary system also allowed for the development of other buffer mechanisms regulating money flows, and, to at least a small degree, the movement of people (during the late colonial period).

The costs of state expansion were still high given the fact that the physical environment was still daunting and the technology and resources

---

M. Kirk-Greene, ed. Terrence Ranger and Olufemi Vaughan (London: Macmillan, 1993), p. 80.

[144] Jürgen Osterhammel, *Colonialism: A Theoretical Overview* (Princeton: Markus Wiener, 1997), p. 68.

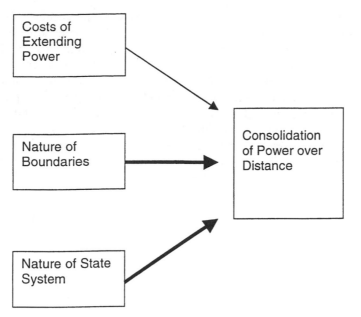

Figure 3.1. Paths to State Consolidation in Colonial Africa

the Europeans were willing to deploy were limited. However, the new state system and the establishment of at least one important buffer mechanism significantly reduced some of the effective costs of state consolidation. Figure 3.1 graphically displays the notion that the boundaries and the state system were the major avenues by which the colonial state was consolidated. The physiology of the colonial state was therefore different in some important respects compared to what was found in precolonial Africa. However, in terms of how leaders actually ruled, the colonial state still shared important similarities with many precolonial systems. In particular, only core areas continued to be ruled through formal means. Beyond the core, the whites continued the tradition of having very weak formal structures of rule. The primary reason for the continuation of so many precolonial practices was that while the state system created at Berlin allowed for absolute external sovereignty (the protection from encroachment by other powers), it did not provide states much assistance with the tasks of actually ruling over internal areas. Inevitably given the same geography, colonial rulers turned to some of the practices that precolonial leaders had devised. However, over the long-term, the colonial design was, as was eventually recognized, a problematic solution because Europeans were not willing to allow the old African practice of continual change in the nature and size of the units—critical responses to the problems posed by low population densities—to continue.

If precolonial Africa was a time when fictions of rule were not allowed, European colonialism was a combination of domestic administrative structures and a state system that went to elaborate lengths to uphold the notion that Europeans were actually ruling Africa. European rule was no fiction. Colonialism was marked by extreme violence, the development of new economic systems, and fundamental changes in many social practices as foreign languages, religions, and ideologies were introduced. However, neither was the case that the Europeans had established states that actually sought to rule over all the territories that were indeed said to be theirs. That would be the stated ambition of their African successors.

Four

The Political Kingdom in Independent Africa

> The new nations of the African continent are
> emerging today as the result of their struggle for
> independence. This struggle for freedom from
> foreign domination is a patriotic one which
> necessarily leaves no room for difference.
>   Julius K. Nyerere, "The African and Democracy,"

AFTER GAINING INDEPENDENCE in the early 1960s, African leaders were faced with an exquisite dilemma. They recognized that the states that emerged from Berlin were artificial and did not, in many cases, actually rule their putative nations other than through the use of exceptional violence. Yet, if the states, with their colonial power gradients, were to change, the new leaders would have to give up many of the newly tasted benefits of power and face considerable uncertainty about their own fate and the fate of their nations. In a rare instance of not muddling through on a question of monumental importance, the Africans decided early and decisively that the colonial map should be retained.

As a result, postindependence African leaders were faced with the problem of how to extend power over their territories given the incomplete and highly variable administrative systems they inherited from the Europeans. Following their colonial predecessors, the new leaders decided against gaining control of African territory through wars of expansion or by claiming control of territory on the basis of the administrative facts on the ground. At the same time, despite much rhetoric about recovering the African past, the new leaders rejected the entire precolonial tradition of multiple sovereignties over land with soft borders. Instead, Africa's leaders devised a set of domestic and international strategies that, much as during the colonial rule, gave maximum flexibility to the leaders when deciding how to expand the actual geographic reach of the state while formally preventing any outside challenge to their territorial control. Therefore, the particular international system and domestic institutions that African countries erected have had profound effects on the ability of the state to consolidate authority, either by collecting taxes or by developing bonds of loyalty through nationalism, which are still apparent four decades after independence.

The critical question unresolved in the literature is the degree to which power practices actually changed at independence. Jackson's well-known view is that the dramatic change at independence was in the nature of sovereignty. He has argued that starting with the famous Harold Macmillan "wind of change speech" in 1960, "empirical statehood went rapidly into eclipse" and a new form of juridical statehood based on a "rights-model of international relations" became dominant. In the new model of international relations, epitomized by United Nations' General Assembly Resolution 2621, states no longer had to earn sovereignty (through the establishment of a national government that could enforce its authority) but deserved it, simply on the basis of being decolonized.[1] There is no doubt that there were changes in international practices surrounding the decolonization process and Jackson is right to highlight them. However, this analysis of power consolidation suggests that, at least in some ways, there were important continuities from the Berlin rules to the modern era that often are ignored.

This chapter explores what is, in many ways, the most revolutionary aspect of Africa's independence: the attempt to build a large number of states during peace. It devotes special attention to the boundaries and state system that the Africans constructed for themselves. Finally, the chapter explores the relative peace that resulted from the decisions made by Africans and how, ironically, the seeds of some countries' destruction were planted in the actions taken by leaders as a consequence of these early decisions.

Units and Boundaries

Many similarities existed between the wave of decolonization, which began with Ghana's independence in 1957, and the process of colonization formalized by the Berlin Conference in 1885. Independence occurred at a time and speed that all of the protagonists, notably the Africans, never expected, much like the colonization of Africa was a shock to all concerned. In both processes, there was almost no attention given to the viability of the units being created. And, perhaps most importantly, after the deed was done, the international community, led by the protagonists, had to create law to justify what had been accomplished and to prevent the new arrangements from being torn asunder by war.

African leaders at independence confronted the states as demarcated by

---

[1] Jackson, "The Weight of Ideas in Decolonization: Normative Change in International Relations," pp. 117, 125.

the Europeans and, at times acting unilaterally and at times collectively, actually made two sets of interrelated decisions: to retain the nation-state as the exclusive unit of organization and to retain the boundaries that the white colonizers had drawn. Although passing reference often is made to the problematic geography of many African states, the particular decisions the early leaders made regarding national design are so fundamental that many analyses of African politics simply begin with an examination of the dramas of domestic politics, as if the design of the stage was irrelevant and no other configuration was possible.[2] This is a significant analytic error, as chapter five will demonstrate, because decisions regarding national design inevitably affected the options available to African leaders on a host of domestic policy issues.

The Nation-State as Organizing Principle

As chapter two documents, in precolonial Africa, a wide variety of political organizations—villages, city-states, nation-states, empires—rose and fell. However, at independence, African leaders turned their backs on this diversity of forms. While borrowing the names of great states from Africa's past (e.g., Benin, Ghana, Mali),

> the educated elites in West Africa—for a long time, it would be much the same in South Africa—saw Africa's own history as irrelevant and useless . . . when it came down to brass tacks, to the question of who should take over from the British when the British withdrew, they demanded a more or less complete flattening of the ethnic landscape.[3]

The retention of the European nation-state was encouraged and welcomed by Africans. Even as trenchant a critic of colonialism as Ghanaian Professor A. Adu Boahen could note that one of the positive aspects of European rule was the creation of new states with clearly defined (albeit inappropriate) boundaries in place of "the existing innumerable lineage and clan groups, city-states, kingdoms, and empires without any fixed boundaries."[4]

In the early 1960s (or now, for that matter), there were few intellectual sentiments that could effectively counter the draw of the nation-state.

[2] Thus, Mazrui could argue that traditionalism was a strong theme in African politics but only examine the retention of traditional leaders such as the kabaka of Buganda, and largely ignoring the rejection of traditional African notions of boundaries and how power was to be demarcated. Ali A. Mazrui, *Africa's International Relations: The Diplomacy of Dependency and Change* (London: Heinemann, 1977), pp. 35–6.

[3] Davidson, *Black Man's Burden*, pp. 102–3.

[4] A. Adu Boahen, *African Perspectives on Colonialism* (Baltimore: Johns Hopkins University Press, 1987), p. 95.

For instance, much of the pan-African movement that sporadically erupted during the twentieth century was based in the West Indies and the United States and did not even have a vision for a postcolonial Africa, much less one that could move beyond the European nation-state. Of the great pan-African Congresses held in the twentieth century, only the fifth, convened in Manchester, England, in October 1945, had significant African representation that might have led to innovative thinking about national design in Africa.[5] However, as colonialism ended, Africa's new leaders did not see foresee an organizing principle for politics other than the nation-state. An examination of the writings of the African nationalists the colonial empires found particularly radical—Kenyatta, Lumumba, Machel, Mugabe, Touré—reveals no desire for any alternative to the state as theorized and designed by the Europeans.[6]

Further, when decolonization happened, it came so quickly and Africans were so intent on seizing power that there was neither the time nor the motivation to develop whole new concepts about the method of national political organization. As a U.S. government intelligence assessment correctly noted in 1961, "The problems of political survival and of maintenance of law and order have kept African leaders from concentrating on their interrelationships."[7]

The international embrace of the nation-state was also an important element in the rapid African rejection of any indigenous alternative. First, the nation-state was seen as the very essence of modernity by nationalists (e.g., Mao, Nehru, Ho) who were part of the post-WWII revolutionary movement that led, for the first time, to one type of political organization having a practical monopoly on organizing political activity across the globe. Second, the United Nations and its related organizations (including the World Bank, the International Monetary Fund, UNICEF, and the World Health Organization) created an extraordinarily powerful template that molded international society by recognizing only nation-states as legitimate actors in the international community. In particular, membership in the General Assembly, the essential gateway to sovereignty, was open to any nation-state that gained independence but was not available to any other form of organization. Thus, exceptionally

---

[5] W. E. B. Du Bois, *The World and Africa* (New York: Viking Press, 1947), p. 244.

[6] See Jomo Kenyatta, *Facing Mt. Kenya* (New York: Vintage Books, 1965); Patrice Lumumba, *Congo, My Country* (New York: Frederick A. Praeger, 1962); Robert Mugabe, *Our War of Liberation* (Gweru, Zimbabwe: Mambo Press, 1983); Barry Munslow, ed., *Samora Machel: An African Revolutionary* (London: Zed Books, 1985); Ahmed Sékou Touré, *Strategy and Tactics of the Revolution* (Conakry, Guinea: Press Office, 1978).

[7] Central Intelligence Agency, "The Probable Relationships of the Independent African States," in *Foreign Relations of the United States: Africa, 1961–1963*, ed. Nina Davis Howland (Washington, DC: Government Printing Office, 1995), p. 299.

small states such as Lesotho, Gambia, and Guinea-Bissau can be members of the General Assembly, but larger units like the Zulu or Ashanti groups, which were previously organized as empires, cannot. This is not merely a debating detail, as membership in international organizations provided important financial benefits that were denied to other forms of organization.[8]

The momentum the nation-state developed was so great that even those who were legitimately committed to true Pan-African structures saw their efforts come to nothing. For instance, Julius K. Nyerere, shortly before becoming Tanganyika's first prime minister, advocated that all of East Africa gain independence simultaneously so that the region could retain the institutions of unity that had been created by the East African Federation. Nyerere, presciently, warned that if each country in East Africa gained independence separately, "the feeling of unity which now exists could . . . be whittled away" as interests reified around the old boundaries.[9] In contrast, Kwame Nkrumah, the most publicly fervent pan-Africanist, argued that it was critical for Ghana to gain independence first and then the elaborate panoply of pan-African structures he envisioned could come into place.

In fact, Nyerere's more pessimistic view of African leaders was correct and Nkrumah's optimism about the willingness of his colleagues to place Africa before their own new countries (however artificial they might be) was misplaced. As Sylvanus Olympio, Togo's first leader, noted in a moment of bitter insight, "political unification is only desired by those political leaders who believe they could come out on top in such unions."[10] Mazrui is thus wrong to blame the "West" for the imposition of rigidly defined national states on Africa.[11] In fact, this is exactly what African leaders decided would be best for their countries and themselves, despite the fact that the colonially inspired units were so at odds with the traditional African practices that had evolved to meet the challenges of low population densities.

So complete was the desire to retain the design of the national units that much of the *internal* colonial apparatus was also retained. As Delavignette notes,

---

[8] On the tendency of international systems to favor like units, see Hendrik Spruyt, "Institutional Selection in International Relations: State Anarchy as Order," *International Organization* 48 (Autumn 1994): p. 546.

[9] Julius K. Nyerere, *Freedom and Unity* (Oxford: Oxford University Press, 1967), p. 85.

[10] Sylvanus Olympio, "Reflections on Togolese and African Problems," in *Africa Speaks*, ed. James Duffy and Robert A. Manners (Princeton: D. Van Nostrand, 1961), p. 75.

[11] Ali Mazrui, "Africa Entrapped: Between the Protestant Ethic and the Legacy of Westphalia," in *The Expansion of International Society*, ed. Hedley Bull and Adam Watson (Oxford: Clarendon Press, 1984), p. 289.

[T]he independence movement maintained the same administrative core as had existed during the colonial epoch. Only the names were changed: the circle was now called the department, and the *commandant de cercle*, the prefect . . . On the eve of independence, French Black Africa had 500-odd basic administrative circumscriptions consisting of circles and subdivisions. The independent republics in 1960 had 576 in all . . . The machinery had changed hands but not the parts.[12]

Critically, there were very few attempts to change the location of the capital as designated by the Europeans to a place that would either be more logical for the administration of the country or would signify a reversion back to precolonial practices. The few countries that did try to move capitals have had very mixed experiences. Malawi relocated to Lilongwe from Zomba after independence, but largely because South Africa financed the project due to the gratitude the white government felt to Hastings Banda for continuing diplomatic relations. Nigeria has moved some offices from Lagos to Abuja but financial problems have caused delays of many years in the timetable. Tanzania's move from Dar es Salaam to Dodoma and Côte d'Ivoire's relocation from Abidjan to Yamoussoukro have gone so slowly that diplomatic offices remain in the old capital.[13] More often than not, old precolonial centers—including Ibadan, Kumasi, Masvingo (the site of old Zimbabwe)—have either been ignored or are seen as competing for loyalty with the (colonially inspired) national capital.

What is most noticeable about the international relations of early African independence is that all of the supranational arrangements, which actually seemed to be divergences from the sovereign nation-state as inherited from the Europeans, failed. The Mali Federation, the East African Federation, the aborted Ghana-Guinea-Mali Union, and "Senegambia" all either did not get off the ground or rather quickly crashed, precisely because they challenged the domestic authority exercised by political elites.[14] Africa is also littered with the carcasses of failed economic unions (e.g., the Economic Community of West African States), and the volumes planning putative continental organizations that were never realized are legion. Thus, the 1980 *Lagos Plan of Action*, the apotheosis of the Organization of African Unity's (OAU) desire to create pan-African institutions, asked for the creation of an African Economic Community, supported by an African Monetary Fund and an African Mutual

---

[12] Delavignette, *Freedom and Authority in French West Africa*, p. 276.

[13] D. Pfaff, "The Capital Cities of Africa with Special Reference to New Capitals Planned for the Continent," *Africa Insight* 18 (1988): p. 193.

[14] Claude E. Welch Jr., *Dream of Unity: Pan-Africanism and Political Unification in West Africa* (Ithaca: Cornell University Press, 1966), p. 356.

Guarantee and Solidarity Fund.[15] Of course, none was even attempted because the hopeful architects of these new creations, like the planners of many aborted groupings, could not offer leaders significant enough incentives to abdicate even small bits of power. The regional organizations failed, despite the fact that many donors were sympathetic to them, because Africa's political fragmentation made aid to individual countries problematic.[16]

Boundary Maintenance

Once it was clear that the European nation-state would serve as the organizing principle for African politics, it was probably inevitable that African leaders would decide to retain the boundaries as created by the colonialists. In the early 1960s, the founding members of the OAU faced the same problems that the colonialists did when they came to power. Again, the demography, ethnography, and topography of Africa made it extremely difficult for new, more "rational" borders to be established. The African nationalists did not advocate returning to precolonial practices because they knew that precolonial practices had nothing to offer them when thinking of how to rearrange "Kenya" or "Guinea." Precisely because precolonial states were not organized on a territorial basis, they could have little resonance in a world organized around hard boundaries.

Similarly, the new leaders had no interest in organizing boundaries around actual territorial control. As noted in chapter three, the colonial state apparatus that had been inherited did not provide for true panterritorial rule and the newly independent states had not had time to expand their administrative nets. As a result, basing boundaries on what each state actually controlled would result in the territory of most states becoming smaller. Further, much of the continent would have to experience a long period of profound uncertainty as administrative presence and territorial claims were, somehow, correlated.

African leaders were also unwilling to resort to war as a way of determining boundaries because the leaders recognized at the onset that violent redrawing of boundaries would threaten their own positions. The partition of the Indian subcontinent in 1947 had provided an astonishingly vivid warning of the human cost of boundary change, especially

[15] Organization of African Unity, *Lagos Plan of Action for the Economic Development of Africa, 1980–2000* (Geneva: International Institute for Labour Studies, 1982), pp. 87, 126.

[16] See, for instance, a paper prepared by the U. S. State Department's Policy Planning Council, "Selected Aspects of U.S. Economic Aid Policy for Africa," in *Foreign Relations of the United States: Africa, 1961–1963,* ed. Nina Davis Howland (Washington, DC: Government Printing Office, 1995), p. 296.

since Africa's leaders were conscious of how peaceful the transfer of power had been.[17] In any case, even if a new state had the desire to change its borders, it probably could not have done so because the armies inherited by the post-independence leaders were generally little more than mechanized police forces.[18]

As a result, among the first acts of the Organization of African Unity was to eliminate any hope that the idea explicit in its name could actually be realized. In particular, the OAU's 1964 resolution on border problems pledged member states, "to respect the frontiers existing on their achievement of national independence."[19] Thus, there was an almost immediate determination that the OAU Charter, written in 1963 and demanding (article III, paragraph 3) the, "Respect for the sovereignty and territorial integrity of each State and for its inalienable right to independent existence"[20] meant the states as mapped by the Europeans.

Therefore, African boundaries have been almost unchanged since independence; the only significant deviation was the secession of Eritrea from Ethiopia. However, even this development was, especially from the perspective of the Eritreans, to a significant degree a question of decolonization rather than secession. Most of the interstate conflicts in Africa that have occurred were not, as in Europe, wars of conquest that threatened the existence of other states, but conflicts over lesser issues that were resolved without threatening the existence of another state. For instance, Tanzania invaded Uganda in 1979 to overthrow Idi Amin, not to annex Uganda. Even South Africa's destabilization efforts against its neighbors in the 1980s were primarily attempts to influence the policies of the majority-ruled countries, not to change the borders of the region. Lesotho or Swaziland would not exist today if South Africa had any real territorial ambitions. Similarly, in the bloody wars over Zaire/Democratic Republic of the Congo in the late 1990s, there was a continued recognition of the old boundaries. For instance, in 1998, Rwanda and Uganda decided to try to oust Laurent Kabila and replace him with a more manageable puppet in order to have their security concerns addressed. They did not try to simply seize territory in eastern D.R.O.C. and declare that their states had grown, even though this would have been far easier than re-

[17] This view is identified and praised by the International Court of Justice in *Frontier Dispute (Burkina Faso/Republic of Mali), Judgment, I. C. J. Reports 1986*, pp. 566–7.

[18] Walter L. Barrows, "Changing Military Capabilities in Black Africa," in *Arms and the African*, ed. William Foltz and Henry Bienen (New Haven: Yale University Press, 1985), p. 101.

[19] Organization of African Unity, "O.A.U. Resolution on Border Disputes, 1964," in *Basic Documents on African Affairs*, ed. Ian Brownlie (Oxford: Clarendon Press, 1971), p. 361.

[20] Organization of African Unity, "Charter of the O.A.U.," in *Basic Documents on African Affairs*, p. 3.

placing the government in far-away Kinshasa. In the few conflicts that did have the potential to threaten fundamentally the existence of states— Somalia's attempt to invade Ethiopia in the 1970s and Libya's war against Chad in the 1970s and 1980s—the aggressor did not succeed.

The growth and structure of African militaries are indicative of the relative peace that they have experienced on their external borders for most of the postindependence period. African armies expanded rapidly after independence and took roughly fifteen years to reach maturity. In 1963, at the dawn of independence, the average African army had 0.73 soldiers for every thousand people. By 1979, that figure had more than quadrupled to 3.10 soldiers per thousand citizens. The size of African armies then began to decrease so that by the mid-1990s, there were only two soldiers per thousand citizens across the continent.[21] African armies are, by comparative standards, small. In 1994, African countries had on average only 57 percent as many soldiers per thousand citizens as the average developing country (2 versus 3.5).[22] In a stunning indication of how little security concerns have affected state actions, African governments cut defense spending disproportionately when they were forced to reduce spending.[23] One of the primary reasons for coups in Africa and the rest of the third world is that soldiers have so little to do. As a result, they seek to carve out a role for themselves in politics.[24]

Thus, the vision in much of the international relations literature of states emeshed in some kind of Hobbesian struggle in a merciless international environment really has very little resemblance to Africa as ruled by the colonialists or Africans. In particular, the realist view of the world is problematic in systems where the use of force between units is not a serious concern.[25] In Europe, as noted in chapter one, there was a long period where open conflict and hostility was the norm but this was due to the presence of a very particular set of geographic and demographic facts. In particular, a defining feature of European international relations was the ceaseless struggle for territory. As a result of this difficult environ-

[21] Calculated from Donald George Morrison, Robert Cameron Mitchell, and John Naber, *Black Africa: A Comparative Handbook*, 2nd ed. (New York: Paragon House, 1989), pp. 167–8; and U. S. Arms Control and Disarmament Agency, *World Military Expenditures and Arms Transfers 1985* (Washington, DC: ACDA, 1985), p. 47; and ACDA, *World Military Expenditures and Arms Transfers 1995* (Washington, DC: ACDA, 1995), p. 54.

[22] ACDA, *World Military Expenditures and Arms Transfers 1995*, pp. 53–4.

[23] Mark Gallagher, "Government Spending in Africa: A Retrospective," *Journal of African Economies* 3 (April 1994): pp. 86–7.

[24] Talukder Maniruzzaman, *Military Withdrawal from Politics: A Comparative Study* (Cambridge: Ballinger Publishing Co., 1987), pp. 114–5.

[25] Robert Powell, "Anarchy in International Relations Theory: The Neorealist/Neoliberal Debate," *International Organization* 48 (Spring 1994): p. 333.

ment, Tilly estimates that the "enormous majority" of states in Europe failed.[26] Even those that survived changed frequently, given the hostility of their environments. For instance, it took between three and five hundred years for the modern French frontier to be established.[27]

However, all of Africa's weak states have survived. Neither the colonial nor the independent state system that have, successively, defined international relations in Africa since 1885 have been hostile to weak states. Rather, both systems have been highly organized and designed to protect the frontiers of countries who could not necessarily defend themselves. While there are many reasons for the relative lack of international war, the fact that territorial competition was not a significant motivation for either the colonialists or the rulers of independent Africa undoubtedly has been a significant factor. For instance, the security dilemma—the notion that each state's effort to become more secure threatens another state—is rooted in a world where armies had to be massed on frontiers in order to protect territory. Thus, Kenneth Waltz notes that, "contact generates conflict and at times issues in violence."[28] Without having to compete for territory, Africans could devise rules by which all could become more secure.

THE END OF SELF-DETERMINATION

One implication of the OAU's solution to the boundary problems faced by the African countries was, as the quote from Nyerere at the beginning of this chapter indicates, to effectively quash the right of self-determination. This right, which all African nationalists had relied upon during the fight to gain independence, posed an extraordinary threat to the leaders of the newly independent countries because it implied that the many disgruntled minorities in these countries had a legal right to destroy the territorial integrity of their states through secession. Of course, self-determination via secession was also the traditional African manner of resolving disputes in many parts of the continent. While the OAU Charter recognizes "the inalienable right to all people to control their own destiny," the OAU Principles are designed to promote the rights of states rather than individuals. The first three items of the principles (in article 3 of the Charter) affirm sovereign equality of all member states, noninter-

[26] Charles Tilly, "Reflections on the History of European State-Making," in *The Formation of National States in Western Europe*, ed. Charles Tilly (Princeton: Princeton University Press, 1975), p. 38.

[27] Malcolm Anderson, *Frontiers: Territory and State Formation in the Modern World* (Cambridge, U.K.: Polity Press, 1996), p. 23.

[28] Kenneth Waltz, *Theory of International Politics* (Reading, MA: Addison-Wesley, 1979), p. 103. See also Robert Jervis, "Cooperation under the Security Dilemma," *World Politics* 30 (October 1977): pp. 168–9.

ference in the internal affairs of member states, and respect for the states' sovereignty and territorial integrity.[29] Self-determination was deemed only to apply to those countries that were still colonies or that were still under white minority control.

The effective elimination of the right to self-determination after independence has occasionally been challenged in Africa. Undoubtedly, the most important protest was the recognition accorded by Tanzania and several other states to the rebel Biafran regime during the Nigerian Civil War (1967–1970). The government of Tanzania said that it understood the need for Africa to prevent the disintegration of existing states. However, it was compelled to go against existing norms because "Africa has watched the massacre of tens of thousands of people, has watched the employment of mercenaries of both sides in the current civil war, and has accepted repeated rebuffs of its offers to help by mediation or conciliation."[30] President Nyerere argued that, "the people must feel that this State, or this Union, is theirs; and they must be willing to have their quarrels in that context. Once a large number of the people of any such political unit stop believing that the State is theirs, and that the Government is their instrument, then the unit is no longer viable."[31] The OAU rejected these sentiments and, in 1967, reaffirmed its respect for the sovereignty and territorial integrity of Nigeria and other African states; condemned attempts at secession anywhere in Africa; and proclaimed that the Nigerian Civil War was an internal affair.[32]

Similarly, the right to Eritrean self-determination was never recognized, despite the fact that the Eritreans had an excellent case for self-rule based on the abrogation of international agreements by successive governments in Addis Ababa and despite the fact that the Eritreans had physical control over at least some of the land they claimed. Instead, Eritrea only was recognized as an independent state once a military victory was won over the government in Addis Ababa, the traditional way that international society has recognized new states.[33]

The project of defeating any internal attempts at rearranging boundaries was undoubedly helped by the strong balance of force in favor of the state compared to African societies. In the early 1960s, while armies

[29] Organization of African Unity, "Charter of the OAU," pp. 2–3.

[30] Government of Tanzania, "Tanzania Recognizes Biafra," in *Crisis and Conflict in Nigeria: A Documentary Sourcebook, 1966–1970*, ed. A. H. M. Kirk-Greene, vol. 2 (London: Oxford University Press, 1971), p. 208.

[31] Julius K. Nyerere, "Why We Recognized Biafra," in ibid., p. 211.

[32] Organization of African Unity, "OAU Resolution on the Situation in Nigeria, 1967," in *Basic Documents on African Affairs*, ed. Ian Brownlie (Oxford: Clarendon Press, 1971), p. 364.

[33] James Crawford, *The Creation of States in International Law* (Oxford: Clarendon Press, 1979), p. 262.

were weak, almost all the guns that were available in Africa were controlled security forces. Power being a relative concept, African states were thus in the most important way classically Weberian because they had a monopoly on the use of force throughout most of their territories.

A FRIENDLY INTERNATIONAL SYSTEM

Several developments at the international level helped African leaders in their effort to continue the inherited state system. First, the Cold War had the effect of providing African countries with patrons when their boundaries were challenged internally or externally. The superpowers were concerned with cultivating clients in all parts of the world and therefore were willing to help African nations crush ethnic rebellions or threats from neighbors. A secret 1963 U.S. document argued that an important U. S. interest, right after keeping Africa free of communists, was "to restrain violence in general and preserve the present territorial order as the most feasible alternative to chaos."[34] Thus, Zaire won crucial aid from the U. S. in turning back the Shaba rebellions; Chad relied on France to retain its territorial integrity in the face of Libyan aggression; and Ethiopia was given critical military support by the Soviet Union in order to resist Somalia's irredentist claims. During the Cold War, the superpowers were actually exceptionally attentive to African sensibilities concerning boundary maintenance. Indeed, despite continual meddling throughout the continent, not once did either superpower, or any other outside power, offer significant support to an African effort to overturn an existing boundary. This deference continued after 1989. For instance, when President Kabila was threatened by a rebellion in eastern D.R.O.C. in 1998, the U.S. immediately said that it wanted, "the Government in Kinshasa to be in a position to control its territory" and therefore "believe[d] strongly in the territorial integrity of the Democratic Republic of the Congo,"[35] in spite of the compelling evidence that such integrity did not exist on the ground.

In particular, the international community embraced the goal of boundary stability established by the OAU to effectively prevent the application of the norm of self-determination to a group of people once their country has become independent.[36] For example, in the case of a border dispute be-

---

[34] "The Strategic Importance of Africa," in *Foreign Relations of the United States: Africa, 1961–1963*, ed. Nina Davis Howland (Washington, DC: Government Printing Office, 1995), p. 331.

[35] Steven Erlanger, "U. S. Sees Rwandan Role in Congo Revolt," *New York Times*, 5 August 1998, p. A8.

[36] Gino J. Naldi, "The Case Concerning the Frontier Dispute (Burkina Faso/Republic of

tween Mali and Burkina Faso, the International Court of Justice stated explicitly that because African states had decided to retain the colonial boundaries, the practices of the region must be respected despite the apparent conflict with the principle of the right to self-determination.[37] More generally, the world community has allowed any country, no matter how underdeveloped its political and economic institutions, to enjoy the full privileges of sovereignty. Thus, a late Eisenhower administration document on Africa recognized that while many West African countries were "sorely lacking in both human and economic resources, this fact does not and will not slow the drive toward self-government and independence." The document noted with approval the desire for African countries to be "accepted as equals and be treated with dignity and respect," sentiments that were to be operationalized partially by membership in the United Nations.[38]

Allocating Legitimacy

While the state system designed by the Africans managed to preserve the units and boundaries as designed by the colonialists, politics at the domestic level quickly demonstrated signs of significant instability, as a large number of governments voted into power in the early 1960s either were overthrown by their own militaries or the leaders themselves moved to fundamentally alter the systems in order to reduce the level of political competition. Some countries (including Ethiopia, Congo, and Ghana) also faced insurgencies of varying strengths that sometimes had physical control of territories far from the capital. Thus, African politics were the exact opposite of traditional political science models of domestic and international politics: the politics between countries was extremely well-ordered (as opposed to the Hobbesian model of international relations) while domestic politics did not evidence many signs of stability.[39] African leaders were therefore forced to develop a set of decision rules that would indicate who was actually in charge of the states that were assumed to be permanent and that could not be interfered with.

Mali): *Uti Possidetis* in an African Perspective," *International and Comparative Law Quarterly* 36 (October 1987): pp. 901–2.

[37] International Court of Justice, *Case Concerning the Frontier Dispute (Burkina Faso/ Republic of Mali)*, p. 567.

[38] National Security Council, "Statement of U. S. Policy toward West Africa," in *Foreign Relations of the United States: Africa, 1958–1960*, ed. Harriet Dashiell Schwar and Stanley Shaloff (Washington, D.C.: Government Printing Office, 1992), p. 117.

[39] See Robert H. Jackson and Carl G. Rosberg, "Why Africa's Weak States Persist," *World Politics* 35 (October 1982): pp. 23–4.

This problem came to a head with the first coup in West Africa when Togolese president Olympio was killed in a military revolt on 13 January 1963. There was significant sentiment to condemn the coup because African leaders were obviously afraid that the same fate might be visited upon them. However, after a brief period of ostracism, Togo was allowed to reenter normal diplomatic relations with other African countries and to sign the Charter of the Organization of African Unity.[40] While the OAU Charter does (article III, paragraph 5) offer "unreserved condemnation, in all its forms of political assassination," leaders were not willing to make judgments about the legitimacy of governments. As Boutros-Ghali noted, there was no attempt similar to the Central American effort (the so-called Tobar Doctrine) to not recognize governments that had come to power via forceful means.[41]

Instead, the OAU established a decision-making rule that preserved African borders and prevented any kind of external competition while requiring only minimal levels of effective domestic sovereignty. To do so, the OAU said, in effect, that if an African government is in control of the capital city, then it has the legitimate right to the full protection offered by the modern understanding of sovereignty. Thus, Olympio's killers were recognized as the legitimate government of Togo because they controlled Lomé, not because they were perceived by the Togolese as legitimate or because they physically controlled the territory of the country. As a result, even if an African country did not have physical control over its own territory, by the rules of the international community, it could not be challenged by other domestic groups or by outsiders. In fact, large countries such as Ethiopia, Zaire, and Angola at various times did lose control of parts of their territories to opponents but the international community always recognized whoever controlled Addis, Kinshasa, and Luanda as the unquestioned leaders of those territories. Thus, Mobutu was recognized as the ruler of Zaire even though he controlled little more than Kinshasa and its environs for the last years of his rule and continued to be recognized as the leader while the forces of Laurent Kabila marched through the country in late 1996 and early 1997. Kabila was only recognized as the legitimate ruler when he captured Kinshasa on 17 May 1997. As William J. Foltz notes, the rule reflects the reality that, "the greatest point in common among those who attend OAU

---

[40] See "No More African Groups," *West Africa*, 1 June 1963, p. 597.

[41] Tobar, foreign minister of Ecuador, set down a principle in 1907 declaring that a state should not recognize a foreign government that comes to power by regicide, popular rebellion, or coup d'etat. This doctrine was included in the 1907 Washington Convention, ratified by five Central American states, and by the 1923 Washington Convention, ratified by the same states. Boutros Boutros-Ghali, "The Addis Ababa Charter," *International Conciliation* 546 (January 1964): pp. 28–9.

summits is that they control capital cities."[42] Indeed, the Charter of the OAU begins, "We, the Heads of African and Malagasy States and Governments" while the UN charter starts with "We, the Peoples of the United Nations." As a result, Boutros-Ghali detected early on the trend toward an "Africa of Heads of State."[43]

This decision rule was popular with the international community. Physical control of the capital (still usually located on the coast) is the easiest indication of political presence for outsiders to discern. It would have been far more difficult for the international community to have recognition rest on measures of popular support or administrative presence throughout a country. Finally, states have relations with other states. The OAU decision rule that territorial control or popular legitimacy was irrelevant therefore meshed nicely with the operational code of international diplomacy.

The Organization of African Unity thus offered a very clear guide to the geographic nature of power gradients after independence. The center, essentially the capital city, has to be controlled but the degree of authority outside the capital could be highly variable. The African leaders were then free to extend their rule throughout their territories as they found convenient. The resemblance between the rule of control of the capitals and the Berlin rules is not accidental. Control of the capital is the analogue to the minimal level of government presence that the Europeans first defined at the Berlin Conference. As with the Berlin rules, the Addis rules (if they can be so named after the city where the OAU charter was signed), allowed the continent to continue to be demarcated in a way that most of the protagonists would agree is irrational while preventing any external challenge to rule. Thus, while Jackson is right that the admission of African states to the community of sovereign nations is in many ways a revolutionary development given their lack of "empirical statehood,"[44] this development also should be seen as a logical progression from the Berlin rules, which did not demand much in the way of an administrative presence for a colonizer to claim control of the territory.

It is telling that the international system, created in good part by the Africans, no longer demanded a theory of rule. As noted in chapter three, colonial governors of the respective European powers were obsessed with the problem of ruling over vast areas with low population densities. They

---

[42] William J. Foltz, "The Organization of African Trouble: How and Why it Works and Does not Work," Report 689-AR, U.S. Department of State, mimeograph, September 1983, p. 18.

[43] Boutros-Ghali, "The Addis Ababa Charter," pp. 25, 45.

[44] Robert H. Jackson, *Quasi-States: Sovereignty, International Relations, and the Third World* (Cambridge: Cambridge University Press, 1990), p. 25.

therefore promulgated all nature of theories of rule as, if nothing else, explanations of how they were trying to cope with an unprecedented administrative problem. No similar fixation is evident in the writings of independent African leaders. The assumption at independence was that the accession to power in the capital was synonymous with the ability to rule their entire territorial expanse, a belief firmly supported by the international community. Thus, Nkrumah famously argued that, with independence, "We have won the political battle. . . ."[45] Similarly, Lugard's eventual successors in independent Nigeria were not obsessed with the problem of extending power over a sparsely populated hinterland because they believed (falsely as it turned out) that independence would solve the problem of broadcasting power. For instance, Alhaji Abubakar Tafawa Balewa, the first Nigerian prime minister said, during the 1959 debate over the motion to ask for independence, that "I am confident that when we have our own citizenship, our own national flag, our own national anthem we shall find the flame of national unity will burn bright and strong."[46] Similarly, Nnamdi Azikwe, the first premier of the eastern region of Nigeria, would claim that, "The North and the South [of Nigeria] are one, whether we wish it or not. The forces of history have made it so."[47]

The Political Consequences of Peace

As with Europe, the particular external environment that African countries confronted had a profound effect on internal arrangements. African countries faced the luxury of escaping the brutal history of continual war that so mars the barbaric European experience in the twentieth century. However, the problem of state-building in times of peace and, in particular, of extending authority, is nonetheless consequential and, given the dominance of the belligerent European experience, largely unexplored. Standard narratives of European state development highlight the crucial contribution of war. Thus, Samuel P. Huntington argued that "war was the great stimulus to state building," and Charles Tilly went so far as to claim that "war made the state, and the state made war."[48] Similarly,

[45] Kwame Nkrumah, "Tenth Anniversary of the CPP," in *Selected Speeches of Dr. Kwame Nkrumah*, ed. Samuel Obeng (Accra: Ghana Advance Press, 1973), p. 4.

[46] Alhaji Tafawa Balewa, *Mr. Prime Minister* (Apapa, Nigeria: Nigerian National Press, 1964), p. 37.

[47] Nnamdi Azikwe, *Zik: A Selection of Speeches of Nnamdi Azikwe* (Cambridge: Cambridge University Press, 1961), p. 102.

[48] Samuel P. Huntington, *Political Order in Changing Societies* (New Haven: Yale Uni-

nomadic states in inner Asia were forced to acquire a higher level of social organization than would have been required to solve their domestic problems in order to defend themselves from their sedentary neighbors.[49]

At the most basic level, war in Europe acted as a filter whereby weak states were eliminated and political arrangements that were not viable either were reformed or disappeared. Weak states do exist in Europe today—Belgium is one example—but the near-constant threat of war prompted most states to become stronger in order to survive. The contrast between this evolutionary development and the current situation in Africa, where even states that are largely dependent on foreign aid will continue to exist for the foreseeable future, in good part because of the protection afforded by the international system they helped to create, is dramatic. More specifically, war in Europe played an important role in the consolidation of many now-developed states in ways that are particularly important to an understanding of how power is broadcast: war caused the state to become more efficient in revenue collection by forcing leaders to dramatically improve administrative capabilities (thereby allowing states to fund nationwide administrative and economic systems), and war created a climate and important symbols around which a disparate population could unify and bond with the state in a manner that legitimized the capital's authority. That African countries have, to date, largely failed to solve these problems has important implications for their ability to consolidate power and has had a significant impact on the evolution of their political economies.

Taxes

There is no better measure of a state's reach than its ability to collect taxes. If a state does not effectively control a territory, it certainly will not be able to collect taxes in a sustained and efficient manner. At the same time, a widely distributed tax base helps guarantee consolidation of the state by generating a robust revenue stream. Perhaps the most noticeable effect of war in European history was to cause the state to increase its ability to collect significantly more revenue with greater efficiency and less public resistance. Given the freedom of European states to attack

---

versity Press, 1968), p. 123, and Charles Tilly, "Reflections on the History of European State-Making," p. 42.

[49] Thomas J. Barfield, *The Perilous Frontier: Nomadic Empires and China* (London: Basil Blackwell, 1989), p. 7.

each other, states that could quickly raise money could successfully threaten neighbors with a war that might lead to significant damage or even complete destruction. Richard Bean writes, "Once the power to tax had been successfully appropriated by any one sovereign, once he had used that power to bribe or coerce his nobility into acquiescence, that state could face all neighboring states with the choice of being conquered or of centralizing authority and raising taxes."[50] While success in war depended on many factors, including technology, tactics, and morale of the troops, raising sufficient revenue was a necessary condition to prevent defeat. As Michael Mann notes, "A state that wished to survive had to increase its extractive capacity to pay for professional armies and/or navies. Those that did not would be crushed on the battlefield and absorbed into others—the fate of Poland, of Saxony, of Bavaria in [the seventeenth and eighteenth centuries]. No European states were continuously at peace. It is impossible to escape the conclusion that a peaceful state would have ceased to exist even more speedily than the militarily inefficient actually did."[51]

War affected state finances for two reasons. First, it placed tremendous strains on leaders to find new and more regular sources of income. While rulers may have recognized that their tax system was inadequate, a war may have been the only prompt that would have forced them to expend the necessary political capital and to deploy the coercion required to gain more revenue. For instance, in Mann's study of taxation in England between 1688 and 1815, he finds that there were six major jumps in state revenue, and that each corresponds with the beginning of a war.[52] The association between the need to fight and the need to collect revenue is perhaps clearest in Prussia, where the main tax collection agency was called the General War Commissariat.[53]

Second, citizens are much more likely to acquiesce to increased taxation when the nation is at war, because a threat to their survival will overwhelm other concerns they might have about increased taxation. In fact, taxation for a war can be thought of as a "lumpy" collective good: not only must the population pay to get the good, but it also must pay a considerable amount more than the current level of taxation, because a

---

[50] Richard Bean, "War and the Birth of the Nation State," *Journal of Economic History* 33, (March 1973): p. 220.

[51] Michael Mann, "State and Society, 1130–1815: An Analysis of English State Finances," in *States, War, and Capitalism: Studies in Political Sociology*, ed. Michael Mann (Oxford: Basil Blackwell, 1988), p. 109.

[52] Mann, *Sources of Social Power*, p. 486.

[53] Michael Duffy, "The Military Revolution and the State, 1500–1800," in *The Military Revolution and the State, 1500–1800*, ed. Michael Duffy, Exeter Studies in History no. 1 (Exeter, U.K.: University of Exeter, 1980), p. 5.

small increase in revenue often is not enough to meet the new security threat facing the state.[54] In this way, taxation for a war is like taxation for building a bridge: everyone must pay to build the bridge and a small increase in revenue will not be enough, because half a bridge, like fighting half a war, is useless.

Thus, war often causes a "ratchet effect," whereby revenue increases sharply when a nation is fighting but does not decline to the ante bellum level when hostilities have ceased.[55] Once governments have invested the sunk costs in expanding tax collection systems and routinized the collection of new sources of revenue, the marginal costs of continuing those structures are quite low and the resources they collect can be used for projects that will enhance the ruling group's support. Ironically, it is under external threat from others that European states were able to consolidate control over their own nations.

War in other societies at other times often played the same kind of role that external conflict did in Europe. For instance, the South Korean and Taiwanese states have been able to extract so many resources from their societies in part because the demands to be constantly vigilant provoked the state into developing efficient mechanisms for collecting resources and controlling dissident groups.[56] A highly extractive state also can cloak demands for greater resources in appeals for national unity in the face of a determined enemy.

It is extraordinarily difficult, outside times of crisis, to reform elemental parts of the governmental system, such as the means of taxation. Since taxes are so consequential to every business decision, over time the tax system reflects a large number of political bargains made by the state with different interest groups. Edward Ames's and Richard Rapp's conclusion that tax systems "last until the end of the government that instituted them" and that tax systems in some European countries survived "almost intact" from the thirteenth and fourteenth centuries until the late eighteenth century may be an exaggeration, but their conclusions suggest just how much inertia a particular system for collecting government revenue can develop over time.[57] Other than war, no type of crisis demands that the state increase taxes with such forcefulness, and few other situations would impel citizens to accept those demands, or at least not resist them as strongly as they otherwise might have. It is therefore hard to counter

[54] "Lumpy" goods are products that are not useful if only part is purchased. Margaret Levi, *Of Rule and Revenue* (Berkeley: University of California Press, 1988), pp. 56–7.

[55] Mann, *Sources of Social Power*, pp. 483–90.

[56] Joel S. Migdal, *Strong Societies and Weak States: State-Society Relations and State Capabilities in the Third World* (Princeton: Princeton University Press, 1988), p. 274.

[57] Edward Ames and Richard T. Rapp, "The Birth and Death of Taxes: A Hypothesis," *Journal of Economic History* 37, no. 1 (March 1977): p. 177.

Tilly's argument that "the formation of standing armies provided the largest single incentive to extraction and the largest single means of state coercion over the long run of European statemaking."[58]

AFRICAN PUBLIC FINANCE

War's effect on the structure of government revenue is important to Africa because the continent's political geography has a profound influence on possibilities for taxation. Given low densities of population dispersed across large hinterlands, it was difficult for precolonial states to tax individuals. It was also hard to derive rents from land the way that feudal governments did in Europe because land had such a low value and because it was easy for the population to avoid land-based taxation.[59] As a result, most precolonial governments were dependent on taxing trade. Gaining revenue from international commerce, which usually originated in the political center, also was easier for precolonial states than to tax individuals, especially given the uncertain sovereignty that so many precolonial states had over their outlying areas. Of course, for many African states, gaining tribute from outlying areas via war or the threat of war was also a significant means of gaining revenue.

Not surprisingly, colonial governments were unable to solve the revenue problem because there was not a fundamental change in the nature of population distribution and because economic development, except in the settler colonies, was extremely slow. As a result, most colonial governments were also highly dependent on revenue from customs duties. Hopkins estimates that customs duties accounted for about two-thirds of the total revenue for the greater part of the colonial period in both the West African anglophone and francophone colonies.[60] Reflecting their modest motivations for ruling in Africa, the states the Europeans created did not develop impressive institutions for collecting revenue.

Aid from the metropole, the other important revenue stream for colonial governments, was, of course, a direct transfer to the capital. As a result, these flows worked to retard additional efforts to gain revenue from the countryside given the low cost of receiving aid versus the high cost of developing rural collection systems. After World War II, when colonial governments finally began a limited focus on development projects, transfers from abroad, especially the metropole, became critical. For

---

[58] Tilly, "Reflections on the History of European State-Making," p. 73.

[59] Anthony G. Hopkins, *An Economic History of West Africa* (New York: Columbia University Press, 1973), p. 62.

[60] Ibid., p. 191.

TABLE 4.1

Structure of Government Revenue (Percent of Total Government Revenue)

Level of Per Capita Income	Taxes on Foreign Trade	Indirect Internal Taxation	Internal Direct Taxes	Other Revenue
Less than U.S.$80	44	22	22	11
Greater than $81 to $199	36	14	29	21
Greater than $200	33	22	28	17

Source: Economic Commission for Africa, *A Survey of Economic Conditions in Africa, 1960–1964* (New York: United Nations, 1968), p. 186.
Note: Data are for three of the years between 1959 and 1964.

instance, in francophone territories, transfers from France accounted for 75 percent of total capital formation.[61]

Independent African countries inherited the fiscal structures their colonial predecessors constructed. In the early 1960s, when the vast majority of African countries were about to receive independence, most governments were still highly dependent on indirect taxation, especially taxes on foreign trade. Table 4.1 provides a snapshot of just how difficult it would be for African leaders to mobilize a consistent revenue stream. In this sample, internal direct taxes accounted for only 22 to 29 percent of government revenue at the dawn of independence. Indeed, indirect taxation, especially taxes on international transactions as a percentage of government revenue, had risen in the 1950s as colonial governments started to undertake large-scale infrastructure projects and quickly exhausted the savings that had accrued over previous decades.[62] At least some African countries also received a significant amount of their revenue from nontax sources, especially from mineral concessions.[63] This statistic is highly variable and, particularly in the 1960s, not well recorded. In 1960, data from the Economic Commission for Africa (ECA) suggests that 16.5 percent of total government revenue was accounted for by nontax revenue.[64]

Finally, foreign aid was also a significant feature for many newly independent governments. In the early 1960s, foreign aid tended to be over-

[61] Economic Commission for Africa, *Economic Survey of Africa since 1950* (New York: United Nations, 1959), p. 186.

[62] Economic Commission for Africa, "Public Finance in African Countries," *Economic Bulletin for Africa* 1 (June 1961): p. 13.

[63] Mark Gersovitz and Chris Paxson, "The Revenues and Expenditures of African Governments," *Journal of African Economies* 5 (June 1996): p. 206.

[64] Economic Commission for Africa, *A Survey of Economic Conditions in Africa, 1960–1964* (New York: United Nations, 1968), pp. 199–201.

whelmingly funneled through the state apparatus. Western powers were skeptical that a significant private sector could develop given their racist perceptions of Africans' entrepreneurial talents (especially after colonial governments had done their best to suppress African entrepreneurs for the previous sixty years). In the early 1960s, a time when the centrally planned Soviet Union was viewed as in some ways more technologically advanced than the U.S., there was also much greater optimism about the efficacy of the state as an economic unit. The World Bank suggested to many African countries that they expand the number and extent of state-owned enterprises in order to increase the vibrancy of the economy. Finally, most foreign aid was directed at large infrastructure projects (ports, hydroelectric projects, roads) that only governments could operate.[65] The ECA estimated that extraordinary revenue and loans, of which foreign aid composed a very large amount, accounted for nineteen percent of total government revenue across Africa in 1960 and eighteen percent in 1965.[66]

TAXES AND PEACE

Even in the 1960s, it was recognized that the structure of government revenue in Africa was highly problematic. First, the revenue streams produced were clearly inadequate. African states were desperately short of revenue to fund even minimal state services (e.g., pay nurses' salaries, buy books for schools, supply transport for agricultural extension services) that their populations had been promised in the heady days after independence. In addition to these recurrent costs, African countries were in need of more extensive and more efficient tax systems because the process of development requires large expenditures on infrastructure (including, of course, roads) to promote economic activity throughout the country.[67] W. Arthur Lewis estimated that the public sector in Third World countries should be spending on the order of 20 percent of GDP on services, exclusive of defense and debt repayment.[68] For the countries the ECA had data for, government expenditures amounted to only 17 percent of GDP in 1960 and only 22 percent in 1968 before defense

[65] For an overall review of the evolution of foreign aid, see Jeffrey Herbst, *U.S. Economic Policy Toward Africa: Promoting Reform in the 1990s* (New York: Council on Foreign Relations, 1992).

[66] Economic Commission for Africa, *Survey of Economic Conditions in Africa, 1970*, pt. 1 (New York: ECA, 1971), p. 138.

[67] W. Arthur Lewis, *The Evolution of the International Economic Order* (Princeton: Princeton University Press, 1978), p. 39.

[68] W. Arthur Lewis, *Development Planning: The Essentials of Economic Policy* (New York: Harper and Row, 1966), p. 115.

(which averaged about 27 percent of government expenditures in both years) and debt payments.[69] While these figures are only rough estimates, given the problems associated with African economic statistics in the 1960s, they illustrate the extent of the fiscal problem facing African states at independence.

By 1968, the Economic Commission for Africa was already warning that public expenditure in many countries was rising ahead of revenue (despite significant economic growth) and that the share of GDP absorbed by taxes was not related to the growth of the overall economy.[70] The ECA recognized that African countries relied on indirect taxes because they were convenient and relatively inexpensive to collect, given the nature of the inherited colonial administrative systems, by then only slightly modified. However, the UN agency noted that income tax still could be applied to some individuals with relatively high salaries and that some people did have substantial savings. It complained with a degree of honesty seldom found in more recent publications that "generally sufficient consideration was not given to the possibilities of developing and strengthening other forms of taxation. The shortage of revenue in most cases was due to the fact that the taxation potential was not fully exploited. In many cases it was not only due to bad tax administration but also the result of resistance from powerful pressure groups who blocked the way to effective tax reform."[71]

In direct contrast to the European experience of states being prompted to collect taxes efficiently due to a threatening external environment, the ECA detected no urgency on the part of African governments to raise money: "the problem of collection lies with the government agency responsible for tax collection. But invariably tax laws are not enforced because of the laxity of government officials." It went on to note that before it was reformed (and undoubtedly since those reforms lapsed), the Liberian tax collection agency, like many others across the continent, was, "woefully disorganised and painfully demoralized."[72] Similarly, the ECA described the reasons for poor tax collection in the midwestern state of Nigeria: "The problem was that a number of leading figures in the society were being allowed to avoid their [tax] obligations. Avoidance has been too easy because big businessmen and self-employed professionals have felt that Government was afraid of them, or that they could 'buy off' tax officials. Sometimes the officials were afraid to take

[69] ECA, *Survey of Economic Conditions in Africa, 1970*, pp. 327–8.
[70] ECA, *Survey of Economic Conditions in Africa, 1960–1964*, pp. 186–7.
[71] ECA, *Survey of Economic Conditions in Africa, 1970*, p. 141.
[72] Economic Commission for Africa, *Survey of Economic Conditions in Africa, 1972*, pt. 1 (New York: United Nations, 1973), p. 232.

TABLE 4.2

Comparative Structure of Central Government Revenue (% of Total Revenue)

Region	Taxes on Income, Profits, and Capital Gains	Taxes on International Trade and Transactions	Nontax Revenue
Africa	23.15	27.75	17.01
Asia	23.98	15.89	21.57
Eastern and Central Europe	17.65	6.53	12.30
Latin America	19.78	18.52	15.01

Source: International Monetary Fund, *Government Finance Statistics Yearbook 1997* (Washington, D.C.: International Monetary Fund, 1997), pp. 4–5.

Note: For "Africa," only sixteen countries are included. Statistics are for latest year available.

action because they felt that the defaulters might use their social connections to victimize them."[73]

Despite these warnings, African governments did not work energetically to change their revenue structure. Guyer notes, in one of the rare studies of direct taxation, that, in Nigeria, "since independence . . . the taxation systems set up by colonial governments have been all but dismantled, particularly at the local level." She explains that the atrophy of direct tax systems came about because of several different reasons, including populist ideology, civil disorder, and "the increased importance of national wealth coming from large, single sources such as minerals and government loans."[74] Income taxes did increase across Africa to 28 percent of government revenue in 1985. However, in the critical period 1985–1996, when many African countries were engaged in economic reform, the percentage of government revenue attributable to income taxes actually declined to 25 percent.[75] Table 4.2 indicates that, in the late 1990s, African countries are still much more dependent on a combi-

[73] Ibid., p. 233.

[74] Jane I. Guyer, "Representation without Taxation: An Essay on Democracy in Rural Nigeria, 1952–1990," *African Studies Review* 35 (April 1992): p. 43.

[75] Data is from ECA, "Public Finance in African Countries," *Economic Bulletin For Africa* 1 (June 1961): pp. 16–8 for 1958, and World Bank, *African Development Indicators, 1997: Data on Diskette* (Washington, D.C.: The World Bank, 1997). Data for the period from 1958 to 1980 on a continental basis are not available and even the more recent information presented here should be viewed with caution, given how poorly many African countries kept their accounts in the 1970s and 1980s. Indeed, one of the manifestations of the reliance on indirect sources of revenue was the retardation of a felt need to make public finance transparent.

nation of taxes on international transactions and nontax revenue than developing countries in other regions.

As a result, African governments were unable to increase their fiscal base. As figure 4.1 indicates, total government revenue as a percentage of gross domestic product did improve in the early 1980s. However, those gains subsequently disappeared so that by the mid-1990s, governments had not substantially increased the amount collected in taxes, as a percentage of the total economy, compared to 1980.

Close observers of African public finance today detect the same lack of seriousness with which the ECA was obsessed with in the 1960s. For instance, Collier notes the political origins of the public finance problem in Africa:

> [Taxation] is normally constrained by two mechanisms: popular consent and the law. . . . [in independent Africa] the two usual constraint mechanisms failed. . . . In some countries, governments collect taxes in an arbitrary fashion, because the lack of trustworthy audited accounts has left governments with the choice of failing to collect revenue on profits or collecting it on an arbitrary basis. In many countries, de facto lump-sum assessments are common and so tax rates have little meaning in practice. . . . Thus the fear of high taxation in the private sector goes hand in hand with very low revenues being collected through taxes in many African countries.[76]

The process of tax collection that Collier describes is suggestive, more than anything, of a tribute system where the state has essentially given up on regular tax collection and instead relies on extracting irregular lump sums from corporations and individuals. The political revolution that Africans experienced starting in the early 1960s has yet to lead to a fiscal revolution.

PUBLIC SPENDING AMONG FRIENDS

The inability to change the structure of the revenue stream had an immediate and obvious impact on overall government finances. In the face of poor revenue growth, African countries have depended on deficit spending for growth in government revenue. Figure 4.2 suggests that, especially for the period of 1985–1996, government expenditures and deficit spending moved in tandem. It is clear that African countries have not been completely dependent on internal revenue flows, even over the medium-term, when making their expenditure decisions.

Normally, governments would not have been able to increase spending based almost completely on borrowing. However, governments south of

[76] Paul Collier, "The Marginalization of Africa," *International Labour Review* 134 (1995): p. 552.

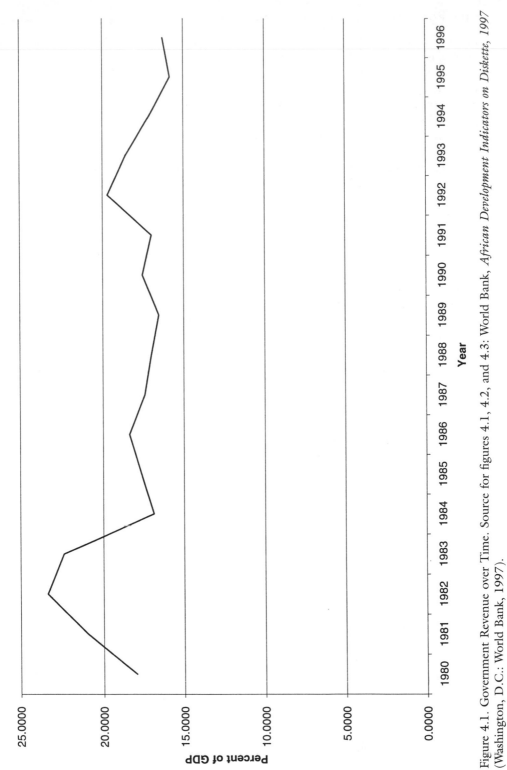

Figure 4.1. Government Revenue over Time. Source for figures 4.1, 4.2, and 4.3: World Bank, *African Development Indicators on Diskette, 1997* (Washington, D.C.: World Bank, 1997).

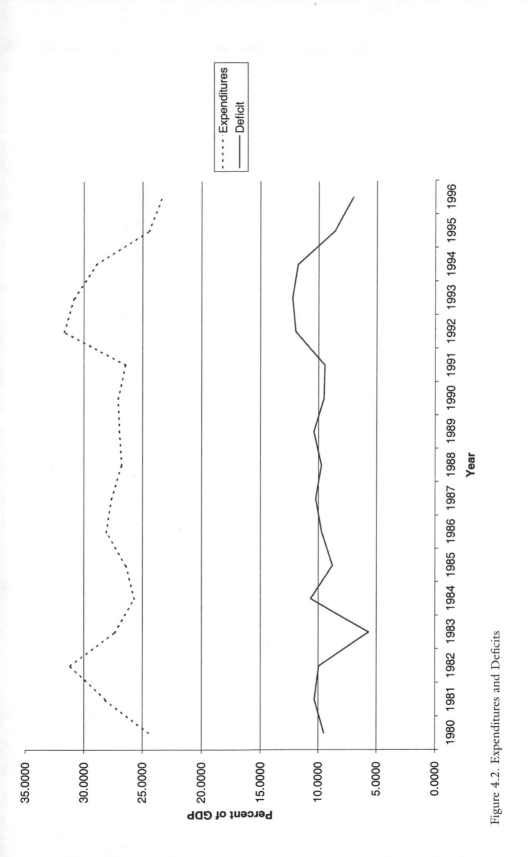

Figure 4.2. Expenditures and Deficits

the Sahara found one revenue stream they had was robust: foreign aid. As figure 4.3 demonstrates, foreign aid increased enough during the period between 1980 to 1995, to allow African governments to spend more than their domestic revenue stream would have allowed. Indeed, donors managed to catch up relatively quickly to African governments when deficits began to increase after 1983. While it is often the case, especially in recent years, that external donors have demanded economic reform and prompted greater economic change than would have been generated internally, looking at the current environment in comparative perspective, it is easy to see how much less threatening the world is today for even weak states in Africa compared to Europe during the formative period of many of those countries. Joseph Stiglitz, in his role as chief economist of the World Bank, has even argued that foreign aid should be treated as a legitimate and predictable source of government revenue.[77] If European states had finances as problematic as many African countries, they may not have survived in an era which punished fiscal failure. Instead, in the era of African independence, the international community kept many governments solvent.

The obstacles posed by large peasant populations, significant non-monetarized sectors, and widespread poverty are, of course, important contributors to the revenue crisis of the African state. However, these problems do not fully explain why poor states do not extract greater resources from society in a manner that is less economically harmful. Factors such as political will, administrative ability, and the population's willingness to be taxed—issues that can be affected by the decisions of political leaders—are also crucial in understanding why states are unable to achieve their potential level of taxation in a benign manner.[78] For instance, Margaret Levi successfully shows that in such diverse cases as republican Rome, France, and England in the Middle Ages, eighteenth-century Britain, and twentieth-century Australia, levels of taxation were affected primarily by political constraints faced by rulers, despite the fact that the structure of most of these economies also posed significant barriers to increased tax collections.[79] Anderson estimates that revenue gains

[77] Joseph Stiglitz, "More Instruments and Broader Goals: Moving Towards the Post-Washington Consensus," 1998 WIDER Annual Lecture, Helsinki, Finland, 7 January 1998, found at: http://www.worldbank.org/html/extdr/extme/js-010798/wider.htm, p. 6.

[78] Raja J. Chelliah, "Trends in Taxation in Developing Countries," *International Monetary Fund Staff Papers* 18, no. 2 (July 1971): p. 312. On the possibility of changing fiscal arrangements in Africa, see Dennis Anderson, *The Public Revenue and Economic Policy in African Countries*, World Bank Discussion Paper no. 19 (Washington, D. C.: World Bank, 1987), pp. 14–5.

[79] Levi, *Of Rule and Revenue*, pp. 104–5.

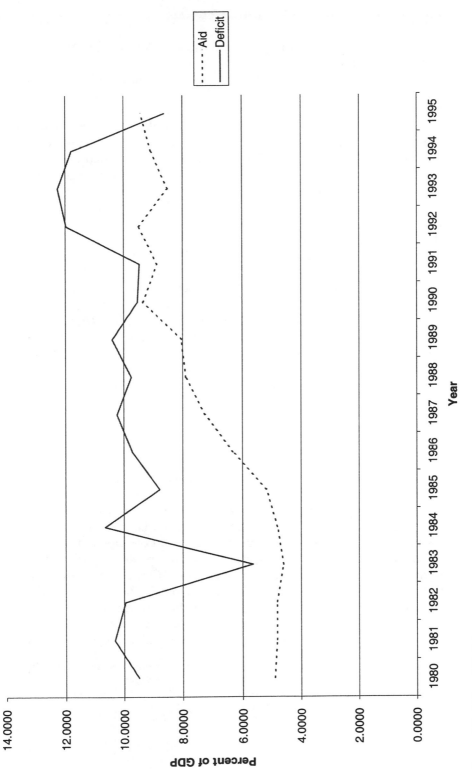

Figure 4.3. Aid and Deficits

in the range of 20 to 30 percent were possible in Africa in the 1980s by increasing charges on public services.[80]

What stands out is that Africa did not face the same kind of security threat as Europe, and, therefore, the pressure to mobilize revenue through efficient administration, including efficient nationwide systems to collect revenue, is much lower. It would be foolish to say that significant interstate war would have solved Africa's many fiscal problems. However, it is obvious that African countries have not solved the problem of how to motivate administrative systems to mobilize the maximum amount of revenue efficiently in times of peace. As a result, the spatial structure of revenue, and thus of the state itself, is very much as during the colonial period: concentrated in the capital and the few other areas of the country where it is easy to tax.

Domestic security threats, of the type African countries face so often, may force the state to increase revenue; however, civil conflicts result in fragmentation and considerable hostility among different segments of the population. Public acceptance of tax increases, a crucial factor in allowing European states to extract greater resources in times of war, will be a much more complicated issue in civil disputes. As Mann notes, "the growth of the modern state, as measured by finances, is explained primarily not in domestic terms but in terms of geopolitical relations of violence."[81]

Nationalism

While critical, taxes are not the only measure of how a state consolidates power. Also important is the far more nebulous idea that the nation and the state are bound together through a series of emotional ties often expressed in the iconic symbols of nationalism. Nationalism can be thought of as another way for the state to consolidate its power over distance not, as with taxes, through the agencies of coercion but through the norm of legitimacy. As such, nationalism is a particularly interesting issue for Africa because it may represent a way of broadcasting state authority that does not require the financial resources that poor countries lack. The dawn of independence in Africa thus presented leaders with another avenue for the extension of state power.

At independence, Africa's new leaders were well aware of just how

[80] Anderson, *The Public Revenue and Economic Policy in African Countries*, p. 18. See generally, Zmarak Shalizi and Lyn Squire, *Tax Policy in Sub-Saharan Africa*, World Bank Policy and Research Series Paper no. 2 (Washington, DC: The World Bank, 1988).

[81] Mann, *Sources of Social Power*, p. 490.

artificial the creations they were about to inherit were. Nationalism, which was never nearly as strong or widespread (especially outside the major cities) in Africa as many had thought, was palpable in the late colonial period because of the excitement generated by the surprisingly sudden prospect of independence. However, there was still the real problem of how to build ties between the population and the state once the euphoria dissipated and the reality of disparate nations facing weak and geographically constrained states became obvious.

European nation-states were hardly natural. As the history of France demonstrates, European states at one time had to deal, and in some cases are still coping with, highly diverse populations that did not have many emotional links with the state. In Europe, this problem was solved in good part by war. Indeed, the presence of a palpable external threat may be the strongest way to generate a common association between the state and the population. External threats have such a powerful effect on nationalism because people realize in a profound manner that they are under threat because of who they are as a nation; they are forced to recognize that it is only as a nation that they can successfully defeat the threat. Anthony Giddens recounts the effects of World War I: "The War canalized the development of states' sovereignty, tying this to citizenship and to nationalism in such a profound way that any other scenario [of how the international system would be ordered] subsequently came to appear as little more than idle fantasy."[82] Michael Howard notes the visceral impact of wars on the development of nationalism throughout Europe:

> Self-identification as a Nation implies almost by definition alienation from other communities, and the most memorable incidents in the group-memory consisted in conflict with and triumph over other communities. France *was* Marengo, Austerlitz and Jena: military triumph set the seal on the new-found national consciousness. Britain *was* Trafalgar—but it had been a nation for four hundred years, since those earlier battles Crecy and Agincourt. Russia *was* the triumph of 1812. Germany *was* Gravelotte and Sedan.[83]

Similarly, in Japan, the Tokugawa Shogunate's armed conquest was "inextricably connected" with the regime's legitimacy.[84] As a result, it is hardly surprising that the critical monuments (e.g., Trafalgar Square, Arc de Triumph, Brandenburg Gates) in so many European capital cities are

---

[82] Anthony Giddens, *A Contemporary Critique of Historical Materialism*, vol. 2 (Berkeley: University of California Press, 1987), p. 235.

[83] Michael Howard, *War and the Nation State* (Oxford: Clarendon Press, 1978), p. 9. Emphasis in the original.

[84] Eiko Ikegami, *The Taming of the Samurai: Honorific Individualism and the Making of Modern Japan* (Cambridge: Harvard University Press, 1995), p. 152.

militaristic. They celebrate the central events that not only preserved the state but also forged its links with the population.

African states, except for the small number (Angola, Guinea-Bissau, Mozambique, Namibia, Zimbabwe) that fought wars of national liberation to gain independence, did not go through the trauma of war that might have resulted in a nationalism that would have made the term nation-state a reality. A reading of the national anthems—songs written and/or endorsed by the state to express the ties between nation and state[85]—make clear that many early leaders understood the particular problem of building nationalism during times of peace. The writers of the Benin national anthem recognized how pacific their new age was:

> Formerly, at her call, our ancestors
> Knew how to engage in mighty battles
> With strength, courage, ardor, and full of joy, but at the price of blood
> Builders of the present, you too, join forces
> Each day for the task stronger in unity
> Build without ceasing for posterity.[86]

The "Song of Abidjan" is even more direct in celebrating Côte d'Ivoire's independence:

> Proud Citizens of the Ivory Coast, the country calls us
> If we have brought back liberty peacefully
> It will be our duty to be an example.[87]

So great was the peace that Africa experienced at birth that some national anthems showed a schizophrenia in calling for devotion both to the nation and to Africa. Thus, the chorus of the national anthem in Mali starts:

> For Africa and for you, Mali.[88]

Indeed, a few national anthems dispense with any call to loyalty to the nation-state and demand general devotion to "Africa." Thus, "God Bless Africa" (more famously known as *Nkosi Sikelel' iAfrika*), which has served, at one time or another, as the national anthem of Namibia, South Africa, Tanzania, Zambia, and Zimbabwe, is actually a hymn rather than a praise song to the nation-state. In fact, it says nothing about any of those states:

---

[85] See, F. Gunther Eyck, "The Setting," in *The Voice of Nations: European National Anthems and their Authors*, ed. Gunther Eyck (Westport, CT: Greenwood Press, 1995), p. xiii.

[86] "L'Aube Nouvelle," in *National Anthems of the World*, ed. W. L. Reed and M. J. Bristow, 8th ed. (London: Cassell, 1993), p. 60.

[87] "L'Abidjanaise," in ibid., p. 271.

[88] "National Anthem of Mali," in ibid., p. 323.

God Bless Africa
Let Her fame spread far and wide
Hear our prayer
May Gold bless us!
Come, Spirit, come!
Come! Holy Spirit!
Come and bless us, her children![89]

In this anthem, there is a clear disjunction between the desire to bless Africa and the needs of national leaders to create ties to their populations by invoking specific national icons. As a result, the development of a national identity is that much more difficult. There is apparently no African national anthem that celebrates the creation of the nation through blood and iron as does the "La Marseillaise":

Arise, children of the fatherland
The day of glory has come
Against us the blood-stained banner
Of tyranny is raised,
The banner of tryanny is raised,
Hear, in the fields, the roar
Of her fierce soldiers.
They come right into our arms
To slaughter our sons and our consorts.
Patriots, to arms!
From your battalions
Let's march, let's march!
May the tyrant's foul blood water our furrow.[90]

France, of course, is one of the outstanding examples of a nation that has managed to overcome significant linguistic and territorial divisions over a short period of time to create a true national identity. This is a task that still eludes most African countries.

Thus, Anthony D. Smith is absolutely right when he writes, "the central difficulty of 'nation-building' in much of Africa and Asia is the lack of any shared historical mythology and memory on which state elites can set about 'building' the nation."[91] Economic development, which early African leaders and the songs they wrote identified as the new struggle that Africa would engage in, and presumably the moral equivalent of war in Europe, has largely been a disaster in much of Africa as large parts of the

---

[89] "God Bless Africa," in ibid., p. 556.
[90] "La marseillaise," in ibid., p. 196.
[91] Anthony D. Smith, "State-Making and Nation-Building," in *States in History* ed. John A. Hall (Oxford: Basil Blackwell, 1986), p. 258.

continent are no richer today than they were at independence. As a result, national identity remains highly problematic in many African countries and often has lower salience than membership in other groups. As Ndeswa writes of Kenya, "the socially enacted relationship between ethnic identity, authority, and legitimacy competes with the legally sanctioned membership, authority, and legitimacy of the nation-state."[92]

This is not to argue that nationalism is absent in Africa or in other parts of the developing world. However, leaders of these states do face a particularly difficult problem in promoting the identification of the nation with the state. Unfortunately, there is no good way to measure nationalistic fervor, much less develop a time series of such sentiments. It is clear that African leaders have yet to systematically develop a strategy of how to build nationalism in times of peace.

Killing the Golden Goose

In Europe there was an almost symbiotic relationship between the state's extractive capacity and nationalism: war increased both as the population was convinced by external threat that they should pay more to the state, and, at the same time, the population united around common symbols and memories that were important components of nationalism. Fighting wars may be the only way in which it is possible to have people pay more taxes and at the same time feel more closely associated with the state. As a result, the state was able to consolidate its power across the breadth of its territory in two ways: by constructing the fiscal infrastructure to fund the administrative apparatus, and by gaining the loyalty of the nation that could be drawn upon through the construction of nationalistic symbols. Ironically, the threat of international war helped solve the problem of the domestic consolidation of power.

In Europe, as taxation fell on individuals and corporations, there was an immediate need for states to reach compromises with the people and the institutions they were taxing. The need to fund warfare only highlighted the connection between taxation and state survival. As Tillly makes clear, the history of Europe is in many ways a series of structured bargains where the state is only allowed to tax more if it makes certain concessions to those being taxed, or when the populations understand that their survival is dependent on paying more to the state.[93] While these bargains were usually in favor of the state, it was clear to rulers that because expenditures were directly tied to taxation, they faced a political

---

[92] Stephen N. Ndeswa, "Citizenship and Ethnicity: An Examination of Two Transition Moments in Kenyan Politics," *American Political Science Review* 91 (September 1997): p. 602.

[93] Tilly, *Coercion, Capital, and European States*, p. 99.

restraint on expenditures. At the same time, since direct taxation is relatively transparent, individuals and institutions could immediately see how much of a burden the state was imposing on them and protest against excessive government spending if the cost to them was becoming too high.[94] In practice, of course, the relationship between taxation and popular sentiment was much more complicated and there are certainly few times in history when populations thought that they were undertaxed. However, leaders understood that there was some relationship between the level of government expenditure that was possible and continued public acceptance of their rule.

A reliance on indirect taxation and nontax revenue streams attenuates, if not eliminates, the link between government taxation and popular support. Indirect taxation makes it exceptionally hard for individuals or groups to understand how much they are being taxed. For instance, indirect taxation in the form of higher prices for certain imported goods is simply much harder to gauge than income or sales taxes. In addition, it is simply easier for the state to tax international transactions because it is not required to interact with individuals but simply control access points on the borders. As a result, the state will be under less pressure to bargain with the population in order to gain revenue. Of course, there is no popular constraint on spending non-tax revenue or on foreign aid. As a result, the kinds of bargains that European governments had to make with significant components of the population in order to ensure fiscal viability are largely absent in African countries. Due to the long peace African countries experienced, they not only did not have to reach accommodation with their populations over taxation policies, but the international community has actually subsidized their highly inefficient attempts at garnering revenue. At the same time, the other means by which the state might identify with the population were highly constrained.

Given that the revenue stream that African countries received was not dependent on making compromises with the domestic population, leaders were able to divert large amounts of revenue to their own purposes and to their own followers. When leaders receive large amounts of money without making compromises with the local population, they are free to spend it in nonproductive ways, especially by enriching themselves and their followers. For instance, the Nigerian experience has been so disastrous because the oil money has flowed in as essentially a windfall. The perhaps inevitable result was depicted starkly by the Nigerian government itself in 1987:

---

[94] A point noted early by J. R. McCulloch in his 1845 classic, *A Treatise on the Principles and Practical Influence of Taxation and the Funding System* (Edinburgh: Scottish Economic Society, 1975), p. 155.

The crucial role of the government in the development of the political economy, converted the government and public bureaucracies into an arena in which politicians and bureaucrats became pawn brokers. As a result of the struggle to control the government and institutions, corruption became part and parcel of the political economy.[95]

Similarly, the Political Bureau, created by General Ibrahim Babangida to review the country's political structure, noted that since oil came online,

Earned revenue was lavished on unviable and grandiose projects which were very poorly thought through, and enormous contracts grossly inflated. Corruption flourished on a scale almost impossible to imagine. . . . All interests converged on the appropriation and consumption of oil revenues.[96]

While the Nigerian experience is exceptional in terms of the amount of money wasted, the general dynamic of governments spending revenue in an unproductive manner when faced with little countervailing pressure is common. There is a marked tendency to overshoot on patronage when there is not a hard political constraint on expenditures. For instance, the Kenyan government eventually spent an extra 1.35 Kenyan pounds for every extra K£1.00 received during the late 1970s coffee boom.[97] More generally, across the continent, elites developed norms which differed drastically from the European determination to build the state in order to ensure their, and the state's, physical survival. Corruption in Nigeria and elsewhere in Africa should not be seen merely as theft by individuals seeking to raid the coffers of the state. Rather, as Richard Joseph has noted, the distribution of state offices "is legitimated by a set of political norms according to which the appropriation of such offices is not just an act of individual greed or ambition but concurrently the satisfaction of the short-term objectives of a subset of the general population."[98]

Thus, a World Bank study of firms worldwide found that private companies in Africa rated corruption the single greatest obstacle to doing business, the only region other than Latin America where corruption featured so prominently.[99] Within many African states, government revenue becomes what Ostrom and her colleagues call a "common pool" re-

---

[95] Government of Nigeria, *Government's Views and Comments on the Findings and Recommendations of the Political Bureau* (Lagos: Government Printer, 1987), p. 8.

[96] Political Bureau, *Report of the Political Bureau* (Lagos: Government Printer, 1987), p. 35.

[97] David Bevan, Paul Collier, and Jan Willem Gunning, *Controlled Open Economies: A Neoclassical Approach to Structuralism* (Oxford: Clarendon Press, 1990), p. 352.

[98] Richard A. Joseph, *Democracy and Prebendal Politics in Nigeria* (Cambridge: Cambridge University Press, 1987), p. 67.

[99] World Bank, *World Development Report 1997* (Washington, DC: Oxford University Press, 1997), p. 42.

source. That is, leaders treat revenue as a resource that can be exploited and, potentially, overexploited unless they reign themselves in, much as farmers have to develop self-regulatory apparatuses not to overuse water in large irrigation schemes. In general, Ostrom and her colleagues are optimistic about the ability of individuals to solve common pool resource problems. However, they note that it is unlikely for the resource problems to be solved in "sparse" environments where, "individuals have no expectation of mutual trust and no means of building trust through communication and continued interaction." Of course, this is precisely the situation caused by a reliance on indirect taxation and nontax revenue in political contexts where nationalism is low. In such instances, even Ostrom and her colleagues believe that the "tragedy of the commons" will be repeated and participants will be likely to over appropriate and under provide.[100]

This is not to argue that the Europeans were inherently less greedy during their critical state-building phase. Rather, opportunities for corruption were limited in Europe by the exigencies created by the need for rulers to physically defend their states. What is often distinctive about rent-seeking in Africa is that it is so high as to be seemingly suboptimal: leaders steal so much from the state that the state itself begins to crumble and, along with it, the opportunities for future rent-seeking behavior. Yet, those states were generally safe from external attack, even as they crumpled internally. Indeed, contrary to what is often said, the post-World War II international system has been exceptionally friendly to weak states. States that had experienced such internal decay in Europe in previous centuries, or elsewhere, would have been destroyed by their neighbors. As a result, Africa has not only poorly performing states but also failed states. Leaders in Zaire, Liberia, Somalia, and elsewhere did not just steal, they stole so much as to cause the state to dissolve. In many other countries, government performance has been so poor that, as chapter one documented, basic infrastructure in many countries is crumbling.

Conclusion: Firm Boundaries and Weak Internal Control

In terms of the model of state authority developed in chapter one, the physical costs of state expansion are still relatively high, especially given the poverty of African states. Indeed, many African leaders were clearly

---

[100] Elinor Ostrom, Roy Garnder, and James Walker et al., *Rules, Games, and Common-Pool Resources* (Ann Arbor: University of Michigan Press, 1993), pp. 319, 328. See also Andrei Shleifer and Robert W. Vishny, "Corruption," *Quarterly Journal of Economics* 108 (1993): especially p. 609.

not successful in expanding the scope of the state so that they could be said to be ruling their entire territories. Some states did make significant gains in the most basic measure of the consolidation of state authority: the collection of taxes. However, continental performance was, on average, extremely poor. Leaders were under very little pressure to expand their taxation systems in particular so that the state would have a physical presence throughout the country. Many African leaders actually engaged in activities that so enriched themselves that the scope of the state contracted. There is also no clear evidence of a growth in nationalist sentiment that would bind states to their populations. Thus, leaders calculate that it is not necessarily beneficial to them to expand the state outward through the process of constructing an elaborate infrastructure of power.

As a result, how power was actually expressed was often similar to the precolonial model of concentric circles of authority. States had to control their political cores but often had highly differentiated control over the outlying areas. Indeed, there was often no immediate imperative to improve tax collection in the hinterlands or to do the necessary work so that those outside of the capital could be bound to the state through symbolic politics.

However, the African states did create hard boundaries that were extraordinarily effective in preserving the integrity of their states. As a result, a divergence could result in how power was mapped and how states were mapped. African politics was no longer in particular harmony with the political geography. Indeed, the hardness of the territorial boundaries (as opposed to their design) was particularly striking. Africa's political geography seemingly favored more nuanced and dynamic demarcations because the broadcasting of power was unlikely to be uniform across space and time, given the generally low levels of population density. Yet the boundaries became institutionalized because of a congruence of domestic and international political factors.

As was the case in the colonial period, Africa's land borders were far from being irrelevant because they were artificial. Rather, the boundaries have been absolutely essential to the particular pattern of state consolidation that occurred across the continent. While they may not appear to be well guarded or to even have a physical manifestation at the frontier of many countries, the borders have performed their essential function: preserving the territorial integrity of nations despite the difficulties that the political center had in expanding its control over territory. In this way, the boundaries were actually more powerful than European territorial boundaries for most of the nineteenth and twentieth centuries because African leaders quickly came to understand that they were under no threat from external attack and that the prospects for attacks on the integrity of the state from within were improbable. European leaders for

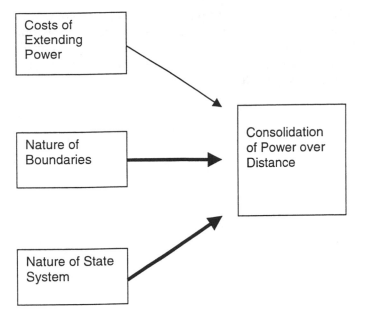

Figure 4.4. Paths to State Consolidation in Independent Africa

the last several hundred years lived in a different world and therefore had altogether different concerns about the fate of their nations.

In an extraordinary use of diplomacy, African leaders were able to arrange a state system that reinforced their own biases to retain the states that the colonialists had demarcated. This success in preserving units and boundaries has been phenomenal from the perspective of leaders. As a result, the international system allowed leaders to have full legal control of the territories that were within their borders. The international system tolerated, and to a limited degree even encouraged, a particular political economy that was biased in favor of providing revenue for patronage and funded the political perquisites of leaders rather than consolidating the state apparatus. Thus the state system created by the Africans was also critical to the consolidation of African states because it defined what control by the central state apparatus meant.

In and of itself, the granting of maximum sovereignty was not nearly as radical a change as Jackson suggests, given how seamlessly the conventions designed at Berlin segued into the Addis rules. What was perhaps more remarkable was that this benign international environment did not lead to improved prospects for the expansion of state authority but, in some very significant ways, retarded the broadcast of power. Independent Africa had thus become a state system with considerable fictions that were in remarkable contrast to precolonial Africa, where control of almost every square mile of land had to be earned and was often challenged. These fictions held for many years but, as chapter nine discusses, by the turn of the century some of the basic failures in state consolidation had become evident to all.

Part Three

NATIONAL DESIGN AND
DOMESTIC POLITICS

Five

National Design and the Broadcasting of Power

The State Stops at PK 12 [12 kilometers from
the capital, Bangui, C.A.R.].
  A Central African Republic official
  quoted in Thomas Bierschenk
  and Jean-Pierre Olivier de Sardan,
  "Local Powers and a Distant State in Rural
  Central African Republic," *Journal of
  Modern African Studies*

THE SHAPE AND SIZE of African nations were received, as chapter four
discusses, almost without change from the colonialists. Except for a relatively few border changes at independence or shortly thereafter (e.g., the
takeover by Cameroon of part of eastern Nigeria, the merging of Tanganyika and Zanzibar), African countries took their national design as a
given. Yet, there has been little systematic discussion of the implications
of the size and shape of African countries on their politics. What discussion there has been of African boundaries has largely been of the few that
have been contested rather than the implications of the vast majority that
quickly became accepted, indeed essential, parts of the political landscape.[1] As the Club du Sahel reported, "the territorial analysis of States is
far less advanced. A few geographical studies allude to the question, usually in terms of regionalization or town-country relations."[2] In many
ways, the ultimate expression of the victory that African leaders achieved
when they managed to get the international community to accept the
boundaries they wanted was to take the discussion of the implications of
national design off the political and intellectual agenda.

As a result, while government policies are routinely discussed as barriers to development, there is almost no mention of the hurdles or oppor-

---

[1] See, for instance, Crawford Young, "Comparative Claims to Political Sovereignty: Biafra, Katanga, Eritrea," in *State Versus Ethnic Claims: African Policy Dilemmas*, ed. Donald
Rothchild and Victor A. Olorunsola (Boulder, CO: Westview Press, 1983).

[2] Club du Sahel, *Preparing for the Future: A Vision of West Africa in the Year 2020* (Paris:
Club du Sahel, 1995), p. 47.

tunities to progress posed by the size and shape of nations. This chapter places the effect of national design on domestic politics back on the agenda by analyzing the ramifications of the size and shape of nations. I will argue that the particular political challenges that African countries face in broadcasting power, combined with the understanding of sovereignty that has developed, cause the calculations regarding national design to be radically different from the conventional wisdom that has developed based on the European experience. In particular, unlike Europe, African conditions privilege nations that are relatively small. Fortunately, the enormous variation in the size of countries across the continent—the largest (Sudan) is 238 times bigger (in terms of square kilometers) than the smallest (Gambia)[3]—makes Africa a particularly good setting to understand the implications of national design on politics.

The Failure to Analyze National Design

The failure to analyze the implications of national design for domestic politics has been evident for some time. For instance, political geographers generally have done little more than divide states into "compact," "irregular," and "divided" shapes; few generalizations about the implications for politics have even been asserted. As East and Prescott note, "It is sufficient for political geographers to be aware that the shape of a state's territory may be significant, and to explore any possible relevance in each particular case."[4] A significant portion of classical political geography also revolved around the assumption that states could actively change their shape, usually via warfare, to address the shortcomings posed by size. Thus, one of the "laws" of the spatial growth of states developed by Friedrich Ratzel, perhaps the founder of political geography, was that "the state strives toward the envelopment of politically valuable positions." Accordingly, he wrote, "if its growth is related to the dispossession of other states, it victoriously captures the good areas and the dispossessed continue in the bad."[5] Of course, while such assumptions are valid for European history, they are not relevant to Africa, or the rest of the developing world, where leaders have usually actively collaborated to ensure stable boundaries.

[3] World Bank, *World Development Report 1998*, p. 232.

[4] W. Gordon East and J. R. V. Prescott, *Our Fragmented World: An Introduction to Political Geography* (London: Macmillan, 1975), p. 57. See also Preston E. James, "Some Fundamental Elements in the Analysis of the Viability of States," in *Essays in Political Geography*, ed. Charles A. Fisher (London: Methuen, 1968), p. 35.

[5] Friedrich Ratzel, "The Laws of the Spatial Growth of States," in *The Structure of Political Geography*, ed. Roger E. Kasperson and Julian V. Minghi (Chicago: Aldine Publishing Company, 1969), pp. 24–5.

Analyzing the implications of the vast majority of boundaries that will not change is especially important because citizens do not undertake perpetual recontracting of their state, constantly examining whether it is the optimal size. Indeed, nearly the opposite is probably true. As chapter four demonstrates, the inertia of the national experience and the incentives posed by international structures and norms that have developed over time combine to make the demarcation of the state a nonissue in most countries most of the time. Here, I differ greatly from writings by economists who seek to find the optimal number of states by assuming that states cooperate to design themselves in a way that will maximize "their joint potential net revenue"[6] or who believe that the size and shape of states is determined on the basis of majority votes motivated by precise calculations of economic interests.[7] Chapter four documents an altogether different way for nations to be created and clearly suggests that precise calculations of economic well-being are far from the minds of those building states. Or as Boris Yeltsin noted as he was dismantling the Soviet Union, "The economy follows politics, after all."[8]

Since realistic discussion of national design has been not been on the agenda recently, many of the assumptions from the critical period of European state-building have been imported to the analysis of developing countries with little hesitation. In particular, what analysis there has been inevitably reflects a European bias in favor of larger states. The nation-state rose to dominance in Europe largely because its unique ability to unite market and population under sovereign rule provided leaders in successive centuries with "economies of scale" in military, economic, and political affairs that could not be achieved any other way. Such economies were especially important given the constant threats that many European states faced and the need for states to garner resources to survive external competition. The comparative advantages of the postfeudal state became progressively more important as warfare became more expensive and increasingly involved the long-term funding through domestic taxes of standing armies conscripted from the national population led by a professional staff that had to be able to adapt to continual changes in military technology. After some failed experiments with mercenary armies, it became clear by 1800 that only the new type of state could support the new

---

[6] David Friedman, "A Theory of the Size and Shape of Nations," *Journal of Political Economy* 85 (1977): p. 60.

[7] See, for instance, Alberto Alesina and Enrico Spolaore, "On the Number and Size of Nations," *Quarterly Journal of Economics* 112 (1997): p. 1033, and Patrick Bolton and Gérard Roland, "The Breakup of Nations: A Political Economy Analysis," *Quarterly Journal of Economics* 112 (1997): p. 1063.

[8] Boris Yeltsin, *The Struggle for Russia* (New York: Random House, 1994), p. 105.

type of warfare.[9] Such were the advantages offered by the nation-state that Joseph R. Strayer was forced to conclude that, "The development of the modern state . . . made possible such a concentrated use of human resources that no other type of social organization could avoid being relegated to a subordinate role."[10]

Similarly, from Adam Smith to current times, economists have argued, in the words of Charles P. Kindleberger, "the state should be large to achieve economies of scale."[11] Economists continue to believe that larger internal markets are intrinsically better because the boundaries of the nation-state, in accord with the theory of comparative advantage, are seen as barriers to economic exchange. As Robinson suggested in 1960:

> The boundary of the nation represents a point of discontinuity; it represents a change in the degree of mobility of almost all the factors of production, of labour more especially, but in hardly less degree also of capital and credit, since currency and banking systems are co-terminous with nations; it represents above all a discontinuity in the mobility of goods.[12]

Similarly, Alesina and Spolaore note, "any model with increasing returns in the size of the economy implies increasing returns in the size of countries."[13] As a result, they worry that, in equilibrium, there could be "an inefficiently large number of countries,"[14] although all of their assumptions regarding the relationship between size and efficiency are unexamined.

In the third world, industrialization through import substitution (ISI), the dominant development ideology from the 1950s until the 1980s, exemplified the fixation with the size of the domestic market. The larger the domestic market, the more viable the strategy became because the approach assumed that growth would be governed by domestic demand. Thus, the Fabian Society argued when it examined the prospects for Eritrean independence, "Looking further ahead, Eritrea is almost certainly not a viable unit on its own. If we are to think in terms of eventual independence, its people can stand no chance unless they link themselves to bigger and more viable neighbors."[15] More generally, the small size of many African countries accordingly has been cited as a structural problem. For instance, Stock complains, "there are forty-six independent

[9] Charles Tilly, *European Revolutions, 1492–1992* (Oxford: Blackwell, 1993), p. 32.

[10] Joseph R. Strayer, *On the Medieval Origins of the Modern State* (Princeton: Princeton University Press, 1970), p. 4.

[11] Charles P. Kindleberger, *Multinational Excursions* (Cambridge: MIT Press, 1984), p. 28.

[12] E. A. G. Robinson, introduction in *Economic Consequences of the Size of Nations*, ed. E. A. G. Robinson (New York: St. Martin's Press, 1960), p. xiv.

[13] Alesina and Spolaore, "On the Number and Size of Nations," p. 1029.

[14] Ibid., p. 1027.

[15] Fabian Society, *The Fate of Italy's Colonies* (London: Fabian Publications, 1948), p. 89.

states, some of which are too small to be considered economically viable."[16] Similarly, Gottmann worried, "The recent proliferation of statehood caused in the patterns of partitioning space and people a puzzle and a fragmentation that may have been desired in a time when self-determination was widely applied, but it certainly also encouraged the frittering away of sovereignty."[17]

The perceived material advantages of size were also translated into virtues by political theorists. Classical political theory stressed the importance of small political units, ideally city-states.[18] Plato calculated the optimal number of citizens at 5,040, while Aristotle believed that all the citizens should be able to assemble in one place and hear a speaker. Later, Montesquieu and Rousseau also stressed the importance of the relationship between size and democracy.[19] The framers of the American constitution were particularly concerned that Montesquieu, who had a profound influence on Jefferson, seemed to be a size determinist, arguing not only that city-states would be democratic but also that larger units would inevitably be ruled by despots.

As a result, starting with the founding of the United States, and especially during the period of great state consolidation in Europe in the nineteenth century, there was a furious effort on the part of theorists and practitioners to prove that the relative largeness of their nation-states was an unambiguous advantage. James Madison brilliantly turned the argument on size and democracy on its head by suggesting not only that large political units were not inherently undemocratic but also that they had substantial advantages over smaller units by being able to limit the damage of "factions."[20] After Madison, there developed a long-term bias in favor of viewing size as positively associated with prospects for viability. Thus, Alexis de Tocqueville famously predicted at the end of the first book of *Democracy in America* that the United States and Russia would be the two great superpowers because they were the only ones that could still expand.[21] In the West, there has been a significant intellectual tradition, exemplified by Marx and Engels, Durkheim, Lenin, Spencer, and

[16] Robert Stock, *Africa South of the Sahara: A Geographical Interpretation* (New York: Guilford Press, 1995), p. 15.

[17] Jean Gottmann, *The Significance of Territory* (Charlottesville: University Press of Virginia, 1973), p. 114.

[18] This discussion relies heavily on Robert A. Dahl and Edward R. Tufte, *Size and Democracy* (Stanford, CA: Stanford University Press, 1973), pp. 4–7.

[19] Especially Montesquieu, *The Spirit of the Laws*, vol. 1, bk. 2, and Jean Jacques Rousseau, *The Social Contract and Discourses* (London: J. M Dent, 1952), pp. 46–55.

[20] Especially, *Federalist* no. 10 in *The Federalist Papers* (Richmond, VA: Westvaco, 1995), p. 61.

[21] Alexis de Tocqueville, *Democracy in America*, vol. 1 (New York: Alfred A. Knopf, 1945), p. 434.

Parsons, that considered a critical part of modernization to be an evolution from small structures based on familial and ethnic identities to larger, more complex social structures such as the nation-state.[22] The increasing scale and complexity of political arrangements as societies moved from *Gemeinschaften* to *Gesellschaften* was perceived as perforce good and desirable, while smaller political units such as the tribe, village, and city-state, which previously were so important to the West, were increasingly seen as anachronistic.

However, while the scholarly commentary during the twentieth century has strongly favored larger political units, political leaders and their followers were making precisely the opposite calculations. The history of the twentieth century is, in good part, the history of the fracturing of large political units. Since 1900, the Austro-Hungarian, Belgian, British, Danish, Dutch, Ethiopian, French, German, Italian, Japanese, Ottoman, Portuguese, Russian, Soviet, and Spanish empires all have collapsed, leaving in their wake a large number of smaller states. For instance, the Eritreans, who number 3.5 million, were unmoved by the Fabians or by later arguments that they should stay within Ethiopia (population 55 million). Undoubtedly, their belief in their own viability was strengthened by the success of other small states. For instance, Dr. Nerayo Teklemichael, head of the Eritrean Relief and Rehabilitation Agency, envisioned that his newly independent country would be successful by emulating the "Asian tigers."[23] Indeed, after independence, Ethiopia's former province became a favorite among foreign aid donors, an irony apparently lost on western officials after decades when they counseled the Eritreans that they would never be viable as a country.

At the same time, as noted in chapter four, African leaders have not been willing to make sacrifices so that proposed political and economic unions, explicitly designed to compensate for the small size of member nations, would work. It is, of course, possible that the leaders have simply miscalculated the relative advantages of size. Or, it could be that leaders and their followers recognized that their circumstances are so different from Europe that a different logic is needed when approaching the desired size and shape of nations.

[22] Marx and Engels, *Manifesto of the Communist Party*, in *The Marx-Engels Reader*, 2nd ed., ed. Robert C. Tucker (New York: W. W. Norton, 1978) p. 477; Emile Durkheim, *The Division of Labor in Society* (New York: The Free Press, 1984), p. 1; V. I. Lenin, "Communism and the East: Theses on the National and Colonial Questions," in *The Lenin Anthology*, ed. Robert C. Tucker (New York: W. W. Norton, 1975), p. 624; Herbert Spencer, *Principles of Sociology* (London: Macmillan, 1969), p. 23; Talcott Parsons, *Structure and Process in Modern Societies* (New York: Free Press, 1960), p. 117.

[23] Associated Press, "Africa's Newest Nation Defies African Stereotypes," 21 August 1994, p.1.

Understanding the Size and Shape of Nations

Political geographers and others have been unable to undertake constructive and systematic analyses concerning the implications of the design of nations because they lack an analytic foundation to approach the problem. However, the perspective developed in this book—especially that population distribution is the critical political challenge facing state-builders in Africa—opens the door to explaining how the size and shape of nations affects the consolidation of power. Shapes and sizes are not important in and of themselves; rather, what is critical is the particular population distribution that they present to national leaders. As Gottmann noted in what became a classic study, "it is the *organization of a territory by its population* that counts more than any other feature of it."[24] In the precolonial era, population distributions yielded boundaries. In the modern era, boundaries define a people.

This analysis begins by developing a typology of African countries based on computer-generated maps that portray the population distribution that the boundaries have enclosed. In the maps that follow, population density is portrayed in a five-category classification: areas with population densities that rank in the highest 20 percent are given the darkest color, areas with population densities in the next fifth of the distribution are allocated the second darkest color, etc. The specific population densities that the colors represent will therefore vary from country to country. For instance, in Benin, the lowest fifth of the population distribution includes areas with up to fourteen people per square kilometer, but only zero to one people in Botswana. The great advantage of this classification is that it allows a comparative analysis of the challenge each state faces in ruling over a given percentage of its population.

States Challenged by Geography

Given population distributions, it is possible to establish three general categories of countries. While there is inevitably some subjectivity in this enterprise, countries can be categorized by their relative size and the nature of the population distribution that their boundaries enclose. The first set of countries are those whose political geographies make it exceptionally difficult to consolidate power. These countries are, with one exception, large (among the top fifteen by size) and have areas of high population density; they are not contiguous, or in many cases, not even near each other (represented by multiple dark spots). Scattered popula-

---

[24] Gottmann, *The Significance of Territory*, p. 107. Emphasis in the original.

TABLE 5.1
African Countries by Size (Thousands of Sq. Kilometers)

First Quartile	Second Quartile	Third Quartile	Fourth Quartile
Sudan (2,376)	Namibia (823)	Côte d'Ivoire (318)	Malawi (94)
D.R.O.C. (2,267)	Mozambique (784)	Burkina Faso (274)	Sierra Leone (72)
Niger (1,267)	Zambia (743)	Gabon (258)	Togo (54)
Chad (1,259)	Somalia (627)	Guinea (246)	Lesotho (30)
Angola (1,247)	C.A.R. (623)	Ghana (228)	Eq. Guinea (28)
Mali (1,220)	Kenya (569)	Uganda (200)	Guinea Bissau (28)
Mauritania (1,025)	Botswana (567)	Senegal (193)	Burundi (26)
Ethiopia (1,000)	Cameroon (465)	Benin (111)	Rwanda (25)
Nigeria (911)	Zimbabwe (387)	Eritrea (101)	Swaziland (17)
Tanzania (884)	Congo-B (342)	Liberia (96)	Gambia (10)

Source: World Bank, *World Development Report 1998* (Washington, DC: Oxford University Press, 1998), pp. 190–1, 232.

tions in a large state present an automatic physical challenge to the extension of state authority over a large percentage of the population. An extensive population distribution also yields a more complex ethnic situation because African minority groups are more highly concentrated in single geographic areas than minorities in other regions. Gurr and his colleagues code 70 percent of black African minorities as being located in one region compared to 61 percent for Latin America and 48 percent in the rest of the world.[25] The combination of large distances and the geographic distinctness of different groups leads, not surprisingly, to the finding that African countries experience extremely high levels of ethnic fragmentation.[26] Thus, African states with difficult geographies face the continual problem of a relatively large number of outlying groups that are not only spatially distinct but that also can be mobilized around ethnic and cultural symbols that can compete with the state.

Democratic Republic of the Congo (the second largest—in terms of square kilometers—of the forty states south of the Sahara included in this book) is perhaps the classic case of an extremely challenging population distribution: the country has a large population density centered around Kinshasa and then other areas of high popoulation scattered throughout its vast landmass, including one area of high population more than eight

[25] James R. Scarritt, "Communal Conflict and Contention for Power in Africa South of the Sahara," in *Minorities at Risk: A Global View of Ethnopolitical Conflicts*, ed. Ted Robert Gurr (Washington, DC: U. S. Institute of Peace, 1993), p. 256.

[26] William Easterly and Ross Levine, "Africa's Growth Tragedy: Policies and Ethnic Divisions," *Quarterly Journal of Economics* 112 (1997): pp. 1219–20.

hundred miles away on the eastern border. In between are areas of extremely low population. D.R.O.C. is an almost classic instance of a "rimland" country: the major population concentrations are found in its border regions while its interior is relatively empty. This particular distribution presents significant political problems because it makes constructing an infrastructure to support the extension of state power difficult, especially given the absolute size of the country, since there would have to be roads that went through vast areas that are relatively underpopulated. It is therefore no wonder that Kinshasa has had such an extraordinarily difficult time consolidating power and that many provinces have informally seceded.

Small areas of high population densities are similarly scattered over the vast land of Sudan, the largest country in sub-Saharan Africa. Not surprisingly, that country has had a long history of civil war, which continues to threaten the viability of the nation. When created, Sudan encompassed "two geographical regions (the North and the South) in which two generically different sets of world-views prevailed."[27] As a result, Khartoum often faces the danger of losing Juba, the major city in the far south of the country, to rebels seeking autonomy, and often has only airlinks to that major agglomeration near the Ugandan border.

In Ethiopia (the eighth largest), a pattern of dispersed areas of high population density in various parts of the country helps explain why Addis Ababa in the end failed to control the civil war that was waged from various regions and why Eritrea, formerly the northern province of Ethiopia, finally gained its independence in 1993. During the 1980s, faced with its particularly severe demographic challenge, the government in Addis tried to change the biological facts on the ground through a program of forced movement of people into controlled villages. The goal was to foster a more favorable population distribution. Five million people were forcibly uprooted through villagization schemes between 1984 and 1986.[28] This effort failed but in so doing inflicted considerable misery on millions of people. In light of the previous failure at social engineering, the post-civil war government in Addis adopted an innovative constitution that grants limited rights of self-determination and secession to

[27] Dunstan M. Wai, "Geoethnicity and the Margin of Autonomy in the Sudan," in *State Versus Ethnic Claims: African Policy Dilemmas*, ed. Donald Rothchild and Victor A. Olorunsola (Boulder, CO: Westview Press, 1983), p. 307. See also Francis M. Deng, *War of Visions: Conflict of Identities in the Sudan* (Washington, DC: The Brookings Institution Press, 1995), p. 9.

[28] Robert D. Kaplan, *Surrender or Starve: The Wars Behind the Famine* (Boulder, CO: Westview Press, 1988), p. 121.

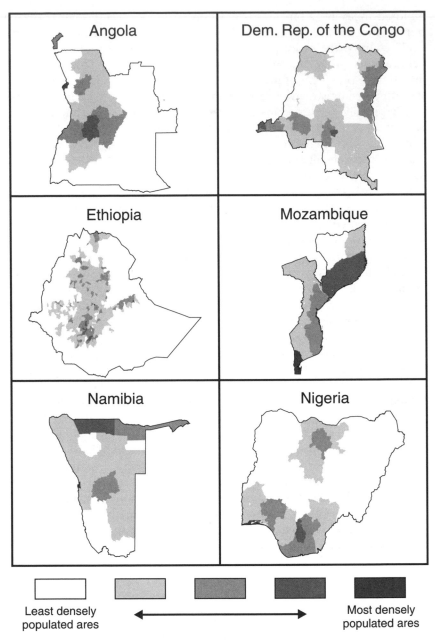

Least densely   ⟵——————————⟶   Most densely
populated ares   populated ares

Figure 5.1. Countries with Difficult Political Geographies

Note: Figures 5.1–5.5, and 5.7 are generated from World Resources Institute, *Africa Data Sampler on CD-ROM* (Washington, DC: WRI, 1992) using ARCVIEW 3.0.

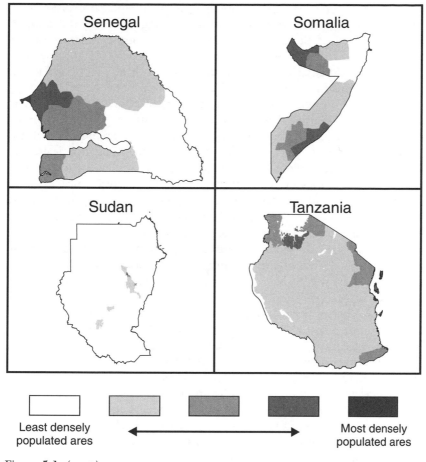

Figure 5.1. (*cont.*)

the provinces.[29] This constitution is important in that it recognizes the geographic problems that Addis Ababa faces in consolidating the Ethiopian state. Instead of simply denying the problems posed by a dispersed population, the constitution seeks to assure all Ethiopians that the capital is serious about devolving power because it grants them a legal way of leaving the country if they are unhappy.

Nigeria (ninth) also has scattered areas of high population density and it fought a civil war as well, to preserve its territorial integrity. As early as 1947, Chief Obafemi Awolowo, one of the great nationalists of his time,

[29] See Fasil Nahum, *Constitution for a Nation of Nations: The Ethiopian Prospect* (Trenton: Red Sea Press, 1997), pp. 154–9.

noted that Nigeria was little more than a "geographical expression."[30] The difficult population distribution has been aggravated by the complex ethnic divisions of the country, coupled with religious polarization between Muslims (concentrated in northern and parts of southwestern Nigeria) and Christians (in the middle belt, southeast, and parts of the southwest). Since independence, Nigerian governments have had to engage in balancing acts aimed at allaying fears of ethnic domination and religious expansionism. The peoples of the south, especially in the oil producing areas, sometimes openly protest the "enrichment" of the "north" via the state at the expense of the "south." This political economy has, in turn, resulted in the gradual impoverishment of the country despite the enormous oil windfall that Lagos has received since 1970.

Similarly, Mozambique (twelfth) is not quite in the top quartile by size but has a strikingly difficult political geography, in good part because it is so long. There are two areas of relatively high population distribution far from each other: one centered around Maputo in the south and one in the northcentral area of the country. Thus, Samora Machel's ambition (never realized) was to have the revolutionary party he led stretch from "Ruvuma to Maputo" and from Tete to the Indian Ocean. Without such an extensive political structure, he recognized, "we shall be isolated like limbs without a trunk."[31] Cognizant of the difficult political geography, Frente de Libertação de Moçambique, once in power, undertook a policy of villagization in order to mobilize the rural population.[32] As was the case elsewhere in Africa, this experiment failed.

Somalia, while not as large as Mozambique (fourteenth), has its highest population density centered around Mogadishu in the middle of the country and also around Hargeysa and Berbera (on the Gulf of Aden) in the north. This region, once known as British Somaliland, has now declared its independence. The difficulty of a government in Mogadishu, should one be formed, exercising power over "Somaliland" is obvious.

Similarly, Namibia (eleventh) also has one large concentration of population around the capital, but almost 50 percent of the population lives in Ovamboland in the far north.

The particular problems posed by peculiar geography also come into focus when population distribution is highlighted. Thus, Angola (fifth) has one center of population density in the middle of the country around Huambo, another around Luanda on the coast, and, by far the most problematic, another concentration of people in the oil-rich enclave of Cabinda, which is physically separated from the rest of the country by a

[30] Quoted in Joseph, *Democracy and Prebendal Politics in Nigeria*, p. 184.

[31] Quoted in Munslow, ed., *Samora Machel*, p. 25.

[32] Economic Commission for Africa, *Measures for Villagization and Resettlement in Selected African Countries* (Addis Ababa, Ethiopia: ECA, 1991), p. 57.

sliver of D.R.O.C. The large territory of Angola has made it extremely difficult for the government to find a military solution to the civil war that began at independence in 1975.

Similarly, while Senegal is not amongst the largest of African countries (only twenty-seventh), it has a particularly problematic geography: high population areas are separated from each other by Gambia. It is therefore hardly surprising that Dakar has faced, and been unable to completely suppress, a secessionist movement in the Casamance area in the southern part of the country.

Other geographic challenges are not as obvious simply from the shape of a country. Tanzania appears, simply looking at the shape of the boundaries, to be an almost classically defined "compact" country, although it is the tenth largest. However, even a cursory examination of its population distribution suggests that it is also a rimland country: the less populated areas are within a circle partially defined by the more populated areas. It is therefore not surprising that the country also attempted one of the more ambitious attempts at social engineering on the continent: the forced movement of large numbers of people into *ujamaa* villages in the late 1960s and early 1970s. Hyden attributes the forced villagization policy to the failure to capture the peasantry because of "the resilience of the peasant mode of production."[33] However, the clear geographical challenges that Tanzania presents to any state-builder are stark and should be taken into account.

Clearly, the geography of these countries is most at odds with the understanding of sovereignty that was developed in Berlin and then enshrined by the OAU. It cannot be assumed that physical control of the capital can be equated with control of these countries because of their size and because there are significant urban areas far from the capital that can serve as a rallying point for political challenges to the capital. Thus, much of D.R.O.C.'s history can be read not only as a dispute between the east, north, and south, but also as a battle between the capital of Kinshasa and the far away cities of Kisangani and Lubumbashi. In Somalia, a central division is between Mogadishu and Hargeysa; in Nigeria it was (and is) between Port Harcourt, Kano, and Lagos; in Ethiopia for many years it was between Asmara and Addis, before the Eritreans won and left. Given the critical masses of population far from the capital, these are the countries most in danger of fracturing. Potential secessionists may believe that the territories far from the capital could be viable if they separated from the capital. As urbanization proceeds and secondary cities grow in size, they become more of a threat to the capital because they risk gaining a critical mass that could finally threaten the

[33] Hyden, *Beyond Ujamaa*, p. 129.

capital. Accordingly, it is not surprising that two of these countries (Nigeria and Tanzania) have attempted to move their coastal capitals (Lagos and Dar es Salaam) to Abujua and Dodoma, both located near the geographic centers of their respective land masses.

Hinterland Countries

Another set of African countries have a particular set of political geographies that I label "hinterland" countries. As figure 5.2 suggests, the large Sahelian countries of Chad (the fourth largest in Africa), Mali (sixth), Mauritania (seventh), and Niger (third) have similar types of political geography. These countries, although exceptionally large by African standards, do not have dispersed areas of high population density. Rather, areas of high and medium population density (by national standards) are in relatively small areas of the country and then there are vast hinterlands where few people live. Unlike the countries with problematic population distributions, the empty areas are not internal to the country but constitute a vast, largely empty, hinterland.

The political geography of these countries offers both profound challenges and perhaps more opportunities than is generally assumed. On the one hand, these countries seem almost impossible to govern. Certainly, no government, given the poverty in Chad, Mali, Mauritania, or Niger is going to be able to exert effective control over the vast, empty areas in these countries. The Club du Sahel complained, "Sahelian states are too large, sparsely populated, and hard to manage."[34] Perhaps more importantly, those who might be alienated by the regimes have a ready-made hinterland in which to escape.

On the other hand, the African construction of sacrosanct boundaries and the assumption that physical control of the capital can be equated with control of the countryside is more appropriate to hinterland countries than those with dispersed areas of high population density. In each of these hinterland countries, the capital will be challenged to control the vast territory. However, given the concentration of population, occupation of the capital automatically means that the government of the day is in close proximity with a large percentage of the population. The extreme example is Mauritania that, despite its vast territory, has 54 percent of its population in urban areas compared to the African average of 32 percent.[35] Further, in the hinterland countries, there is essentially only one city, or at least only one urban agglomeration. Bamako, N'Djamena, Niamey, and Nouakchott do not face any challenges by a distant city to

[34] Club du Sahel, *Preparing for the Future*, p. 47.
[35] World Bank, *World Development Report 1998*, pp. 192–3.

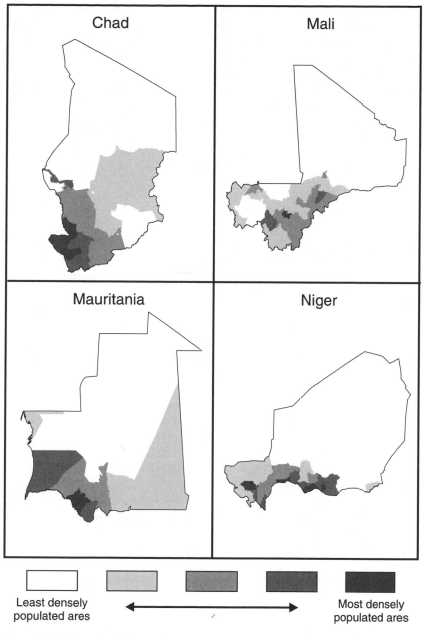

Least densely
populated ares

Most densely
populated ares

Figure 5.2. Hinterland Countries

their supremacy. Greater urbanization only will enhance the importance of the capital city because it is unlikely that people will migrate anywhere else. As a result, the only path to power for an ambitious man is to seize the capital; secession is not a particularly appealing option. For instance, the rebel Tuareg groups in Mali's north recognized that an independent Azawad was not viable.[36] The rebels and an enlightened Malian government eventually signed a peace treaty in 1992, one of the few instances of a successful resolution of an African civil war without one side destroying the other. It is true that those who seek to escape the state can do so but, perhaps paradoxically, the fundamental political battle in these countries must be located in the capital despite the vast territories.

Countries with Favorable Geography

In contrast, the third general shape of African countries, examples of which are portrayed in figure 5.3, is much more conducive to the consolidation of power. In these countries, the highest concentration of power is found in one area, usually around the capital, and then population densities become lower as distance from the capital increases. Not surprisingly, these countries tend to be quite small. For instance, in some ways Benin (ranked twenty-eighth) has the ideal population density given current African understandings of power: the concentric rings of population density correspond to the current understanding of sovereignty; the largest concentrations of people are closest to the capital, where it is easiest for the state to rule them, and population density conveniently declines as distance from the capital grows. Countries such as Botswana (ranked seventeenth in size), Burkina Faso (twenty-second), Central African Republic (fifteenth), Eritrea (twenty-ninth), Gabon (twenty-third), Guinea (twenty-fourth), Sierra Leone (thirty-second), and Zimbabwe (nineteenth) do not have quite as obvious concentric circles emanating away from the capital but there is a clear decline in population density as distance from the capital grows. Distances between areas of relatively high population density are not large. There are one or two hinterlands far from the capital where the fewest people live but these hinterlands are not so vast as to be unmanageable.

There is also a set of countries so small that their population distributions are almost irrelevant because the geographic mass of the state is so limited that it does not pose any obstacle to the extension of authority. Roughly, these are the countries that are in the last fifth of the size distribution with land masses no larger than fifty-five thousand square miles:

[36] Robin-Edward Poulton and Ibrahim ag Youssouf, *A Peace of Timbuktu* (New York: United Nations Institute for Disarmament Research, 1998), p. 31.

no bigger than the state of West Virginia or about 2.3 percent the size of Sudan. From largest to smallest, this includes: Togo (thirty-third), Lesotho, Equatorial Guinea, Guinea-Bissau, Burundi, Rwanda, Swaziland, and Gambia. Given their small size, their population density distributions are obviously quite favorable to political consolidation.

Obviously, these last two sets of countries have geographies that are in greatest accord with the OAU understanding of sovereignty and power. Not only are the capital cities close to a very large percentage of the population, but the capital is also relatively close to a significant percentage of the territory. Further, the countries' designs do not pose any seemingly intractable problems to the broadcasting of authority.

This is not to argue that all will go well in small countries. As Max Liniger-Goumaz notes in his aptly titled book about Equatorial Guinea (*Small Is Not Always Beautiful*), even very small countries can have fantastically corrupt and incompetent regimes that impoverish their nations. Under Macías Nguema (1968–1979) and Teodoro Obiang Nguema (1979–), Equatorial Guinea has become more impoverished, and one-third of the population has gone into exile. Similarly, Burundi and Rwanda have both experienced genocides. However, the type of decline experienced by small countries is different from that of large countries because even in decline, small countries can exercise considerable authority over their populations. Liniger-Goumaz quotes one State Department description of Equatorial Guinea in 1986: "Professional and labor organizations are non-existent; the country is under absolute rule of the President."[37] The 1997 State Department's Annual Human Rights Report also noted an exceptional degree of governmental control even in the midst of decline: "Government authorization must be obtained for meetings of more than 10 persons in private homes for discussions that the regime considers political."[38] Similarly, the genocides in Burundi and Rwanda required high degrees of control over the entire territory. In contrast, Young and Turner describe a very different type of decay for then Zaire: "During the phases of ascendency and expansion, the state exuded an appearance of force and power . . . This imagery was then exploded by the period of decay and crisis, in which the infirmities of the state again became conspicuous."[39] Even if it had wanted to, the state in Zaire could not have arranged the kind of genocide that Rwanda experienced in 1994: there was simply too much land for people to escape away from the reach of the state. Due to the difficulties of geography, large states

[37] Max Liniger-Goumaz, *Small Is Not Always Beautiful: The Story of Equatorial Guinea* (London: C. Hurst, 1988), p. 168.

[38] U.S. State Department, *Country Reports on Human Rights Practices for 1997*, found at: www.state.gov/www/global/human—rights/1997—hrp—report/eqguinea.html.

[39] Young and Turner, *The Rise and Decline of the Zairian State*, p. 77.

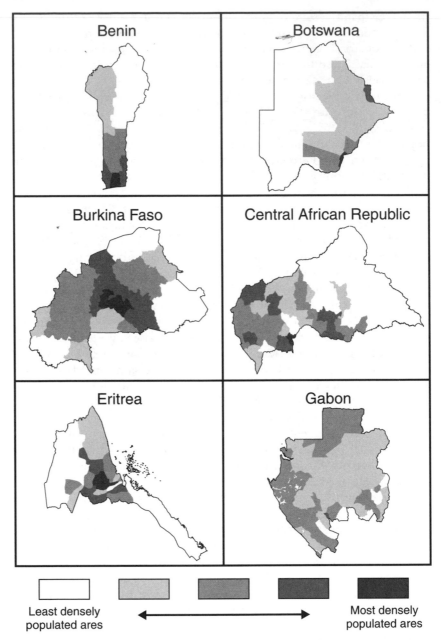

Figure 5.3. Countries with Favorable Geographies

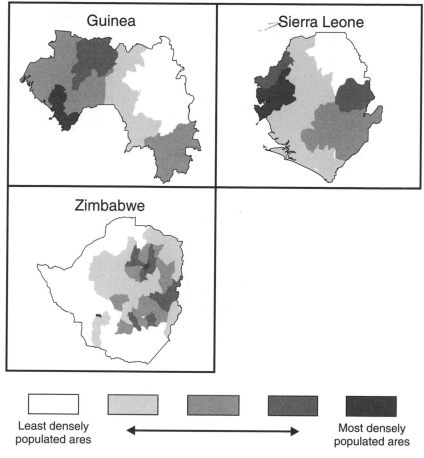

Figure 5.3. (*cont.*)

with difficult population distributions find that the liabilities of their size and shape are more readily apparent than those of small states, which continue to exercise authority over their more limited land masses even in times of decline.

As a result, wars in big countries with problematic geographies often take a different course than in countries where it is easier for the state to reach the hinterland and vice-versa. It is particularly notable that in small wars, the capital itself becomes the battleground: Bissau, Brazzaville, Freetown, and Maseru were all destroyed between 1997 and 1999 because it was so easy for combatants to get to the center of power. In contrast, wars in larger states have the potential to end with a territorial division (as was the case with Ethiopia when Addis was saved in 1991 by

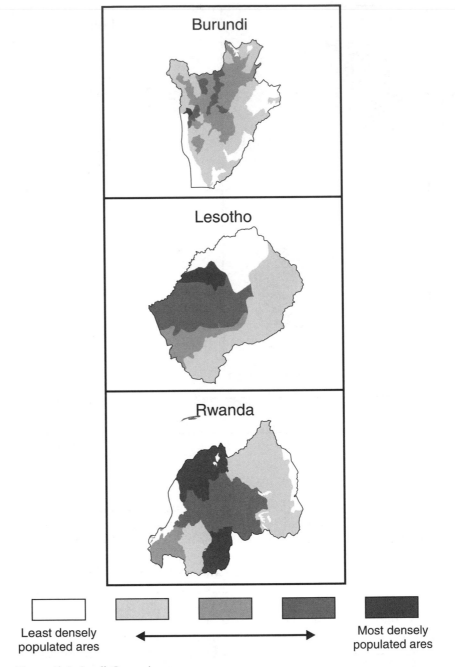

Least densely
populated ares

Most densely
populated ares

Figure 5.4. Small Countries

granting Eritrea its independence) or simply drag on because the capital cannot reach the rebels in the countryside and they cannot march on the central state in, say, Luanda or Khartoum. The size and shape of African countries does not guarantee a particular outcome but does determine the contours the conflict may follow.

Of course, few typologies can be comprehensive and there are some countries that escape obvious classification. Countries whose geography is neither particularly favorable nor unfavorable to state consolidation include Cameroon (eighteenth), Côte d'Ivoire (twenty-first), Ghana (twenty-fifth) Kenya (sixteenth), Malawi (thirty-first), Uganda (twenty-sixth), and Zambia (thirteenth). These countries, all in east and southern Africa and coastal West Africa, have dispersed populations, but the distributions are not so discontinuous as to compare with the countries identified above as having particularly difficult geographies. Nor are their hinterland areas so large as to present insurmountable problems, but they are certainly not among the microstates of Africa. For instance, Zambia does have an extensive population distribution, but Lusaka is located in the geographic center of the country. The central spatial conflict in that country has always been pictured as one between the surface (the government eager for revenue) and the underground (the mines that produce copper) rather than between regions of the country. Similarly, Malawi is elongated, but small enough so that its north-south orientation is not obviously problematic. Uganda has had governments that have demonstrated their ability to sow terror throughout much of the territory and has had a rebel movement (in 1986) win control of the capital. However, it has also had a history of low-level conflict in parts of the country that the state has not been able to suppress. Thus, it is categorized as a country with a neutral political geography although, perhaps even more so than with the others, there is a significant amount of subjectivity in that classification.

Geography and Destiny

Geography is only a given. There is no clearer evidence that geography is not destiny than the fact that while Botswana, Burkina Faso, Congo-Brazzaville, and Sierra Leone may have similar political geographies, their political histories since independence have varied markedly. Botswana has been a well-functioning, multiparty democracy, while Sierra Leone has gradually receded into the category of failed states because it could not contain the civil war that spread from Liberia. Burkina Faso and Congo-Brazzaville epitomize the African pattern of incomplete authoritarianism appearing in different forms. Burkina has an authoritarian government that has adopted democratic trappings while Brazzaville was largely

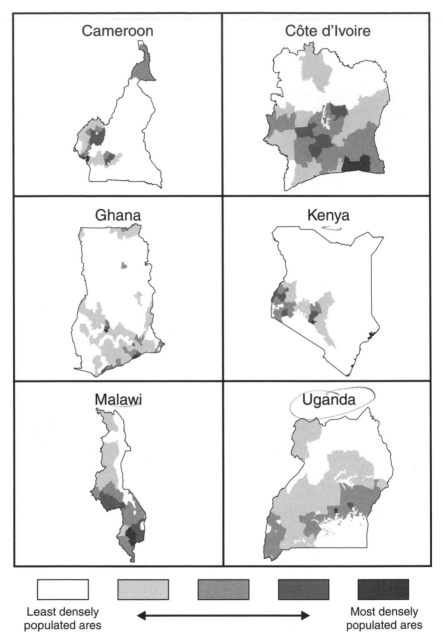

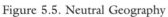

Figure 5.5. Neutral Geography

TABLE 5.2
African National Design

Countries with Difficult Political Geographies	Hinterland Countries	Countries with Favorable Political Geographies	Countries with Neutral Political Geographies
Angola	Chad	Benin	Cameroon
D.R.O.C.	Mali	Botswana	Côte d'Ivoire
Ethiopia	Mauritania	Burkina Faso	Ghana
Mozambique	Niger	Burundi	Kenya
Namibia		C.A.R.	Malawi
Nigeria		Congo-Brazzaville	Uganda
Senegal		Equatorial Guinea	Zambia
Somalia		Eritrea	
Sudan		Gabon	
Tanzania		Gambia	
		Guinea	
		Guinea Bissau	
		Lesotho	
		Liberia	
		Rwanda	
		Sierra Leone	
		Swaziland	
		Togo	
		Zimbabwe	

destroyed in a civil war in 1997 when the old leader (Denis Sassou-Nguesso) overthrew Pascal Lissouba, who had been elected in 1992.

A full understanding of the implications of the size and shape of nations must therefore consider how leaders confront their geographic and demographic endowments by constructing the infrastructure of power. In this chapter, roads will again serve as a proxy for the broadcasting of authority. Precolonial leaders, as noted in chapter three, who needed to physically extend their power were obsessed with roads as were early colonial leaders, like Earl Grey, who operated under the old African rules. Those leaders in Africa—such as Laurent Kabila, the successor to Mobutu—who are desperately concerned about their ability to broadcast power have also identified road construction as one of their most important priorities.[40] Roads are as vital as ever to the workings of African states: approximately 80 to 90 percent of Africa's passenger and freight

[40] One of the few promises that Kabila made during his march to Kinshasa in 1997 was to build roads. James C. McKinley, "Zaire Rebel Leader Spurns Cease-Fire and Sets Sights on Capital," *New York Times*, 23 March 1997, p. 10.

TABLE 5.3
Road Density over Time (Countries with difficult political geographies are highlighted)

Country	Road Density 1963	Road Density 1997	Average Change
Rwanda	0.21	0.56	173
Burundi	0.21	0.52	143
Gambia	0.12	0.25	105
Swaziland	0.13	0.22	67
Nigeria	0.08	0.21	152
Côte d'Ivoire	0.10	0.17	62
Malawi	0.11	0.17	57
Ghana	0.13	0.16	23
Lesotho	0.06	0.16	171
Sierra Leone	0.09	0.16	73
Guinea	0.03	0.13	305
Kenya	0.08	0.13	70
Togo	0.05	0.13	144
Uganda	0.08	0.13[b]	71
Average	**0.06**	**0.11**	**82**
Liberia	0.02	0.10	383
Tanzania	0.04	0.09	133
Cameroon	0.03	0.07	129
D.R.O.C.	0.07	0.07	5
Senegal	0.07	0.07	0
Median	**0.05**	**0.07**	**69**
Benin	0.06	0.06	4
Angola	0.06[a]	0.06	0
Zambia	0.05	0.05	5

traffic travel by road and road transport, "provides the only form of access to most rural communities."[41] Thus it is not surprising that the great geographer Derwent Whittlesey noted, "Efficient transportation consolidates political areas, whether the Roman Empire or the United States of America. The lack of ready means of circulation is a source of political weakness whatever the density of population, as the plight of China proves."[42] Or as Eugen Weber noted in his magnificent history of rural France, "Until roads spread, many rural communities remained im-

[41] Ian G. Heggie, *Management and Financing of Roads: An Agenda for Reform* (Washington, DC: The World Bank, 1995), p. 1.
[42] Whittelesy, *The Earth and the State*, p. 11.

TABLE 5.3
(*Continued*)

Country	Road Density 1963	Road Density 1997	Average Change
Burkina Faso	0.06	0.04	−37
C.A.R.	0.03	0.04	32
Congo	0.03	0.04	16
Mozambique	0.05ª	0.04	−20
Botswana	0.01	0.03	109
Chad	0.03	0.03	18
Gabon	0.02	0.03	33
Somalia	0.02	0.03	41
Ethiopia	0.02	0.02	−6
Mali	0.01	0.02	97
Mauritania	0.01	0.01	76
Niger	0.01	0.01	69
Sudan	0.00	0.01	183

ªData from 1974.

ᵇData from 1992, the most recent available.

Data are for all countries independent before 1980. Data for 1963 are for year closest to 1963. Data for Equatorial Guinea and Guinea Bissau are not available.

Numbers have been rounded to two decimal places. However, percentages were calculated off the raw numbers.

Source: For 1963 data, see table 3.1. Data for the former Belgian and French territories have been disaggregated. Data for 1974 statistics for Mozambique and Angola from International Road Federation Union, *World Road Statistics, 1974–1978* (Geneva: International Road Federation Union, 1979), pp. 15, 17. Statistics for road density for 1997 are for year closest to 1997. Source for 1997 statistics: International Road Federation Union, *World Road Statistics 1993–97* (Geneva: International Road Federation Union, 1999), pp. 10–15.

prisoned in semi-isolation, limited participants in the economy and politics of the nation."[43]

Across Africa, during the independence period, overall road-building performance has been poor. As table 5.3 indicates, the thirty-five African countries that gained independence in the 1960s and 1970s for which data are available (no statistics appear to exist for Equatorial Guinea or Guinea Bissau) had, on average, only increased their road stock (as measured by road density: kilometers of roads divided by square kilometers of land) by 82 percent by 1997. The median increase was only 69 percent,

[43] Eugen Weber, *Peasants into Frenchmen: The Modernization of Rural France* (Stanford, CA: Stanford University Press, 1976), p. 195.

suggesting that a few countries with relatively successful road-building programs are distorting the already unimpressive average.

As roads generally do not often disappear (except, apparently, in Burkina Faso, Ethiopia, and Mozambique), road construction is additive and understanding the relationship between the road stock in 1963 and 1997 should be a first step in understanding the different paths that countries have taken. This is a long enough period so that African countries could reasonably be expected to make a significant imprint on their inherited infrastructure. I would have also included Zimbabwe (independent since 1980), but its road density appears particularly difficult to calculate due to the large number of secondary and tertiary roads.[44] Namibia and Eritrea are excluded from the statistical analysis because they received independence in the 1990s and therefore have not yet had a chance to profoundly influence their infrastructure. As figure 5.6 shows, there is a very strong relationship between the density of roads at or close to independence (in 1963 for all but Angola and Mozambique and in 1974 for those two countries) and in 1997. Across thirty-three countries, about 70 percent ($R^2 = 0.70$, Prob $> F = 0.0000$) of the variance in road stocks in 1997 can be explained by what was present at independence.[45] This relationship can reasonably be assumed to be causal because the 1997 road systems are built out from the colonial backbones. As figure 5.6 suggests, this relationship holds across the board: countries with both very low and very high stocks of roads are profoundly influenced by their colonial inheritance.

Interestingly, the sign of the relationship between road stocks at independence and road stocks in 1997, as is clear from figure 5.1, is positive. As a result, there was relatively little change in the rank order of countries by road density between the end of the colonial period and 1997. It might have been expected that countries with relatively poor infrastructure inheritances from the colonialists would have been unusually energetic road builders, but that is not the case.

That road stock at independence is a relatively good predictor of road stock in 1997 and that those unusually badly off at independence did not do relatively well during the next three decades are both indicative of Africa's overall poor economic and political performance. The failure of African countries to significantly enhance their rather pathetic colonial inheritance suggests one reason for the general lack of progress in political and economic consolidation across the continent. The absence of sig-

[44] The International Road Federation's Statistics are too inconsistent between years to use. See International Road Federation, *World Road Statistics 1999* (Geneva: International Road Federation, 1999), p. 15.

[45] Burundi and Rwanda were dropped from the equation because they are outliers. $R^2 = 0.84$ with Burundi and Rwanda.

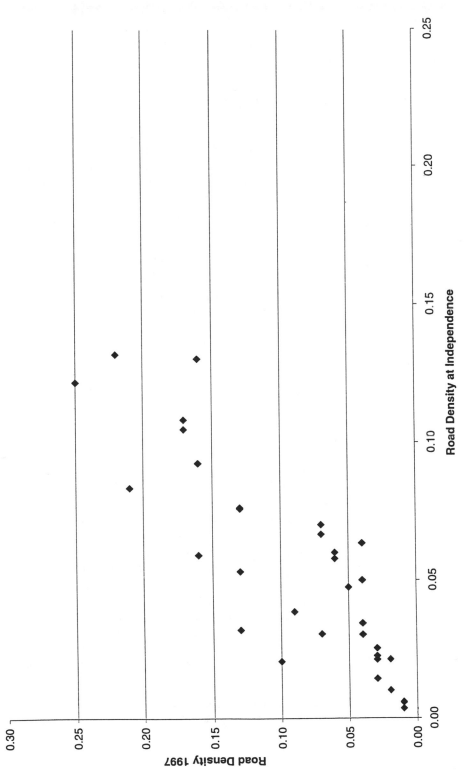

Figure 5.6. Road Density over Time

nificant changes in rank order is also depressing: countries did almost uniformly poorly in building roads.

Road Building and Difficult Geography

The most striking result of the comparison between geography and road-building efforts is that those countries most in need of road networks did not build them and those with the least problematic geographies built the most roads. Only three of the countries with the most problematic geographies (Nigeria, Sudan, and Tanzania) achieved greater than the median increase of 69 percent between independence and 1997. Of the others that were independent for the entire period, D.R.O.C. increased its road stock by only 5 percent, 6 percent of Ethiopia's roads seem to have disappeared, Senegal did not add appreciably to its road stock, and Somalia's roads increased by only 41 percent. Angola and Mozambique have only been independent since 1975, but in the first twenty-two years of independence, neither managed to increase their road densities.[46]

As a result of this poor performance since independence, the overall road stocks of African countries with truly problematic geographies are unimpressive. Table 5.3 indicates that of the nine countries with problematic geographies independent before 1980 (Namibia is excluded), only Nigeria and Tanzania are above the African median for road density in 1997. All of the other countries with problematic geographies that were independent before 1990 (Angola, D.R.O.C., Ethiopia, Mozambique, Senegal, Somalia, and Sudan) have road stocks that are only at or below the median despite the challenges they face. Some of the performances are strikingly bad. For instance, Sudan's 183 percent increase in road stocks was not able to make up for its poor colonial endowment. As a result, it had the lowest road density of any African country in 1997, despite its obvious need for more roads to consolidate authority.

Overall, there is a strong negative relationship between road density and country size. Country size (as measured in square kilometers) explains about 28 percent of road density ($R^2 = 0.28$, Prob>F= 0.0015) while the sign of the coefficient is negative.[47] Of course at some level, there is a mathematical association between road density and size because size is also the denominator in the road density calculation. However, the fact that the mathematical association is allowed to be significant is caused by the failure of African countries to overcome their colonial inheritance.

[46] International Road Federation, *World Road Statistics 1999*, p. 10–13.
[47] This regression again excludes Burundi and Rwanda.

The poor road-building performance of countries with problematic geographies can be tied to the understanding of how power was broadcast over the last century. The colonialists essentially built the minimum number of roads necessary to rule given the Berlin rules. Using the scheme developed in chapter one, they only addressed the fixed costs that had to be paid immediately in order to rule the capital. That meant that colonies with large geographic masses had relatively low road stocks because most of the road building under white rule was concentrated around the capital and efforts were not made to consolidate far-flung populations. Since independence, large countries have not overcome their inheritance. The explanatory power provided by size is completely washed out if the colonial inheritance is taken into account.[48] Indeed, the size of a country explained less of its road density at independence ($R^2 = .20$) than in 1997. Large countries with problematic population distributions have found only the capital, and perhaps some adjoining areas, necessary to control through the creation of a dense road network.

It is certainly not the case that a significant road-building performance would have been beyond the reach of these countries. The increase in road density achieved by the high performers is simply not that impressive that more countries could not have significantly changed the rank ordering if they had a more determined road-building project. It cannot be said that the large countries were too poor as road construction and economic development are not related. In general, the demand for road infrastructure is most clearly related to national income for middle-income countries rather than low-income African countries.[49]

Roads and the Hinterland Countries

Chad, Mali, Mauritania, and Niger all have road density statistics that are well below the continental average. However, national road density statistics for these countries are somewhat misleading because their political geography allows them to consolidate rule over much of their population without extensive road systems. The road construction that did occur in these countries may have significantly enhanced the capital's reach to a large percentage of the population, even if most of the national territories

[48] A regression using both road density in 1963 and size of country to explain road density variation in 1997 has almost no more explanatory power ($R^2 = 0.73$) than road density in 1963 alone ($R^2 = 0.70$).

[49] World Bank, *World Development Report 1994: Infrastructure for Development* (New York: Oxford University Press, 1994), p. 15. There is a clear overall relationship between road infrastructure and income that is not apparent for low-income countries by themselves. Generally, see Cesar Queiroz and Surhid Gautam, *Road Infrastructure and Economic Development: Some Diagnostic Indicators*, (Washington, DC: The World Bank, 1992), p. 4.

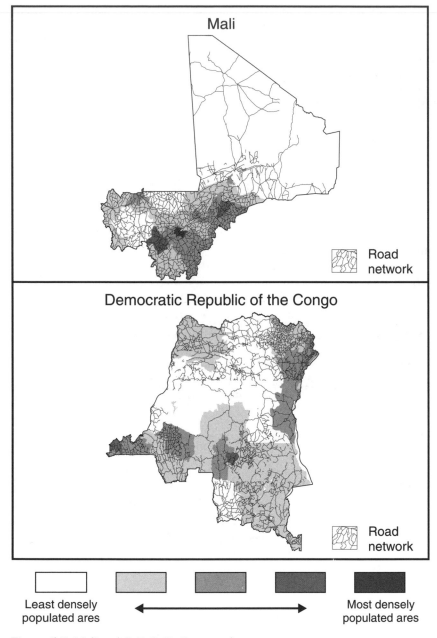

Figure 5.7. Mali and D.R.O.C. Compared

are still not served by extensive transport systems. Table 5.7 compares Mali and D.R.O.C. by overlaying functional (at least in theory) road networks over population distributions. Both are extremely large countries. However, while D.R.O.C.'s road density is statistically three and half times Mali's, Mali has a more compact road system that is more amenable to the extension of state power because its people are not nearly as widely dispersed as in D.R.O.C. In D.R.O.C., many roads have to be built through unpopulated areas just to get to the populated regions. Only a nuanced analysis of population distribution and geography allows for the insight that the power infrastructures of the hinterland countries can be significantly different from other countries that, while also large, have population distributions that present an altogether different political challenge.

Roads and Power in Countries with Favorable Geography

Consistent with the above analysis, it is also clear that those countries with less problematic geographies have more impressive road stocks after thirty years of independence. The four countries with the highest road densities are four of the very smallest countries in Africa (Rwanda, Burundi, Gambia, and Swaziland). The explanation for the seeming paradox of why those least in "need" of roads, given the continental African experience, can be traced back to the evolution of sovereignty. These countries had relatively high road densities in 1963 because the Berlin rules forced the colonialists to build roads around the capital and these countries are not much more than the capital and relatively small adjoining areas. Again, state consolidation is not necessarily a good thing for the population in the short-term. Rwanda's exceptionally high road density (.56 compared to the African median of .07) undoubtedly made the quick killing of almost eight hundred thousand Tutsi in 1994 possible. Similarly, the extraordinary repression that Robert Mugabe's government visited on Matabeleland (in southwest Zimbabwe) in 1983 and 1984—including food embargoes and bans on the use of transportation—was possible because the area the government sought to repress was not that large, especially given the relatively good infrastructure that had been inherited from the Rhodesians.[50]

---

[50] For details on the Matabeleland atrocities, see Catholic Commission for Justice and Peace, *Report on the 1980s Disturbances in Matabeland and the Midlands*, pt. 2 (Harare, Zimbabwe: Catholic Commission, 1997), pp. 5–6.

Roads to Power

The failure of those who most needed roads to develop them is not surprising given the analysis in chapter four that suggests that the particular international environment that African countries face is very different from that of Europe. As noted in chapter one, countries that face external threats have to tie their forward areas that have direct responsibility for confronting enemies to the political core. As a result, they have a profound incentive to build roads. For instance, Namibia has a high road density (.08, above the African median)[51] despite its vast empty regions because, while it was ruled by Pretoria (independence was in 1990), it was perceived by the white government as a forward theater in the struggle against external aggressors, primarily the African National Congress, who wanted to overthrow white rule. In contrast, there is no strategic reason why most African countries would necessarily have to build roads in order to defend themselves from internal threats, as the Addis rules award sovereignty to those who control the capital. Not a few leaders will have recognized that building roads is quite literally a two-way street: roads allow the capital to reach outward but also allow those in the hinterland to march more quickly to the center of power. In fact, a not illogical strategy for many leaders confronting vast territories would be to try not to reach out to outlying areas and let those areas that want to threaten the state live in relative isolation, rather than face the choice of having to be governed by the center or seizing it themselves. Instead of spending money on roads to secure their authority, African leaders, as chapter four suggests, have strong incentives to engage in patronage politics at the center.

Reevaluating the Political Advantages of Size

It is easy to see that the traditional bias in favor of large states is irrelevant to Africa because the strategic and economic environments are so different. The fundamental problem European states faced was survival given external threats and they therefore developed a particular morphology. Size was a tremendous advantage in both garnering military assets and providing strategically important buffers between core areas and boundaries. However, African countries do not face external aggressors and therefore gain no advantage from larger size when confronting their external environment. Rather, due to their particular demographic circumstances, African states find it difficult to broadcast power and must worry

---

[51] International Road Federation, *World Road Statistics 1999*, p. 13.

continually about internal threats. Therefore, small size is an advantage given the particular challenges faced by African countries. However, size must be understood in relationship to population distribution.

A large size is not advantageous for solving domestic political problems. Madison, in many ways the pivotal figure in the debate about the advantages of size, argued for large countries because he recognized that larger countries have more factions, an assumption that is accurate for Africa given the geographic distinctness of minority groups. He therefore believed that size was an advantage because the larger a state, "you take in a greater variety of parties and interests; you make it less probable that a majority of the whole will have a common motive to invade the rights of other citizens; or if such a common motive exists, it will be more difficult for all who feel it to discover their own strength, and to act in unison with each other."[52] However, this analysis only makes sense if the central concern is limiting the authority of both the state over groups (i.e., factions) and groups over other groups. Obviously, if the primary consideration is the broadcasting of state authority, the analysis is turned on its head and size becomes a disadvantage precisely because, everything else being equal, it is more difficult to exercise authority over more than fewer groups.

Conclusion

This chapter develops a perspective on the desirability of the size and shapes of African countries based on political challenges that state-makers confront. It seems relatively clear that smaller states face fewer political challenges in consolidating their rule, although size is not a uniform barrier to broadcasting authority. Indeed, broadcasting authority in some of the relatively large states (those labeled as "hinterland") may be easier than their sheer size suggests because of their peculiar population distributions. Given the lack of external threat, power will be broadcast in Africa at least somewhat like it was during the precolonial period and as it is now encouraged by the Addis rule: profoundly at the political core and radiating out with decreasing authority. However, unlike the precolonial period, the territorial boundaries are fixed. As a result, those countries with population distributions that are congruent with the OAU's vision of sovereignty in Africa will find it easiest to consolidate authority. Those countries with either very large territories and/or difficult population distributions find it exceptionally hard to consolidate authority. There are no guarantees, of course, because the final consolidation of authority is

[52] Madison, *The Federalist Papers*, p. 64.

still dependent on wise state policies. However, understanding the ramifications of the design of nations is critical to understanding state-making. Indeed, while small size is no guarantee of success, it seems clear that large size, in the current impoverished African context, may be a sufficient reason for a country's failure unless the population is not distributed across the vastness of a large state's hinterland.

Six

Chiefs, States, and the Land

Mafumu *Ndi* Boma [Chiefs *are* the
Government].
  Malawian chiefs quoted at a
  democratization seminar. National Democratic
  Institute for International Affairs,
  *Chiefs: Traditional Authority and
  Democratic Governance in Malawi*

THE INABILITY of African states to project power over distance has meant
that one of the most contentious issues in the politics of the continent
has been the relationship between central authorities and local leaders.
"Chiefs"—to use one word for a group of leaders who vary considerably
and whose titles alone include emir, *oba, obi, eze, obong, amayanabo,
shehu, ovie,* and *otaru* (to use only the *Nigerian* terms)[1]—can often trace
the basis of their authority back to the precolonial period, have sometimes benefited from colonial attempts to strengthen certain local institutions, and still control the allocation of many critical resources at the
local level. As a result, they are often competitors to the centralized African state and are viewed as such by national leaders. The loyalties that
citizens have toward these leaders, often expressed in a complex network
of ethnic relations, is a significant challenge to African countries still having great difficulty (as chapter four notes) in creating a nationalist ethos.
Ethnic fragmentation is arguably the single most important threat to
many African countries as widescale ethnic violence has been symptoma-
tic of many of Africa's failing states and ethnic politics has paralyzed
many others.

This chapter reviews how far the centralized states in Africa have been
able to broadcast power into rural areas by examining ongoing disputes
over land tenure. The role of local elites in the distribution of land is
critical to their autonomy from the state. As a result, states have continually sought to alter property rights in order to disempower local elites.
However, given the uneven ability of African states to implement contro-

[1] Eghosa Osaghae, "The Role and Functions of Traditional Leaders and Indigenous
Groups in Nigeria," in *The Rights of Indigenous People: A Quest for Coexistence,* ed. Bertus
de Villiers (Pretoria, South Africa: Human Science Research Council, 1997), p. 105.

versial policies in the hinterlands, national authorities have had varying success in their efforts to supplant chiefs in controlling the process of allocation of this critical resource. This chapter explores the reasons why some states are more successful than others in implementing changes in property rights that supplant chiefs and, by extension, are better able to broadcast power over distance.

By examining changes in the legal infrastructure that furthers the reach of the state, this analysis is an appropriate companion to chapter five, which examines the development of the physical infrastructure needed to extend state power. Of course, given this book's focus on the spatial elements of power, how the land itself is allocated is a pivotal issue to study. Finally, to some extent, African states' ability to determine the method by which their own land is distributed is the domestic analogue to winning the right to control boundaries at independence.[2]

The Complicated Dance between States and Chiefs

The relationships between states and chiefs have been among the most complicated in African politics. Many African nationalists yearned to overturn traditional structures in rural areas that had survived colonial rule. Thus, Tafawa Balewa argued as early as 1950 when he announced a new era of native administration in Nigeria, "Lord Lugard, whom we shall always respect . . . surely never intended that the expedient of the hour should remain the unchanging authority of all time."[3] To the young men who led the new parties seeking independence, very few of whom were of high status at birth,[4] the traditional authorities were seemingly the very antithesis of the modern revolution that they sought to lead. In turn, traditional authorities generally had played a highly ambiguous role during the run-up to independence because they did not know and did not trust the young turks who, seemingly overnight, appeared on their way to capturing political power in a revolutionary manner. Abrahams tells a common story of neighborhood groups in parts of Tanzania emerging as important grassroots supporters of TANU (the leading na-

[2] Kwamena Bentsi-Enchill, "Do African Systems of Land Tenure Require a Special Terminology?" in *African Law and Legal Theory*, ed. Gordon R. Woodman and A. O. Obilade (New York: New York University Press, 1995), p. 117.

[3] Quoted in in A. H. M. Kirk-Greene, introduction to *The Principles of Native Administration in Nigeria*, ed. A. H. M. Kirk-Green (London: Oxford University Press, 1965), p. 17.

[4] Henry S. Bienen, "The State and Ethnicity: Integrative Formulas in Africa," in *State Versus Ethnic Claims: African Policy Dilemmas*, ed. Donald Rothchild and Victor A. Olorunsola (Boulder, CO: Westview Press, 1983), p. 121.

tionalist party) and beginning to exercise jurisdiction over local activities (e.g., enforcing a boycott against an Asian trader). In this process of self-assertion, he writes, "both the chiefs and the colonial government were challenged. Indeed, the two of them were merged in some people's minds."[5]

However, there was still a profound need for the new nationalists to come to terms with the traditional leaders. The politicians recognized that their parties did not extend fully into rural areas and that their appeal was therefore spatially limited. Also, African states came to independence with almost no local state structures besides those that were intertwined with traditional authorities. Or as Deschamps was willing to admit, "the new nations in our sector inherited rudimentary or worthless substructures."[6]

After independence, the ambivalence toward traditional leaders continued. As van Rouveroy van Nieuwaal correctly notes, "Most heads of state, both reactionary and revolutionary, were suspicious of the chief." He goes on to cite many examples of post-independence suppression of traditional rulers, including the undermining of the Guinean chiefdoms by Sékou Touré (despite the fact that he claimed descent from the great nineteenth-century chief Samory Touré), the formidable legal constraints enacted by Nkrumah, the abolition of chiefdoms in Tanzania, and the marginalization of Mogho Naba, ruler of the Mossi, in then Upper Volta.[7] The critical year was probably 1966 when Ugandan prime minister Milton Obote sent the army to invade the palace of the kabaka of Buganda—among the most storied of Africa's traditional leaders—and forced Kabaka Sir Edward Mutesa into exile. In the same year, Mwambutsa IV, king of Burundi, was deposed (by his son who would be overthrown shortly thereafter) and Sir Ahmadu Bello, Sadauna of Sokoto and premier of Nigeria's Northern Region, was killed in a coup d'etat.

Further, traditional leaders were at odds with the operating code of the one-party state that African leaders across the continent began to adopt in the mid-1960s. While there were many reasons for the adoption of one-party states—including a favorable reading of the Soviet experience, a distrust of western democratic institutions that had been planted in the last few moments of colonial rule, and a fear that divisive party politics could distract governments from the critical goal of economic development—it was clear that African states were trying to compensate for their weaknesses by attempting to consolidate authority through the creation

---

[5] Ray Abrahams, "Law and Order and the State in the Nyamwezi and Sukuma Area of Tanzania," *Africa* 59 (1989): p. 360.

[6] Deschamps, "Association and Indirect Rule," p. 176.

[7] Emile A. B. van Rouveroy van Nieuwaal, "Chiefs and African States: Some Introductory Notes and an Extensive Bibliography of African Chieftaincy," *Journal of Legal Pluralism and Unofficial Law* 25–26 (1987): pp. 3–4.

of a formal monopoly on political power that tolerated no competitors. Traditional leaders, who held positions of authority in rural areas—precisely the areas that the new states were most worried about—did not have a place in the new parties. The failure, noted in chapter four, of African leaders to develop a theory of rule hurt the new states, especially in this area, because there was no theoretical or ideological perspective that would allow for the incorporation of traditional authorities. In contrast, the question of how to co-opt traditional authorities had obsessed British and French officials during the colonial period.

At the same time, African leaders knew that they simply could not crush traditional leaders. In fact, they coveted the legitimacy that traditional leaders had because, if harnessed by the central state, those sentiments could be an extraordinary means of getting around their own administrative weaknesses and the physical and emotional distance from their populations. Chief Awolowo, while well aware of Tafewa Balewa's sentiments, deftly summed up the dilemma:

> In spite of agitation here and there against this or that Oba or Chief, the institution of Obaship and Chieftaincy was still held in high esteem by the people. But the traditional rights and privileges which the Obas and Chiefs wished to preserve were antithetic to democratic concepts and to the yearnings and aspirations of the people . . . The problem which faced me, therefore, was that whilst I must strive to harness the influence of the Obas and Chiefs for our purposes, I must, at the same time, take the earliest possible steps to modify their rights and abrogate such of their privileges as were considered repugnant, to an extent that would both satisfy the commonalty and make the Obas and Chiefs feel secure in the traditional offices.[8]

African leaders were also well aware that it would be odd, and probably unsustainable, if they called upon the great traditions of the past when naming their countries (e.g., Mali, Ghana) while not coming to an accommodation with those at the local level who were seen to embody these traditions.[9] There is certainly no better proof of the failure of African countries to develop pan-territorial nationalist sentiments (see chapter four) than the felt need of leaders to gain legitimacy by associating with those traditional authorities who seemed to represent the very antithesis of the modern state.

As a result, postindependence African states were often schizophrenic in their approach to chiefs. Thus, Bienen notes that in Tanzania, chiefs were deposed as government officials after independence; however, head-

---

[8] Obafemi Awolowo, *Awo: The Autobiography of Chief Obafemi Awolowo* (London: Cambridge University Press, 1960), p. 261.

[9] See generally Anthony D. Smith, *The Ethnic Revival* (Cambridge: Cambridge University Press, 1981), p. 143.

men often became the new village executive officers in their own communities, contrary to the policy of transplanting traditional rulers when they were to become local officials. The government was aware that the "deposition of chiefs, sub-chiefs, and headmen could break the link between a traditionally oriented people and the district administration."[10] Similarly, in Mauritania, Niger, and Chad, states abolished or marginalized chiefs after independence only to invite them back a few years later in the face of extraordinary difficulties in governing the rural areas.[11]

The new militaries that came to power in the 1960s faced similar problems. The military elites had few ties to the civilian population and were seldom ethnically representative of their populations.[12] Further, by and large, African militaries did not try to develop their own means for mobilizing the population, especially in rural areas. There were few parties that emerged out of military rule that were analogous to the Kemalist model in Ataturk's Turkey. The soldiers in power were, if anything, more isolated from the population than the one-party states, which came to power in almost all countries that did not have military rule. The militaries were sometimes conscious of their weaknesses in the rural areas and also tried to both disempower and to co-opt tradtional leaders. Thus, shortly after having come to power in August 1966, General Yakubu Gowon, the new Nigerian leader, released Awolowo from jail and made him "Leader of the Yorubas" and head of the "Leaders of Thought" in the western region. The Leaders of Thought were civilian elites who were asked to debate issues regarding the constitutional review and to provide insight on other political issues facing Nigeria.[13]

The political liberalizations that have swept the African continent since 1990 once again have placed in sharp relief the uncertainties of how African states should approach civilian leaders. On the one hand, as rulers sometimes still tainted by colonialism who are mainly chosen either by heredity or by other elites, traditional leaders are seemingly the very antithesis of democratic rule. On the other hand, those who head weak African states still crave the legitimacy associated with traditional rulers and, again conscious of their limited reach into rural areas, want to find a place for those who exercise local power. Thus Museveni, a leader not known for his enthusiasm in devolving power, allowed Mutebi II, Mutesa's son, to return to Uganda and assume his duties as kabaka in 1993.

[10] Henry S. Bienen, *Tanzania: Party Transformation and Economic Development* (Princeton: Princeton University Press, 1970), p. 353.

[11] Van Rouveroy van Nieuwaal, "Chiefs and African States," pp. 20–21.

[12] Samuel DeCalo, *Coups and Army Rule in Africa*, 2nd ed. (New Haven: Yale University Press, 1990), p. 5.

[13] See Henry S. Bienen, *Armies and Parties in Africa* (New York: Africana Publishing Company, 1978), p. 218.

In a starkly Weberian speech at Princeton, Mutebi II outlined a vision where traditional leaders and national politicians could co-exist: "African Leaders who enjoy national-legal political legitimacy based on being elected in a fair manner, must supplement it with the traditional legitimacy which traditional leaders like Kings possess." He suggests further that while traditional leaders should not become involved in partisan politics (one of the reasons for the downfall of his father), these leaders should have control over their own resources and enjoy "some autonomy from the state."[14]

Modern Chiefs and Modern States

Academic research has only begun to explore the relationships between chiefs and states. For the most part, analysis has not evolved from in-depth studies of one or a few polities to systematic cross-national comparisons. The overwhelming number of studies on the relationship between chiefs and states still focus on one country. In addition, there has been uncertainty regarding how to approach traditional leaders, given that at least some appear to have been "invented" during the colonial period. Mamdani describes the administrative chief as emerging during the colonial period "as the full-blown village-based despot, shorn of rule-based restraint."[15] While this description is a profound exaggeration, the general sentiment did deter many from studying chiefs. Certainly, far more academics have been interested in the theories of socialist or communist leaders in the 1960s and 1970s than in understanding how seemingly anachronistic chiefs wielded power. However, whether or not they are legitimate in the eyes of researchers, whether or not they were created by colonial officials, local rulers are an important factor in African politics that cannot be ignored. As Richard Sklar noted in the bluntest possible terms, "The *kgotla*, the *Alake* of Egbaland, and the marabouts of Senegal exert power in their societies regardless of one or another academic interpretation of their roles."[16]

Given the ambivalence of African leaders and the complicated and evolving relationship between authorities in the center and periphery, it is hardly surprising that there is considerable controversy about the balance of power in African countries. Van Rouveroy van Nieuwaal argues that

[14] The speech is reprinted as Mutebi II, "Traditional Leaders and Democracy in Africa," *West Africa*, 15 April 1996, p. 577.

[15] Mamdani, *Citizen and Subject*, p. 43.

[16] Richard Sklar, "The African Frontier in Political Science," in *Africa and the Disciplines: The Contributions of Research in Africa to the Social Sciences and Humanities*, ed. Robert H. Bates, V. Y. Mudimbe, and Jean O'Barr (Chicago: University of Chicago Press, 1993), p. 94.

there is no clear trend in the complicated conflict between states and chiefs.[17] For him, local factors are critically important: "the maintenance of authority by the chief, now and in the future, is linked to his having a good relationship with his people."[18] In comparison, von Trotha is more willing to predict a shift in the balance of power in favor of the chiefs:

> it seems that the idea of the state is losing ground at a fast rate, particularly in Africa. We might call this process the "political tribalization" and "cultural ethnicization" of social order. In it the institution of chieftaincy could play a leading role, becoming the center of new political orders drawing on the experiences and the political, cultural and social resources of both precolonial and administrative chieftaincy.[19]

There is, for instance, considerable discussion about new parliamentary institutions that would allow chiefs to participate in Africa's nascent democracies.

However, Geschiere believes that the chiefs are not alternatives to the state because the chiefs, to maintain themselves, increasingly look like the state elite: they have academic degrees and are involved in modern businesses.[20] This is the more traditional view that contact with the state inevitably contaminates those whose basis of power is outside the formal political apparatus. In addition, there are still concerns that some of the attributes of modernity that many countries in Africa possess will inevitably diminish the power of local authorities. For instance, Kgosi Linchwe II, paramount chief of Bakgatla-Ba-Kgfela (in Botswana), argues that the power and prestige of the chieftaincy is being eroded by migration to urban areas and by increased levels of education.[21]

In contrast, there is a consensus in the literature regarding the effect of colonial heritage on traditional authorities. Kirk-Greene argues that chiefs in anglophone Africa are at least potentially vigorous and still able to launch rearguard actions against the state, while in francophone Africa, "the colonial administrators had shown themselves, by the single-minded continuity of their policy of destabilizing the traditional rulers, to be far more effective firemen. There are few better ways of preventing conflagration than by removing the matches."[22] Similarly, Ayittey argued that

[17] Emile A. B. van Rouveroy van Nieuwaal, "States and Chiefs: Are Chiefs Mere Puppets?" *Journal of Legal Pluralism and Unofficial Law* 37–38 (1996): p. 69.

[18] Van Rouveroy van Nieuwaal, "Chiefs and African States," p. 26.

[19] Trutz von Trotha, "From Administrative to Civil Chieftaincy: Some Problems and Prospects of African Chieftaincy," *Journal of Legal Pluralism and Unofficial Law* 37–38 (1996): p. 91.

[20] "Chiefs and Colonial Rule in Cameroon," p. 169.

[21] Kgosi Linchwe II, "Chieftainship in the 21st Century," in *Democracy in Botswana*, ed. John Holm and Patrick Molutsi (Gaborone, Botswana: MacMillan, 1989), p. 399.

[22] Kirk-Greene, "'Le Roi est Mort! Vive le roi!'" p. 28.

chiefs in francophone West Africa had lost their authority over land, a critical part of their power, when land laws were changed.[23]

Land Tenure as the Critical Resource

In order to gain a systematic perspective on the changing balances between centralized states and local leaders in Africa, this study examines the evolution of property rights in the allocation of land. Part of the problem in understanding the evolving role of chiefs vis-à-vis the central state is that it is not clear what to study. Much of the chiefs' power seems to stem from popular legitimacy, a notoriously difficult concept to operationalize. As with the study of national design in chapter five, the perspective of this book allows for a new understanding of how the conflict between chiefs and the state should be viewed. Earlier chapters indicated that the most difficult challenge African states face is the control of land. The precolonial tradition did not emphasize controlling land via strict demarcation and the colonial and postcolonial states that have evolved constructed boundary and state systems so that they would not necessarily have to physically control land in the hinterland. Instead, land is often controlled by local authorities. Indeed, Miller's claim in 1968 that, "the chiefdom itself has remained the broadest political unit with which a rural African is directly concerned"[24] does not seem anachronistic at the turn of the century. Thus, the design of land tenure processes that describe property rights is at the very center of why the state is weak in Africa.

However, there are few issues in the study of Africa that have generated a more confusing literature than the study of property rights in land. It does seem clear now that the old notions of "communal tenure" and the related concerns about insecurity of property rights were incorrect. "Traditional" practices in many places and at many times were quite dynamic and did provide security in the context of local environments. In addition, there is a wide variety of traditional practices in Africa, given differences in agroecological conditions, population densities, and precolonial and colonial history. Given this diversity and dynamism, John W. Bruce provides the most accurate and useful description of land tenure in Africa and the role of local authorities:

> In most of Africa land has been plentiful. Where shifting cultivation has been practiced or groups have migrated to settle new territory, traditional authorities

[23] George B. N. Ayittey, *Indigenous African Institutions* (New York: Transnational Publishers, 1991), p. 443.

[24] Norman N. Miller, "The Political Survival of Traditional Leadership," *Journal of Modern African Studies* 6 (1968): p. 195.

have often had an important land allocation function . . . Once cultivation stabilizes, the role of land authorities is primarily that of making first allocations of previously unused land. Where population pressure on land is heavy, chiefs or elders sometimes have the right to take land from larger holdings for new households, though this is unusual . . . Eventually, when all the arable land has been allocated and holdings become so small that reallocation loses its point, land passes from generation to generation in accordance with the customary rules of succession and the land authorities' role is increasingly limited to dispute resolutions.[25]

Changing this pattern of land tenure is, not surprisingly, the most contentious issue between central states and local leaders. As Migdal correctly notes,

> In striking at existing land tenure patterns, the new policies hit at what was inevitably the critical set of rules of the game in agrarian societies. Property rights consist of the rules for employing productive factors in a society. What better way to assure the unviability of the old ways of producing than to attack the most important property rights of all in such societies, those involving land?[26]

The stakes are especially high for the state. There are a variety of arguments made for changes in land tenure practices, including the greater efficiency of land markets, increased security of tenure, greater transparency, and perhaps greater fairness for those excluded by traditional systems from owning land, especially women. As a result, reforms proposed by the state typically include title registration and land demarcation by surveying as well as other efforts to promote land markets.[27] Finally, land is simply too important a resource for states not to be vitally concerned about. North argues that "the state attempts to act like a discriminating monopolist, separating each group of constituents and devising property rights for each so as to maximize state revenue."[28] Pressure to raise revenue, amplified by the concerns of donors, has been a critical reason for states to replace variable local practices with national land tenure regulations.[29]

Land tenure is also critical for local authorities. Earle got it exactly

---

[25] John W. Bruce, "A Perspective on Indigenous Land Tenure Systems and Land Concentration," in *Land and Society in Contemporary Africa*, ed. R. E. Downs and S. P. Reyna (Hanover, NH: University of New England Press, 1988), p. 25.

[26] Migdal, *Strong Societies and Weak States*, p. 57.

[27] Richard Barrows and Michael Roth, "Land Tenure and Investment in African Agriculture: Theory and Evidence," *Journal of Modern African Studies* 28 (1990): p. 265.

[28] Douglass C. North, *Structure and Change in Economic History* (New York: W. W. Norton, 1981), p. 23.

[29] See, for instance, D. W. Bromley, "Property Relations and Economic Development: The Other Land Reform," *World Development* 17 (1989): p. 867.

right when he argued that "the evolution of property rights by which chiefs control primary production can be seen as basic to the evolution of many complex stratified societies."[30] Mike Oquaye thus provides a not uncommon description from Ghana: "The land tenure system underscores the position and authority of the chief in the Ghanaian traditional system."[31] It has thus long been recognized that changes in tenure, especially to individual freehold, weaken the power of chiefs.[32] For instance, changes in customary tenure practices allow outsiders, including government officials and wealthy nonlocals, to gain access to land that had previously been controlled by local authorities.[33]

There is considerable controversy as to whether land tenure reform in Africa is beneficial for individual farmers. However, irrespective of the absolute or net effects, it seems certain that all African states will continue to pursue tenure reform in the future. The political incentives (especially to supplant local authorities) and the fiscal imperatives (especially to increase revenue flows) are too powerful to ignore. Thus, the Land Tenure Center noted that the majority of West African countries are increasingly favoring "individualized landholdings as economies based on the production of commodities become more developed, as populations and land pressures increase, and as international donors support widespread legal reform."[34]

Actual Existing Land Tenure in Africa

In order to gain a perspective on land tenure patterns in Africa, I have categorized countries according to the extent of the disruption of customary practices. Individual freehold is obviously one challenge to customary practices and is the avenue that many African countries, sometimes at the behest of donors, are currently attempting to pursue. It is felt that agrarian development will be accelerated if individuals can have

[30] Timothy Earle, "Property Rights and the Evolution of Chiefdoms," in *Chiefdoms: Power, Economy, and Ideology*, ed. Timothy Earle (Cambridge: Cambridge University Press, 1991), p. 74.

[31] Mike Oquaye, "The Role of Traditional Authority in the Politics and Development of Ghana," in *The Rights of Indigenous People: A Quest for Coexistence*, ed. Bertrus de Villiers (Pretoria, South Africa: Human Sciences Research Council, 1997), p. 88.

[32] See, for instance, the early statement by the Colonial Office Summer Conference on African Administration, *African Land Tenure* (Cambridge: Colonial Office, 1956), p. 22.

[33] See, for instance, Catherine Besteman, "Local Land Use Strategies and Outsider Politics: Title Registration in the Middle Jubba Valley," in *The Struggle for Land in Southern Somalia*, ed. Catherine Besteman and Lee V. Cassanelli (Boulder, CO: Westview Press, 1996), pp. 42–3.

[34] Kent Elbow et al., *Country Profiles of Land Tenure: West Africa* (Madison: Land Tenure Center, 1996), p. 4.

certain knowledge that their property rights to particular pieces of land are secure. The second type of land tenure that challenges traditional practice is state ownership. While state control of land today is viewed as inefficient and potentially a strong disincentive to investors, some colonial states and many African countries after independence took control of vast amounts of land. In some countries, such as Angola and Mozambique, all land was nationalized after independence. In many others, the state tried to expand its control over land just as state ownership in other sectors was growing. Because of the tremendous difficulties in changing land tenure laws and the problems African countries have had in privatizing significant assets, these state holdings often remain long after the ideological and economic justification for them has expired. Tanzania, for instance, is, in the late 1990s, still attempting to change its laws after the disastrous villagization experiments in the 1960s and early 1970s.[35]

The third measure of how well a state has succeeded in challenging traditional land tenure practices concerns whether the state has recognized customary practices in formal law. Contrary to what may be thought, the true challenge to customary practices is when the state formally recognizes them. When customary practices are acknowledged, states can "tier" the land and thereby make clear demarcations where customary practices apply and where they no longer are relevant. In its most formal guise, recognition results in the creation of "tribal authority lands," as has occurred in Liberia, Sierra Leone, Gambia, and Ghana, as well as in several southern Africa countries.[36] As the analysis in chapter two notes, customary practices cannot be readily mapped, and chapter three demonstrates that the British preoccupation with demarcating the writ of traditional authorities helped delegitimate them. If states manage to define where customary practices apply, they pose a profound threat to the very existence of these practices. Recognition of customary practices thus is the first step in a process of eventual co-optation that will render local authorities less powerful.

States that either do not recognize or that actively oppose traditional practices might conventionally be seen as posing more of a direct challenge to customary practices. However, given the limited ability of most African countries to deploy entire administrative systems in the countryside and the local power of traditional authorities, it is more likely that measures that seek the wholesale replacement of local practices will simply be futile.[37] For instance, the attempt by successive Nigerian govern-

---

[35] Land Tenure Center, *Country Profiles of Land Tenure: East Africa* (Madison: Land Tenure Center, 1996), p. 57.

[36] Elbow et al., *Country Profiles of Land Tenure*, p. 10.

[37] A point made early by Miller, "The Political Survival of Traditional Leadership," p. 185.

ments through the Land Use Decree of 1978 to "replace the authority of customary leaders over land tenure" failed because Lagos does not have the ability to enforce the law. As a result, "Rural communities continue to rely on community-based systems, and not the state system, to govern tenure practice. By alienating the support of traditional authorities through undercutting their power, the government simultaneously eliminated its most effective means of extending rule to the grassroots."[38] Similarly, in Mozambique, the state

> Attempted to replace [indigenous tenure practices] with more "modern" state institutions and regulatory practices. In reality, due to insufficient state capabilities and war-imposed constraints, the state has permitted indigenous tenure systems to operate in many rural communities.[39]

In most instances, policies of blanket opposition to traditional tenure arrangements probably have precluded more serious attempts to challenge local practices because leaders feel that they can abolish local practices by administrative fiat, much as their sovereign control over the entire territory was simply proclaimed, not earned.

There is, in fact, a consensus in the literature that states only will succeed in land tenure reform if they move slowly while recognizing traditional practices. Thus, Bruce, Migot-Adholla, and Atherton note that radical plans that attempt to completely overturn traditional arrangements or that ignore local practices often are worse than doing nothing: "Unsuccessful attempts to substitute state titles for customary entitlements may reduce security by creating normative confusion, of which the powerful may take advantage."[40] They are therefore more optimistic about incremental plans that seek to work with traditional practices.

States and Land Tenure

A continental overview of how African countries have performed in challenging local tenure arrangements is provided in table 6.1 (see pp. 186–87). The table indicates if private or state leasehold is absent, whether such leaseholds at least exist to the extent that they affect national land tenure policy, and whether such leaseholds are significant. The table also indicates where the state recognizes local tenure practices. Such indica-

[38] Elbow et al., *Country Profiles of Land Tenure*, pp. 125–6.

[39] John W. Bruce et al., *Country Profiles of Land Tenure: Southern Africa* (Madison: Land Tenure Center, 1997), p. 36.

[40] John W. Bruce, Shem E. Migot-Adholla, and Joan Atherton, "The Findings and their Policy Implications: Institutional Adaption or Replacement?" in *Searching for Land Tenure Security in Africa*, ed. John W. Bruce and Shem E. Migot-Adholla (Dubuque, Iowa: Kendall/Hunt, 1994), pp. 260–1.

tors are obviously very general and do not do justice to exceptionally complicated situations on the ground. In addition, the "no," "exists," or "significant" gradation is hardly nuanced. However, the broad banding of countries reflects the current lack of information, given the great variety of local circumstances in even any one country, and the fact that cross-national data are only slowly becoming available. A more nuanced grading would not be supported by the data. The great advantage of these three indicators is that they combine a general description of the formal legal framework with an evaluation of what is actually happening in land markets. These categories are a significant advance on previous scholarship, which has been criticized for not being based on primary research and for assuming that there was a correlation between laws made in capitals and actual practices on the ground.[41]

It is therefore possible to identify, in a rough manner, the African countries that have, at least relatively, disrupted traditional local tenure arrangements. For both the state and private leasehold categories, countries were given two points if significant holdings exist, one point if some such holdings are present, and no points if such holdings are absent. Countries were given one point if they recognized customary tenure practices and no points if they did not. Again, such coding is rough but is all that can be supported by the quality of the data.

There is considerable reason to believe that the coding at least ranks countries correctly given the narratives in table 6.2. The table lists those countries that scored either a "4" or "5" but does not differentiate between those scores given the problems inherent in the data. Also included in the table are those countries that scored a "1" and were therefore at the bottom of the rankings (no country scored "0").

In addition, I have included Kenya among those countries that are scored as high disrupters, even though technically Kenya only has a score of "2." However, Kenya was among the first countries to experience comprehensive land reform and has, in many ways, gone the farthest in promoting individual freehold. It is therefore, "unique in the scope of its conversion to freehold."[42] As a result, Nairobi has not had to resort to state leasehold to disrupt customary tenure and its policy has been so encompassing that it chose largely to ignore customary tenure. This adjustment is simply a recognition that the coding scheme, while useful, is by no means perfect.

The high scorers are all anglophone countries in southern and eastern Africa, except for Mauritania. Mauritania, as a hinterland country with

---

[41] John M. Cohen, "Land Tenure and Rural Development in Africa," in *Agricultural Development in Africa*, ed. Robert H. Bates and Michael F. Lofchie (New York: Praeger, 1980), pp. 381–2.

[42] Land Tenure Center, *Country Profiles of Land Tenure*, p. 31.

TABLE 6.1
Land Tenure Patterns

Country	Private Ownership	State Leasehold	Explicitly Recognizes Customary Tenure
Angola	No	Significant	No
Benin	Exists	Exists	No
Botswana	Exists	Significant	Yes
Burkina Faso	No	Exists	No
Burundi	Exists	Significant	No
Cameroon	Exists[a]	Significant	No
C.A.R.	Exists	Exists	No
Chad	Exists	Exists	No
Congo-B	No	Exists[b]	No
Côte d'Ivoire	Exists	Exists	No
D.R.O.C.	No	Exists	No
Ethiopia	No	Significant	No
Gabon	Exists	No	No
Gambia	Exists	Exists	Yes
Ghana	Exists	Exists	Yes
Guinea	Exists	No	No
Guinea-Bissau	Exists	No	Yes
Kenya	Significant	No	No
Lesotho	No	Significant	No
Liberia	Significant	Unknown	Yes
Malawi	Significant	Significant	Yes
Mali	Exists	Exists	No
Mauritania	Significant	Significant	No
Mozambique	No	Significant	No
Namibia	Significant	Exists	Yes
Niger	Exists	Exists	Yes
Nigeria	No	Exists	No

one of the highest urbanization rates on the continent (see chapter five), is physically closer to a much larger percentage of its population than most African countries. In addition, Mauritania is unusually small when it comes to how much land is actually being used for agricultural purposes: only .2 percent of the land area is under crops or pasture, compared to an average of 6.5 percent for Africa.[43] Mauritania's land under agricultural use is exceptional even by the standards of other Saharan countries. Chad (2.6 percent), Mali (2.8 percent), and Niger (3.9 percent) have at least

[43] All figures on land under agriculture in this and the following paragraphs are from Food and Agricultural Organization, *FAO Production Yearbook 1996* (Rome: FAO, 1996), p. 3.

TABLE 6.1
(*Continued*)

Country	Private Ownership	State Leasehold	Explicitly Recognizes Customary Tenure
Rwanda	Exists	Exists	Yes
Senegal	No	Exists	No
Sierra Leone	Exists	Exists	Yes
Somalia	No	Significant	No
Sudan	Exists	Exists	No
Swaziland	Significant	Exists	Yes
Tanzania	No	Significant	No
Togo	Exists	Exists	Yes
Uganda	Exists	Exists	Yes
Zambia	No	Significant	Yes
Zimbabwe	Significant	Exists	Yes

Note: Information is not available for Equatorial Guinea and Eritrea.

ªCountries were coded conservatively. Thus, a country listed in the sources as having between "significant and "exists" for the extent of state leasehold is coded as "exists."

ᵇChanged from the source coding of "significant" because private ownership is not apparent in large parts of the country where customary land tenure is still critical.

Tables were constructed from the following publications from the following publications: John W. Bruce et al., *Country Profiles of Land Tenure, Southern Africa 1996* (Madison, WI: Land Tenure Center, 1997); Land Tenure Center, *Country Profiles of Land Tenure, East Africa 1996* (Madison, WI: Land Tenure Center, 1996); Kent Elbow et al., *Country Profiles of Land Tenure: West Africa, 1996* (Wisconsin: Land Tenure Center, 1996). John Bruce of the University of Wisconsin's Land Tenure Center kindly gave permission to quote from the country profiles the LTC had produced for Africa.

Data for the tables for countries in West and southern Africa are taken directly from tables in the above reports. Data for countries in East Africa are taken from individual country profiles.

an order of magnitude more land, as a percentage of total land mass, devoted to agriculture. As a result, Nouakchott has been able to reach out and affect traditional tenure arrangements in a way that could not have been predicted given Mauritania's absolute size. Further, as a result of persistent droughts, Mauritania's entire land tenure system has been disrupted. Given this demographic and ecological context, the state has made some attempts to change land tenure to the benefit of agriculturists and to the detriment of herders. It has also sought to abolish or limit land rights of Senegalese who have traditionally had access to land on both sides of the Senegal River (a rare moment when security and land tenure concerns coincided).[44] It was not the (quickly abandoned) attempt in the 1960s to abolish chiefs that expanded the reach of the Mauritanian

[44] Elbow et al., *Country Profiles of Land Tenure*, pp. 110–4.

TABLE 6.2
High and Low Land Tenure Scores

High Scorers	Rationale
Botswana	Role of chiefs has been phased out and replaced with decentralized land boards.
Kenya	Massive program during colonial period to create "yeoman" farmers. Postindependence government embraces individual tenure to an unprecedented degree.
Malawi	Highly dualistic tenure structure with large estates occupying large tracts of land. Estates date back to early settler colonialism when white farmers took over large tracts of land.
Mauritania	Traditional land tenure disrupted by government policies and traumatic drought.
Namibia	Dispossession of indigenous people during colonial rule results in white commercial farmers owning 74 percent of potentially arable land.
Swaziland	Highly dualistic land structure where approximately 43 percent of land is controlled by foreign concessionaires and private land owners.
Zimbabwe	Land tenure profoundly disrupted by settler colonialism. A small number of white farmers control a large perentage of the arable land and an even higher percentage of the best land.
Low Scorers	Rationale
Burkina Faso	Government does not have manpower to staff local councils and are, for the most part, based on traditional local power structures.
Congo-Brazzaville	Government reforms have stalled.
D.R.O.C.	Ninety-seven percent of all land is governed by community tenure. Reforms aimed at overturning local practices have been defeated.
Gabon	Land conflicts are limited as there is still available land. Traditional practices still govern the majority of land.
Guinea	1992 Law Code applies only to the more urbanized areas of lower Guinea and not to the other three regions where more traditional practices still apply.

TABLE 6.2 (*cont.*)

Low Scorers	Rationale
Nigeria	Government has been ineffective in changing local practices.
Senegal	Guidelines for national land tenure decisions are unclear and rural council actions have been minimal.

Source: See table 6.1.

state but a combination of political events and ecological catastrophe in the 1980s that changed the balance of power.

Botswana scores exceptionally high on the scale due in good part to its almost unique ability to disrupt local practices. Botswana was classified in chapter five as a country with a favorable political geography; as a result, the capital is physically close to a large proportion of the population. In addition, Botswana, like Mauritania, has an extremely small amount (.6 percent) of its land under crop or pasture so it not only has a good population distribution but, for the purposes of land tenure, the area the state must operate across is also exceptionally small. Of course, Botswana is also the outstanding development story in Africa, having increased its per capita income considerably while its neighbors stagnated. Botswana's per capita income at $3,260 is approximately six times the African average.[45] It thus is more likely to have the resources to fund administrative systems in the rural areas to compete with local authorities. Given this context, Gaborone has made steady and determined progress in a long-term project to disrupt local tenure practices:

> The role of chiefs in making land allocation decisions has been phased out and replaced with a decentralized system of Tribal Land Boards which are linked to the national Ministry of Local Government, Land and Housing . . . By employing an adaption rather than replacement strategy, the government has been more attentive to the evolving needs of its citizens . . . At the same time, it has eliminated distinctions between citizens from different tribes and subtribes and provided all Botswana citizens a right to land where they live.[46]

The other countries that are scored as high disrupters of local tenure practices (Kenya, Malawi, Namibia, Swaziland, and Zimbabwe) all had unusually traumatic colonial histories that saw exceptionally large amounts of land alienated during white rule for the benefit of white settlers. In the colonies with settlers, there were at least some efforts by the colonialists to enact fundamental changes in the rural areas. As a result, local constituencies developed a profound interest in the state extending

---

[45] World Bank, *World Development Report 1998*, pp. 191, 232.
[46] Bruce et al., *Country Profiles of Land Tenure*, p. 13.

its reach in order to alienate large amounts of land from Africans. Colonial states were therefore pressured into taking costly actions for the benefit of local settlers and white business interests. In Kenya there were also significant attempts to create individual African freehold during the colonial period, a policy that was intensified after independence. These patterns of white or foreign land ownership have continued through the independence period, no doubt helped by the fact that all of these countries are near South Africa. South African whites or South African multinational corporations are actually the owners of much of the land in these countries.

For instance, while Swaziland is still governed by a king, a very substantial portion of its land is controlled by foreigners. Similarly, in Namibia and Zimbabwe, land systems were completely disrupted by powerful white settler colonial states that managed to penetrate far into the countryside. Indeed, these were two of a very limited number of colonial states that fought a protracted war during their terminal colonial periods. They are also the two countries where the white settlers managed to secure the most concessions from their black successors because the whites were not defeated on the battlefield but managed to negotiate the transfer of power. In comparison, the whites in Angola and Mozambique fled their former colonial homes in 1975 after the Salazar government was overthrown and military opposition to African nationalists simply collapsed. Malawi is something of an exception because, while it experienced significant (by African standards) land alienation during the colonial period, it is the growth in private sector leasehold since independence that has contributed to challenging customary tenure practices. However, at least the practice of large-scale white landholdings was established during the colonial period. While the chiefs may think, apropos of the frontispiece to this chapter, that they are the government in Malawi, they are actually "ruling" over a diminishing territory.

In contrast, in many African colonies without settlers, the colonial authorities did not attempt to disrupt local tenure practices. Indirect rule was interpreted to call for, in some places, vesting local authorities with control over land.[47] As a result, Bentsi-Enchill concluded that, "the overwhelming bulk of the land remained under African occupation and under the regime of the traditional systems of land law [during the colonial period]."[48]

The countries that have been most ineffective in disrupting land tenure also share some commonalties. All are francophone countries except

[47] Robert H. Bates, "Some Conventional Orthodoxies in the Study of Agrarian Change," *World Politics* 36 (1984): p. 243.
[48] Bentsi-Enchill, "The Traditional Legal Systems of Africa," pp. 2–129.

Nigeria and Somalia and all are in West Africa except for Democratic Republic of the Congo and Somalia. France was notable for its unusually unsuccessful efforts to disrupt customary tenure during the colonial period, despite its sweeping laws that theoretically made wholesale changes in land tenure. It did not, of course, have settlers in its West African colonies who would have a direct economic interest in seizing land from traditional authorities, as was the case with several anglophone Southern Africa countries. Instead, France relied on administrative fiat to try to change customary tenure procedures. The hope in France's territories was that title and registration systems eventually would result in widescale private ownership, after a period of state leasehold when the future owners fulfilled requirements regarding exploitation and development of the land (the *mise en valeur* regulations). Not surprisingly, given the analysis in chapter three regarding the variability of colonial rule, across West Africa, this policy was a failure:

> Indigenous populations made extremely little use of legal provisions governing state leasehold or freehold land. Later attempts by French colonial administrators to make land registration more accessible to indigenous populations—such as the introduction of a less cumbersome method of land registration known as the *livret foncier* appearing in French West African legislation in 1925—did little to change the situation.[49]

In addition, some of the francophone countries are relatively large in terms of the amount of land that they have under crops. Thus, Burkina Faso (12.5 percent) and Senegal (11.8 percent) both have very extensive agricultural lands that the capital, by necessity, has a harder time reaching out to than is the case for political authorities with less extensive agricultural lands. There is probably also less land pressure in parts of West Africa due to better agroecological conditions than in the drier southern Africa region.

The failure of Democratic Republic of the Congo and Somalia to significantly change traditional land tenure arrangements is hardly surprising given the tenuousness of rule by Kinshasha and Mogadishu. Of course, these two countries were also among those that chapter five classified as having particularly difficult political geographies, making state extension into the rural areas especially unlikely. The failure of Nigeria is more complex to explain, although that country also has an extremely difficult political geography, as in chapter five notes. Further, Nigeria also has an high percentage of its land under some kind of crop or pasture (36.1 percent), making the state's task of changing tenure arrangements particularly difficult. Finally, the maximalist attempt by the Nigerian authorities to

[49] Elbow et al., *Country Profiles of Land Tenure*, p. 3.

TABLE 6.3
Countries Arrayed by Land Tenure Score

Country	Score	Country	Score
Malawi	5	C.A.R.	2
Botswana	4	Chad	2
Mauritania	4	Côte d'Ivoire	2
Namibia	4	**Ethiopia**	2
Swaziland	4	Guinea-Bissau	2
Zimbabwe	4	Kenya	2
Burundi	3	Lesotho	2
Cameroon	3	Mali	2
Gambia	3	**Mozambique**	2
Ghana	3	**Somalia**	2
Liberia	3	**Sudan**	2
Niger	3	**Tanzania**	2
Rwanda	3	Burkina Faso	1
Sierra Leone	3	Congo-B	1
Togo	3	**D.R.O.C.**	1
Uganda	3	Gabon	1
Zambia	3	Guinea	1
Angola	2	**Nigeria**	1
Benin	2	**Senegal**	1

Note: Countries with difficult political geographies are in boldface.
Source: See table 6.1

change land tenure regulations was a failure because it played to the state's own weaknesses, especially its increasingly attenuated presence and competence in rural areas after oil came on line in the early 1970s.

Between the extremes there is a range of countries whose land tenure conditions are mixed and highly complicated. Table 6.3 arrays all of the countries in Africa (except Equatorial Guinea and Eritrea) according to their scores on the three indicators listed above. It is obvious that the countries identified in chapter five as having particularly difficult political geographies have generally fared poorly in disrupting traditional land arrangements, even in comparison to other African countries. All of the countries with difficult political geographies score a "two" or lower except for Namibia whose traumatic colonial history featured widespread tenure disruptions by white settlers. Generally in these countries, nothing more than state or private leaseholds exist, while the state sometimes does not recognize customary tenure arrangements. The average score of countries with a difficult political geography is 1.9 compared to the overall African average of 2.4.

Land Tenure and the Status Quo

What stands out from the analysis of attempts to reform land tenure is how starkly African countries have failed. Thus, in West Africa, "whether officially recognized or not, community-based tenure systems predominately dictate who has access to land and natural resources."[50] Botswana and Mauritania are the only clear instances where states have apparently managed to replace customary tenure and only then in an environment where the amount of land under consideration was low, the political geography favorable, and the state's access to resources (at least in the case of Botswana) exceptional. In the other instances of significant reformers, the critical actions were performed during the colonial period.

It seems exceptionally difficult for African countries under "normal" circumstances to disrupt customary tenure. Returning to the fixed cost analysis in chapter one, changing customary land tenure is a particularly difficult challenge for most African countries. Unlike roads, land tenure reformers cannot even build out incrementally from the capital: The kind of nuanced and persistent reform operation that seems to work best requires a dispersed presence across vast parts of the hinterland. Indeed, the mild liberalization that some African countries have experienced has actually made it harder to implement land reform because citizens are able to "shop" between different forums to argue their case, thus putting an especially high premium on institutional coherence.[51] Thus, when reforming land tenure, there are significant fixed costs that are entirely separate from those that states have to address as they seek to control the capital. Under the Addis rules, African states face no security imperatives to control formally the land far from the capital. Given the extreme poverty of most African states, it is not surprising that African states have not made more inroads into changing rural practices: it is simply too costly for them to do and there is no security imperative (because their boundaries are secure) that would cause them to ignore the cost-benefit calculations. Finally, in contrast to the former settler colonies, in most postindependence African countries, there is no powerful elite who pressured the state to control land far from the capital at a loss. Rather, as chapter four discusses, the elite is intertwined with the state and earns most of its wealth from economic activities at the center.

Given the overall inability of states to disrupt local tenure practices, it is hardly surprising that national design considerations, especially whether a country has an unfavorable political geography, play an important role in

---

[50] Ibid., p. 5.
[51] See, for example, Christian Lund, *Law, Power, and Politics in Niger: Land Struggles and the Rural Code* (Hamburg: Lit Verlag, 1998), p. 222.

relative performance. All other things being equal, it is simply more difficult for the state to affect rural tenure practices when the capital is physically distant from a relatively large segment of the population. In addition,
large countries with low population densities, almost by definition, have
more variation in land tenure practices across their territories, making it
harder for capitals to devise models that would effectively compete with the
relatively large number of local authorities in the hinterlands.

Chiefs: Rising and Declining

The data only provide a snapshot of land tenure arrangements so it is
difficult to make concrete judgments about how chiefs have done over
time. It is certainly the case that customary land tenure arrangements
have survived to a greater extent than most would have predicted when
many African countries were receiving independence in the early 1960s.
African states have been inept enough and chiefs sufficiently resilient that
the notion of wholesale replacement of customary tenure has been largely
defeated.

There is no evidence that chiefs are losing power vis-à-vis states in the
crucial land tenure area. The fact that those states that have been relatively
successful in replacing customary tenure have been able to do so primarily
because of particular ecological conditions (Mauritania and, to some extent, Botswana) or because of a particular traumatic colonial history suggests that states have found few successful ways to make inroads into land
allocation processes. Malawi, Namibia, Swaziland, and Zimbabwe have
been trying to overturn their colonial land legacies so they can hardly be
viewed as models for other countries. The fact that national design is at
least somewhat correlated with success in disrupting customary tenure is an
indication that domestic policy has mattered much less to date than externally imposed structures inherited from the colonial period.

Whether chiefs can increase their power vis-à-vis the central state is a
separate issue. As most states have failed to significantly disrupt local tenure arrangements, there is no way for local authorities to increase their
power by taking back from the state what the state does not have. Also,
the power that chiefs have over land is a particular type of resource control. Land tenure arrangements often have not been affected by states
because this is an enormously complex and nuanced issue that is played
out in countless locations in a decentralized manner far from the capital.
Chiefs often can circumvent national land design because of the local
legitimacy they have based on local traditions By design then, land tenure
is hard for states to even monitor, much less control. However, land
tenure, for precisely the same reasons, is hardly a platform for local authorities to mobilize around. Control over land tenure provides local

power but it is hard to see how politicians could aggregate that power in any meaningful way.

Further, if chiefs do mobilize beyond the local level, they become much more visible to the state and are therefore vulnerable to a strategy that many African states are particularly good at: decapitation. While African states may not have the capability to compete with chiefs when it comes to land allocation, they can suppress chiefs or other politicians who emerge from the rural areas to challenge leaders for authority at the political core. One of the more notable aspects of independent Africa is that the state has failed to disrupt local land arrangements but, at the same time, there are very few examples of political parties that have managed to come to power with an explicitly rural base. Most African countries lack a William Jennings Bryant. A rough equilibrium therefore has developed whereby the state, in many countries, has not been able to penetrate into the rural area but the rural areas have not been able to challenge the state on its own turf through conventional politics.

It is, of course, possible for the state and traditional leaders to come to other accommodations. One of the more interesting developments in nascent African democratic theory is how national institutions can come to some kind of accommodation with chiefs. The agreement between the Ugandan government and the kabaka (where Mutebi II has explicitly agreed to stay out of national politics) is one such example. Others include the so-called "Houses of Chiefs" that some countries are exploring, which could be analogous to the House of Lords. Finally, in South Africa, the government has agreed to pay the salaries of traditional leaders both to sustain them and to undercut the base of the Inkatha Freedom Party that has traditionally looked to rural KwaZulu/Natal for support. Whether these arrangements allow the central state apparatus to share in the legitimacy accorded traditional leaders remains to be seen. However, it is probably the case that, when it comes to these national arrangements, Geschiere is right: traditional leaders will lose some aspect of their power base if they begin to look more like the state. Thus, it is hardly surprising that some traditional leaders have tried to avoid the new embrace of the state, even if it is now with the best of intentions, and instead try, as Mutebi II noted, to retain some degree of autonomy. While chiefs are not becoming weaker, theirs is not a base that can be used to become more powerful.

Francophone versus Anglophone Chiefs

The data presented in this chapter, among the first collected on at least a somewhat systematic basis across the continent, also show a fascinating variation between anglophone and francophone countries. The average rank across the anglophone countries is 2.9 and there is only one anglophone country (Nigeria) that scores a rank of "1." In addition, there are several anglophone African countries, as noted above, that score a "4" or higher. In contrast, the average rank of francophone countries is 2.0, almost a full point below anglophone countries. The only francophone country that scores a "4" is Mauritania, which has had a unique postindependence history for reasons explained above, while several of France's former colonies score "1." The lusophone countries also have an average rank of 2.0, while Belgium's former colonies score 2.3.

It appears then there is no evidence to support the widespread contention that chiefs in francophone countries have fared relatively poorly compared to anglophone countries. Quite the opposite appears to be true: in anglophone countries, on average, there has been greater disruption of customary land tenure practices than in francophone countries. As a result, the position of chiefs, at least in regard to land, appears to be stronger in francophone countries. The notion that chiefs have done well in anglophone Africa is largely a Nigerian story (Kirk-Greene's evidence mainly concerned Nigeria) where customary tenure still seems to be very much intact. Where anglophone chiefs have conspiciously lost ground, as it were, is in southern and eastern Africa where settler colonialism did tremendous damage to traditional practices. While it is true that indirect rule, at least as proclaimed, may have theoretically left anglophone chiefs in a better position, other factors seem to have intervened. First, given the failure of postindependence states during business as usual to disrupt customary tenure patterns, land alienation brought about by white settlers—overwhelmingly an anglophone phenomenon—remains exceptionally important. Second, while anglophone chiefs may appear more powerful than their francophone counterparts, francophone states are even weaker than anglophone authorities. As a result, the relative balance of power has shifted in favor of francophone chiefs and anglophone states. The fact that many analyses focus on chiefs and states in West Africa precisely because southern African conditions are so different may have caused scholars to miss the underlying continental pattern. Finally, as indirect rule was not always practiced even where it was preached (see chapter three), theoretical statements about how chiefs emerged from a particular type of colonialism run into trouble when they are compared to descriptions of the much messier empirical reality.

Conclusion

The terrain of struggle for the reform of land tenure is perhaps uniquely difficult for African states, given how they evolved. To be successful, reform takes a significant administrative presence in the rural areas, nuanced policies, and significant resources. African states tend not to have strong networks in many rural areas, usually use extremely blunt instruments of power when forced to operate far from the capital, and are poor. Therefore, it has been exceptionally difficult for African countries, without exceptionally traumatic ecologies or colonial histories, to diminish the power of local authorities by changing patterns of land allocation. Of course, in the very long-term, African countries probably will develop land markets that profoundly undermine traditional practices. However that day, which probably seemed relatively close at hand as many countries gained independence in the 1960s, is farther away at the turn of the century. Thus, the rough equilibrium in conventional politics between the state and traditional leaders—where neither makes significant inroads on the other's turf—appears likely to be relatively stable for many countries for many years. In turn, the conventional wisdom on land tenure increasingly favors incremental measures because states are not capable of doing more.

The great irony of the stalemate between chiefs and states over land is that African states, to some extent, have continued the precolonial tradition of unbundling ownership and control of the land by adopting the modern notion of soveriegnty. Even in African countries where the state claims to own the land, local elites control its allocation on a day-to-day basis. In other countries, the fact that the state claims to regulate land allocation is challenged by the facts on the ground on a daily basis. It is thus in the hinterlands where the fundamental contradiction of states having sovereign authority but not actual control it is most evident. And those states that have the most problematic geographies face the most serious obstacles to usurping the power of the chiefs.

Part Four

BOUNDARIES AND POWER

Seven

The Coin of the African Realm

When I went out [to Nigeria] there was no
currency. I instituted a currency.*
  Frederick Lugard

THE ESSENCE of sovereignty is negative: states are given the right to make
decisions about issues within their own boundaries without interference.
They are, however, assigned very few powers. One of the unquestioned
powers a sovereign nation state does have is the ability to mint currency,
although the value of the currency vis-à-vis other currencies (the exchange rate) can only be decreed, not enforced. For instance, no one
questioned the right of the government of President Mobutu to replace
the Congolese franc with the zaire in June 1967. The replacement of the
zaire with the new zaire in 1993 was also seen as a sovereign right, even
though many of the new notes were largely regarded as worthless and
some outlying provinces of Zaire retained the old currency (and thereby
insured monetary stability in those areas). Similarly, President Mobutu
was seen as well within his rights to import thirty-one tons of banknotes
from a German company to pay his troops in 1992.[1] Finally, it was perceived as not only natural but fully appropriate for Laurent Kabila, after
he overthrew Mobutu in 1997, to replace the new zaire with . . . the
Congolese franc.

This chapter will focus on the politics of the currency in West Africa
from the beginning of the twentieth century. A focus on West Africa is
particularly appropriate and useful because a very public series of debates
over the nature of the currency occurred in the region during both the
colonial and independence periods. In addition, a focus the politics of the
currency in West Africa is especially useful because of the juxtaposition of
anglophone countries, which quickly adopted their own currencies after

---

*Testimony of Frederick Lugard in West African Currency Committee (Barbour Com-
mittee), *Report, Minutes of Evidence and Appendices*, (London: Colonial Office, 1900), p.
16. Hereafter cited as Barbour Report. The Barbour Report and the accompanying evidence were never published. They can be found in the U.K. Public Record Office file,
Confidential Print-Africa, CO 879:62.
  [1] Steven Metz, *Reform, Conflict, and Security in Zaire* (Carlisle, PA: U.S. Army War
College, 1996), p. 16.

independence, and francophone nations, which have struggled to retain a link between their common currency, the CFA (Communauté Financìere Africaine) Franc, and the French franc. Finally, since 1983, West African countries have been pioneers in Africa in developing new strategies to combat overvaluation of the currency and, very much related, reduce the control of government over the currency supply.

The chapter will trace the evolution of West African currencies as boundaries and highlight their relationship to state consolidation. A study of West African monetary developments over the twentieth century reveals that leaders (both white and black) in African capitals did manage to make the units they ruled increasingly distinct from the international and regional economies. However, the greater salience of the currency did not end up promoting state consolidation. Rather, in one of the great tragedies of African economic history, winning the ability to determine the value of the currency led to a series of disastrous decisions that severely weakened the states themselves. Only when states gave up part of their control over the currency did they become stronger.

Money and Politics

Understanding the politics of the exchange rate is critical to analyzing state consolidation. There are few signs of the center extending its reach that are as profound as a currency minted in the capital being accepted in the rural areas. The phenomenon of paper currency, itself intrinsically worthless, being seen as a store of value is as substantive an economic vote of confidence as a state can receive. Successful adoption of the currency links all parts of the country together in a way that is powerful and relatively difficult to reverse. Likewise, failure to integrate the country through the adoption of a single currency, demonstrated by the presence of black markets or the use of other currencies as stores of value, is perhaps the most damning sign that a central government does not have the confidence of the country. Thus, the use of gold was very much tied up with the rise and decline of various Akan states in what is now Ghana.[2] Similarly, the adoption of coin currencies by the British was used as a way of reducing the slave trade in West Africa because slaves were sometimes treated as a store of value and were also vital to transporting the commodity currencies that dominated in the precolonial period.[3] Not surprisingly, across the world, the adoption of national moneys has

[2] Timothy F. Garrard, *Akan Weights and the Gold Trade* (Bristol: Longman, 1980), p. 66.

[3] Allen McPhee, *The Economic Revolution in British West Africa* (London: George Routledge, 1926), p. 235.

coincided with centralization of political power within borders.[4] Yet, the relationship between the currency and national identity has been understudied.[5]

The politics of the currency is also critical to understanding two sets of political conflicts that are often central to the extension of state authority. First, an important aspect of the conflict between African states and business has traditionally been over who has control over the money supply. African states, both colonial and post-colonial, naturally wanted the ability to mint currency at their convenience, in good part because of fiscal pressures, while businesses feared the loss of asset value if the keys to the currency printing press were turned over to government officials. This dispute is no less real today than at the turn of the century because international society still issues harsher condemnations against property seizure than against inflationary monetary policies that diminish asset value, although the two may in some cases may be different means to the same end. Taxation via inflation has always been a more attractive option for governments who did not want to become entangled in the legal and political complications of nationalization, much less operate the assets that were seized, especially after the disastrous experience of African nationalizations in the 1960s.[6]

Second, the conflict over the value of the currency vis-à-vis other currencies has an important spatial dimension. The forests, farms, plantations, and mines that produce goods for export in African countries are in the rural areas. The areas outside the cities are thus net exporters. In contrast, the urban areas are strongly net importers because city residents tend to buy foreign food and consume other goods produced abroad. As a result, failure to adjust to the consequences of currency creation, especially allowing the exchange rate to become overvalued, hurts the rural exporters but aids urban consumers. Correspondingly, an exchange rate correctly valued is of enormous benefit to the rural areas. In the 1960s, there were few more telling indications of the accumulation of power by African governments vis-à-vis rural asset holders (be they peasants or multinational corporations) than the establishment of government allocation of foreign exchange (and the accompanying black markets) instead of market-based systems of exchange rate determination.

Finally, the politics of the currency is an important window to understanding how African countries have become more, or less, integrated

---

[4] Benjamin J. Cohen, *The Geography of Money* (Ithaca: Cornell University Press, 1998), pp. 32–3.

[5] Eric Helleiner, "National Currencies and National Identities," *American Behavioral Scientist* 41 (August 1998): p. 1410.

[6] Young and Turner discuss the catastrophic Zairian nationalization in *The Rise and Decline of the Zairian State*, chapter 11.

into the world economy. The dependency literature was the most volu-
minous scholarly effort to understand the relationship between African
countries and the international economy. This school portrayed African
countries as becoming, especially after World War II, more integrated
with the world economy because of the demands of the outside world for
raw materials, and it was suggested that there was very little these countries could do to reverse this trend.[7] Similarly, the more recent literature
on globalization takes it as a given that African states, like all others, are
being increasingly integrated into the world economy.[8]

However, both these literatures are flawed because they fail to devote
enough attention to the institutional structures of African countries, especially indigenous efforts to moderate the impact of the international
economy. Focusing on the currency and the exchange rate, the critical
and most visible buffer between the domestic and international economies, provides a more complex and interesting analysis of how Africa in
particular became economically integrated with the rest of the world than
is possible with existing perspectives.[9] Indeed, as will become clear, a
comprehensive examination of the politics of the currency suggests that,
in many ways, African countries have become progressively less integrated in the world economy compared to the early colonial period when
the Imperial Treasury in London feared that monetary developments in
West Africa could destabilize the metropole. It is impossible to imagine
similar concerns today. The omnipresent declarations of globalization of
all markets are largely based on unthinking application of the American
and European experiences to very different parts of the world.

The Politics of the Currency in Colonial West Africa

By the early part of the twentieth century, a large part of West Africa had
changed over to colonial currencies.[10] For instance, by 1912, British gold

[7] See, among many examples, Samir Amin, *Neo-Colonialism in West Africa* (New York:
Monthly Review Press, 1973), pp. xiv, 274.

[8] See, for instance, Richard O'Brien, *Global Financial Integration: The End of Geography*
(London: Royal Institute of International Affairs, 1992); Richard B. McKenzie and Dwight
R. Lee, *Quicksilver Capital: How the Rapid Movement of Wealth has Changed the World*
(New York: Free Press, 1991); Frances Cairncross, *The Death of Distance: How the Commu-
nications Revolution Will Change our Lives* (Cambridge: Harvard Business School Press,
1997).

[9] Here I agree with Robert Bates, who argues that understanding how institutions struc-
ture political games in open economies is of central importance. Robert H. Bates, *Open-
Economy Politics: The Political Economy of the World Coffee Trade* (Princeton: Princeton
University Press, 1997), p. 165.

[10] There is a significant debate over exactly why this changeover occurred. See J. C. de

and silver coin was legal tender without limit in Sierra Leone, the Gambia, the Gold Coast and its Dependencies (the colony of Ashanti and the northern territories protectorate), and in all of Nigeria. In Sierra Leone and the Gambia and in the western province of Nigeria, certain French, Spanish, and American gold coins were also legal tender. However, imperial silver had undoubtedly become the single most important means of payment.[11] Thus, while the quote from Lugard at the front of the chapter is technically inaccurate, as West Africa has a long currency history that predates the Europeans, he was correct in asserting that he established a currency specific to the area he ruled, a signal development in the region.

The Search for Seigniorage

Certain peculiarities of the British silver coinage brought about a major jdebate concerning the currency exchange mechanism at the end of the nineteenth century. This currency was technically overvalued because the amount of silver in the coin was only (at the turn of the century) 50 percent of the face value of the coin. This overvaluation was preserved, in good part, because it was widely believed that the Imperial Treasury would convert the silver currency to gold at the face value. However, the treasury was only legally required to convert up to £2 of the coin's face value.

The overvaluation of the currency soon prompted colonial authorities to realize that the treasury was reaping significant amounts of seigniorage (the revenue collected when the face value of the coin is higher than the value of the materials used to mint it) from the production of silver coins for West Africa, and to demand a share of the "profit." As early as 1897, Sir Harry McCallum, governor of Lagos, noted that the price of silver had decreased and asked for a percentage of the seigniorage that the treasury in London was reaping. The "profits" from minting silver looked particularly attractive because the contingent liability that had to be covered in case the coins were ever redeemed did not appear to be large. A great deal of silver was being absorbed by the countryside, to be used either as jewelry or permanently circulated in the internal market, so it was unlikely that many coins would ever be redeemed for gold.[12]

Graft-Johnson, "Some Historical Observations on Money and the West African Currency Board," *Quarterly Economic Bulletin of the Bank of Ghana*, 11 (1967): p. 4, and Walter Ibekwe Ofonagoro, "The Currency Revolution in Southern Nigeria, 1880–1948," (UCLA African Studies Center Occasional Paper no. 14, Los Angeles, 1976), p. 19.

[11] J. B. de Loynes, *A History of the West African Currency Board* (London: Eyre and Spottiswoode, 1974), pp. 7–8.

[12] Clement Nyong Isong, "Currency and Credit in Nigeria, 1850–1955" (Ph.D. diss., Harvard University, 1957), pp. 44–5.

Colonial officials were always searching for greater revenue because they were constantly trying to fund infrastructure projects and also had high personnel costs while their income streams, as discussed in chapter four, were limited. Hancock's plea dramatically captured the position of many colonial officials when they considered their finances:

> How can governments enlarge their programmes of public works and welfare services when they can no longer be confident of their capacity to finance them? Adam Smith seems to be deserting West Africa when he has only scratched the surface of his West African task.[13]

A constant stream of income from the minting of the currency therefore looked particularly attractive.

However, the imperial treasury was unwilling to simply devote part of the seigniorage to the colonies without assigning them some of the risk if the coins were redeemed. The treasury did note that it was willing to have the colonies issue their own token coinage but that "great care would need to be exercised to restrain the several Governments from the temptation to overissue, with its consequent dangers to their commerce and to their finances."[14] The treasury seemed to understand immediately the fiscal pressures that the colonies were under and the implications for the currency unless money supply was carefully regulated.

The Colonial Office continued to monitor monetary developments and managed in 1899 to have a committee established under Sir David Barbour to examine the possibility of establishing a separate coinage for West Africa in order to capture some of the seigniorage from the treasury. At the hearings, the most straightforward view was taken by then Colonel (later Lord) Frederick Lugard, who advocated not only developing a separate West African currency but also banning all other currencies in the area so as to maximize the seigniorage.[15] Other colonial authorities were less certain. Their primary concern was that Africans would not accept the changes in the currency, and this fear appeared to outweigh the potential for gains through seigniorage.[16] Certainly, there is no better evidence of the problematic nature of colonial control of West Africa in the years immediately following the conquest than the uncertainty of the British authorities about their ability to impose a new currency on the territories they nominally controlled.

British merchant interests who operated in West Africa were opposed

---

[13] W. K. Hancock, *Problems of Economic Policy, 1918–1939*, part 2, vol. 2 of *Survey of British Commonwealth Affairs* (London: Oxford University Press, 1942), p. 323.

[14] Quoted in W. T. Newlyn and D. C. Rowan, *Money and Banking in British Colonial Africa* (Oxford: Clarendon Press, 1954), p. 29.

[15] Lugard in Barbour Report, p. 18.

[16] G. C. Denton in ibid., p. 13.

to any change in the form of currency in West Africa. The merchants had two particular fears about a change in currency. First, along with the colonial officials, they were concerned that Africans would not readily accept a new currency. Second, and more important, they shared the treasury's worry that the colonial authorities would, driven by the need for seigniorage, mint an increasing number of coins without retaining a sufficient reserve. Eventually, they believed, a West African colonial currency would not be directly convertible into gold and their own assets would become less valuable, if not worthless. For instance, John Holt, a businessman who founded one of the great commercial enterprises in West Africa (John Holt and Company), said, "I am sure there is no better coinage than the Imperial coinage. There I have got something I can bring home, and convert into sovereigns when I need to . . . if I contemplate getting a colonial coinage I naturally want to know what security I am going to have if I should ever want gold."[17] The views of individual businessmen were supported by the Liverpool Chamber of Commerce, the London Chamber of Commerce, the Bank of British West Africa, and the African Association.[18]

The Barbour Committee recognized the advantages of diverting a portion of the seigniorage to the colonies. The committee recommended that, if a system that guaranteed the value of a new colonial currency could be established, one-half of the seigniorage should be devoted to creating a gold reserve to back the currency and the other half be declared profit for the colonies.[19] Yet, the committee did not clearly endorse a new currency system because of objections from merchants. The Barbour Committee also endorsed a system whereby the treasury would continue to supply West Africa with coins, but the colonies would get one-half of the seigniorage.[20]

The recklessness of the Barbour Committee in proposing such a high seigniorage rate and its attempts to try to satisfy both the interests of the Colonial Office and the merchants caused the report to be ignored. The treasury was still adamantly opposed to allocating seigniorage without assigning responsibility. In addition, colonial officials were not willing to lobby strongly for a change to a West African currency system.[21] Given the opposition from the treasury and the merchant interests, and the weak support from the putative beneficiaries, the Barbour Report experienced a quick death.

[17] Holt in ibid., p. 41.

[18] See the letters in "Protests Against the Introduction of a Special British West African Currency," in ibid., p. 53.

[19] Ibid., p. xi.

[20] Ibid., p. xii.

[21] See A. G. Hopkins, "The Creation of a Colonial Monetary System: The Origins of the West African Currency Board," *African Historical Studies*, 3 (1970): p. 123.

However, after the Barbour Committee Report, the amount of silver going to West Africa continued to increase and therefore remained an issue for several parts of the British government. By 1910, the Colonial Office estimated that the "profit" from silver minting was £180,000 a year, while in 1900 the same office had estimated a "profit" of only £116,000 annually.[22] The increase in silver caused the Colonial Office to become even more enthusiastic about establishing a separate West African currency. As G. V. Fiddes, assistant under-secretary in charge of crown colonies, noted,

> we have never entirely lost sight of the desirability of annexing this profit for the benefits of the [Colonial] Governments concerned . . . we do not issue coins for the sake of profit, and to do that would be a detestable financial operation; but the profit is there, and the profit may legitimately be intercepted by one administration instead of another.[23]

At the same time, the treasury began to be very concerned that the British government was becoming too successful, too quickly, in its effort to promote the use of silver. By 1910, West Africa consumed a very large percentage of the sterling issued for circulation. For instance, during the period 1886–1890, West Africa accounted for only 2 percent of sterling issued while other territories accounted for 21 percent and Great Britain for 77 percent. Twenty-one years later, in 1911, West Africa imported 37 percent of sterling issued, other territories only 12 percent, and Great Britain 51 percent.[24] The Treasury was very worried that the sudden repatriation of large amounts of silver from West Africa could seriously disrupt the money supply in Great Britain.[25] It was probably at this time, when West Africa was suddenly absorbing a significant amount of Great Britain's money supply, that the anglophone portion of West Africa was more integrated with the world economy than at any other point in the century.

The treasury's concerns propelled the establishment of a committee in 1910 led by Lord Emmott to alter, in the terms of this chapter, the currency exchange mechanism. At these hearings, the officials, representing the interests of the individual colonies, were much more strongly in

[22] Barbour Report, p. xi, and G. V. Fiddes in Departmental Committee appointed to Inquire into Matters Affecting the Currency of the British West African Colonies and Protectorates (Lord Emmott Committee), *Minutes of Evidence* (cited here as Emmott Evidence), Cd. 6427 (London: His Majesty's Stationary Office, 1912), p. 2.

[23] Fiddes in Emmott Evidence, pp. 2, 5.

[24] See Departmental Committee appointed to Inquire into Matters Affecting the Currency of the British West African Colonies and Protectorates (Lord Emmott Committee), *Report to the Right Honorable Lewis Harcourt, M.P., Secretary of State for the Colonies*, Cd.6426 (London: His Majesty's Stationary Office, 1912), pp. 6, 22.

[25] de Loynes, *A History of the West African Currency Board*, p. 11.

favor of shifting the seigniorage to their territories. After having the face of three different sovereigns on the coinage in ten years, they no longer worried that trade would be hindered because Africans would not accept a new currency. Rather, the fiscal pressures they faced drove them to seek a share of the seigniorage. For instance, G. B. Haddon-Smith, colonial secretary for Sierra Leone, said, "My sole idea of being an advocate of a special coinage would be for the Colonies to get the profit on it which the Mint at present gets."[26] Similarly, C. L. Temple, chief secretary to the government of northern Nigeria, said, "I am strongly in favor of the proposal [to allow the Colonies a special currency]. I am afraid the point of view I take, coming from a very poor district and protectorate, is rather the revenue point of view."[27]

As they had in 1900, some merchants testified against disturbing the status quo, but there was much less concern that a change in the form of currency would affect trade. However, the merchant interests were still extremely worried that a colonial coinage would be ruinous for their interests because the colonial officials would be driven to debase the currency. For instance, Arthur Bett, manager of John Holt and Company, said that, despite the fact that the silver currency was not technically redeemable in full, "We feel very safe with the Imperial currency, and I think we would take the risk rather than face perhaps some of the difficulties which we think we shall have to face with the new currency."[28]

In the hearings before the Emmott Committee, merchants reluctantly admitted that there would be no substantial change in their business operations if the new West African coinage was directly convertible into gold. However, at least some merchants seemed concerned that because they did not have nearly as good a relationship with the Colonial Office as they did with the treasury, once a West African coinage was established, they would be unable to rely on, and pressure, colonial authorities in the same way that they did with the treasury in London. For instance, Lord Emmott persistently stated to Bett that the continuation of the system might harm merchant interests because a sudden return of silver to Great Britain could cause the government to suspend the redemption of the overvalued currency. However, Bett was adamant in saying that "The Imperial Government would not let their silver depreciate" and noted that merchant interests felt safe even if there was a sudden disruption of the monetary system because "We take it that the Government

---

[26] G. B. Haddon-Smith in Emmott Evidence, p. 22.

[27] C. L. Temple in ibid., p. 37. The same views were expressed by the colonial secretary of the Gold Coast (p. 15), the former provincial commissioner of Southern Nigeria (p. 30), and the chief commissioner of the northern territories of the Gold Coast (p. 31).

[28] Arthur Bett in ibid., p. 60.

would see us out of the difficulty."[29] He did not seem nearly so sanguine about the colonial governments preserving merchant interests.

In good part, merchants' perception that they might lose out if they had to deal with the colonial authorities was due to the fact that many of the owners actually lived in Great Britain or Europe and carried out their business in West Africa through paid agents. The Colonial Office rather pointedly noted that there were no prominent businessmen who actually lived in West Africa.[30] The merchants therefore had only limited leverage vis-à-vis colonial officials, especially in an age when the slowness of communications meant that officials on the ground had a substantial amount of autonomy.

In addition, there was a tradition of mistrust between colonial officials and businessmen that continued through the 1930s. Part of the problem was class differences between Oxbridge-educated colonial officials and businessmen from Birmingham, Liverpool, and Manchester. More generally, the colonial officials in West Africa, wedded in the early years of the century to the system of indirect rule, did not see promoting the business interests of Britain-based firms as central to their mission; indeed, the Colonial Office did not even establish an economic section until the 1930s.[31] As J. M. Lee noted, "the Colonial Office itself was unlikely to be swayed easily by metropolitan business interests . . . [each colony] became suspicious of pressure groups in Whitehall whether they were from capitalist manufacturers or humanitarian societies."[32] The complexity of the relationship between business and the colonial state make it clear that, far from having a "hegemonic project," colonial authorities were highly conflicted about promoting metropolitan interests. Businessmen did not fully trust colonial authorities to advance their own interests and therefore repeatedly turned to the more familiar institutions in London.

However, by 1912, the treasury was firmly on the side of the colonies, despite the fact that it would lose the "profit" from minting the silver coins if West Africa issued its own currency. The merchant interests simply were not powerful enough, given the fears the treasury had about the possibility of the home economy being disrupted if West Africa continued to absorb large amounts of silver. To try to satisfy both treasury and merchant interests, the Emmott Committee recommended the establish-

---

[29] Ibid., p. 60.

[30] Fiddes in ibid., p. 7.

[31] Josephine F. Milburn, *British Business and Ghanaian Independence* (London: University Press of New England, 1977), p. 28, and Hancock, *Survey of British Commonwealth Affairs*, p. 265.

[32] J. M. Lee, *Colonial Development and Good Government* (Oxford: Clarendon Press, 1967), p. 74. See also Frederick Pedler, *The Lion and the Unicorn: A History of the United Africa Company, 1787–1931* (London: Heinemann, 1974), p. 188.

ment of a new West African currency that was to be backed by reserves derived from the seigniorage.

The West African Currency Board

Accordingly, the West African Currency Board, the first institutionalized currency exchange mechanism in the region, was established in 1912. While the merchant interests had lost out in their struggle to retain the imperial currency, they were able to influence the design of the currency exchange mechanism sufficiently so that their vital interests were preserved. The board itself noted that the impetus for the Barbour and Emmott Committees had been the Colonial Office's raising of the seigniorage question. However, the board stated clearly that its own first priority was to allay the concerns of the treasury and the merchants by establishing a sound currency backed up by a reserve.[33] The home government seemed to go out of its way to stress that the West African Currency Board could not be used by colonial officials to print money and thereby derive greater amounts of seigniorage. In a gesture heavily laden with symbolism and, given the location of most businesses, important to practical politics, the West African Currency Board established its headquarters in London, rather than in West Africa.

The entire structure of the West African Currency Board was designed so that the revenue needs of West African colonies could not be met through manipulation of the currency. The board eventually came to interpret its mandate as requiring a 100 percent cover of the coins it issued, even though it was obvious that much of the currency would never be redeemed.[34] The only "profit" that the colonies could receive was from the interest on the reserves that the board had established, despite the fact that officials in the colonies continued to express the desire for British coins in West Africa with the seigniorage going to the colonies.[35] Much to the relief of the merchant interests,

> In 1922, when the system was fully established, the currency was really just as much sterling as it had been ten years previously, before the new system was introduced. The public had coins with exactly the same values as they had before . . . They could put their coin and notes in the bank and get sterling

[33] See West African Currency Board, *Report of the West African Currency Board*, Cd. 7791 (London: HMSO, 1915), p. 2.

[34] The board was able to establish a 100 percent cover in 1926 and after that usually retained a cover over 100 percent. Jan S. Hogendorn and Henry A. Gemery, "Cash Cropping, Currency Acquisition, and Seigniorage in West Africa, 1923–1950," *African Economic History*, 11 (1982): p. 16.

[35] As Lugard makes clear in *The Dual Mandate*, p. 491.

credits overseas on a £ for £ basis, less a commission which was probably lower than that charged by the banks for a similar transaction ten years earlier.[36]

The board was therefore able to establish a currency that always traded at parity with the British pound. The board did not release additional currency for imports unless there was a corresponding increase in exports. In reality, the board did not manage the exchange rate at all. As Ida Greaves noted,

> It is the function of a Currency Authority [such as the West African Currency Board] to satisfy the demand for local currency, not to regulate it; controlling the supply of currency in a colony is entirely a technical matter of providing for local requirements while guarding against losses from theft and forgery; it means deciding what types and denominations of currency are to circulate and issuing them on demand, not exercising discretionary authority over the total amount that is available.[37]

The United Africa Company, one of the most important multinationals operating in West Africa, stated clearly how well this system, which did not allow colonial officials any discretion in the determination of monetary policy, benefited merchant interests,

> The beauty of this system of currency and credit is that it requires no control, other than that of a rigid set of regulations to be followed by the Currency Board. West Africa is linked by this system to the important money market of London, and there is no let or hindrance, apart from the transfer charge, to the free flow of funds . . . West Africa is no more remote than, for example, Wales or Scotland.[38]

The West African Currency Board continued to further the essential merchant interest of having a convertible currency through the end of the colonial period, despite the fact that the Colonial Office managed to staff the board.[39] The only marked change occurred when Great Britain formally created the sterling area and imposed exchange controls on payments to areas outside of the empire after World War II.[40] This move meant that the West African colonial currency was no longer directly

[36] G. L. M. Clauson, "The British Colonial Currency System," *The Economic Journal* 44 (April 1944): p. 7.

[37] Ida Greaves, *Colonial Monetary Conditions*, Colonial Research Studies no. 10 (London: HMSO, 1953), p. 12.

[38] "The West African Currency Board," *U.A.C. Statistical and Economic Review* 18 (1951): p. 16.

[39] On the staffing dispute, see John M. Carland, "Bureaucrats and Imperial Finance: The Colonial Office, the Treasury, and the West African Currency Board, 1911–1914" *Historical Papers* (1982): pp. 65–8.

[40] Yusuf Bangura, *Britain and Commonwealth Africa: The Politics of Economic Relations, 1951–1975* (Manchester: Manchester University Press, 1975), p. 3.

convertible into currencies other than the pound. However, the interests of British firms were not hurt by the change because the link between the colonial currency and the pound was preserved. The establishment of the sterling area probably gave British firms an advantage in anglophone West Africa because they were the only ones who could automatically exchange the colonial currency for their home currency.

In contrast to the British, the French, the other dominant colonial power in West Africa, never felt the need to establish a separate currency in West Africa. Currency boards were very much an invention of the British empire.[41] The much more centralized nature of the French empire meant that their colonial officials did not generate the same kind of pressures for a portion of the seigniorage that the more distinct units of the colonial governments in the British empire did. The fear that the home economy might be threatened by a return of West African silver would probably have also seemed strange to the French who saw the colonies and France as "complementary parts of a single economy."[42] The French established a system of chartered banks to issue money in Africa. However, these banks were under strict metropolitan control with the result that the francs circulating in Africa were also tied and directly convertible to the home currency.[43]

The Politics of the Currency in Independent West Africa

The West African Currency Board succeeded in its primary mission of preserving parity with the imperial currency by backing its currency with reserves generated by the seigniorage. Its extremely conservative reserve policy combined with the boom in the colonies' exports after World War II meant that, by the 1950s, the board had developed very large reserves in London. Inevitably, the large reserves became a political issue as Africans already looking to independence began to wonder why the receipts from their exports were being held outside West Africa rather than used to benefit their own countries. For instance, Kwame Nkrumah noted at independence the large contribution that Ghana had made to Great Britain's sterling and gold balances.[44] Nationalists in West Africa also seized

[41] John Williamson, *What Role for Currency Boards?* (Washington, DC: Institute for International Economics, 1995), p. 5.

[42] D. K. Fieldhouse, "The Economic Exploitation of Africa: Some British and French Comparisons," in *France and Britain in Africa*, ed. Prosser Gifford and Wm. Roger Louis (New Haven: Yale University Press, 1971), p. 598.

[43] Ibid., pp. 610–1.

[44] Kwame Nkrumah, *I Speak of Freedom* (Westport, CT: Greenwood Press, 1976), p. 100.

on the currency as a potent nationalist symbol. Thus, Chief F. S. Okotie-Eboh, the Nigerian minister of finance, said in 1962,

> so long as our currency is linked with sterling we cannot exercise any direct control over its official exchange rate, which automatically follows any changes in the official rate of the pound sterling. . . . However, I am sure it is much more in accordance with our status as an independent sovereign nation . . . that we ourselves should be free to decide our own official rate of exchange.[45]

After the WACB

As successive anglophone countries gained their independence, they left the West African Currency Board, which eventually distributed its remaining assets and folded. In many ways, the leaders of newly independent African countries were simply doing what their colonial predecessors had wanted to do but were stopped from implementing because of the concerns of the Imperial Treasury: they established a new currency in order to try to capture the right to control the money supply. Douglas Rimmer was prescient in calling this change the loss of innocence for Ghana and other African countries that had previously been in the WACB.[46] Politically, the creation of national currencies was seen as an important step toward making the new countries' boundaries an economic reality, especially when the WACB had been used to prevent local actors from affecting the money supply. While Nkrumah and other leaders were publicly committed to pan-Africanism, they were moving quickly to strengthen their own national distinctness at the expense of regional economic arrangements.

The delinking of the newly independent anglophone countries' currencies from the sterling meant that there had been a fundamental change in the currency exchange mechanism. Instead of currency conversion being essentially automatic and therefore inaccessible to local officials, the money supply and the exchange rate were to be determined by the newly independent governments themselves. Therefore, unless another institutional structure was established that would regulate the money supply in a nonpolitical manner, as the WACB had, there was the possibility that the fiscal needs of the new states could at last begin to affect the money supply and thereby have an impact on the currency. Correspondingly, those actors with an interest in not seeing the currency debased, notably multinational corporations and rural producers, would for the first time

---

[45] Quoted in F. A. Olaloku, "Monetary System and Policy," in *Structure of the Nigerian Economy*, ed. F. A. Olaloku (London: MacMillan Press, 1979), p. 186.

[46] Douglas Rimmer, "The Crisis in the Ghana Economy," *Journal of Modern African Studies* 4 (1966): p. 17.

have to try to exercise their political power in West Africa in order to see their businesses protected. They would no longer have the comfort of relying on an institution based in London that automatically prevented fiscal pressures from being translated into the printing of more money.

In fact, soon after independence, the countries in West Africa experienced increasing fiscal pressures that were in sharp contrast to their histories in the 1950s when the colonies ran consistent budget surpluses.[47] The independent governments ran deficits for obvious reasons: they had ambitious development projects (on a much greater scale than what the colonial governments had planned) and their revenue, still based on customs duties and nontax revenue, was inadequate. The new rulers therefore took the option that had been attractive but unavailable to the colonial governments: manipulate the currency to try to meet the ever-increasing fiscal demands.

As deficit financing increased, the countries in the region began to experience significant balance of payment deficits and a consequent loss of reserves. Ghana, for instance, due to balance of payments deficits, reduced its international reserves from five hundred forty-four million cedis in 1960 to fifty-nine million cedis in 1965 (only slightly more than five weeks worth of imports).[48] Of course, under the West African Currency Board, a significant balance of payments problem never occurred because imports were funded from the earnings of exports.

As their foreign reserves decreased, anglophone West African countries were therefore faced with the need to regulate their imports. In general, they chose to regulate imports administratively through the use of quotas and licenses rather than through an outright devaluation of the currency. For example, the Ghanaian authorities extended the exchange controls that had previously applied to the non-sterling area to all their trading partners and eventually imposed import licensing in December 1961.[49] In part, the resort to administrative controls in the 1960s and 1970s rather than a market solution (i. e., devaluation) was a reflection of the times when the ability of the state to regulate the economy was thought of much more highly than it is now.

However, the administrative solution was convenient for several other reasons. Import regulations allowed the Nkrumah government to shift control of a significant portion of the nation's foreign exchange from the

[47] For Ghana, see Ghana, *Economic Survey, 1968* (Accra: Central Bureau of Statistics, 1968), p. 37. For Nigeria, see F. A. Olaloku, "Fiscal System and Policy," in *Structure of the Nigerian Economy*, ed. F. A. Olaloku (London: MacMillan Press, 1979), pp. 213–5.

[48] M. M. Huq, *The Economy of Ghana: The First Twenty-Five Years since Independence* (London: MacMillan Press, 1989), p. 213.

[49] J. Clark Leith, *Foreign Trade Regimes and Economic Development: Ghana* (New York: Columbia University Press, 1974), pp. 5–6.

private to the public sector, something that would have been much more difficult if the price of foreign exchange had been regulated by the market.[50] In Ghana and elsewhere in West Africa, the administrative allocation of foreign exchange also quickly became a way of distributing government patronage. Those favored by the government could make enormous profits if they had a license to buy foreign currency at the official rate and then sell imported goods, which had become extremely scarce. Inevitably, the contradiction between the economic rationale for import regulations and the political advantages of administrative allocation of foreign exchange became too great, with the result that licensing became hugely inefficient.[51]

The increases in the money supply to meet fiscal demands, the reliance on administrative controls to control imports, and the failure to adjust exchange rates led, in the anglophone countries, to an overvaluation of the currency. The emphasis on import regulations with ever-greater controls and regulations misled government officials into believing that they could regulate imports without adjusting the official exchange rate. For the twenty years after independence, Ghana and Nigeria had exchange rates that became increasingly overvalued.[52] Sierra Leone followed a similar pattern.[53] During the early 1980s, the black market premium on foreign exchange (the best measure of overvaluation) was almost 300 percent in Africa, the highest in the developing world.[54]

The profound distortions in the foreign exchange market eventually had significant effects on African economies. The overvalued currencies contributed to the African inability to diversify export portfolios (because new export ventures faced a daunting obstacle in the overvaluation of the currency) and they therefore remained dependent on one or two raw material exports. African agricultural exports became even more concentrated on a few commodities between the 1960s and the 1980s, even while non-African agricultural exporters diversified. The World Bank estimates that the 200 percent overvaluation of the currency in Ghana caused the economy to contract by 3 percent a year, a disastrous performance for an already poor country.[55]

[50] Tony Killick, *Development Economics in Action: A Study of Economic Policies in Ghana* (New York: St. Martin's Press, 1978), p. 266.

[51] Killick's analysis and evidence on this point are authoritative. See ibid., pp. 278–86.

[52] Adrian Wood, *Global Trends in Real Exchange Rates, 1960 to 1984*, (Washington, DC, The World Bank, 1988), pp. 122–31.

[53] Douglas Rimmer, *The Economies of West Africa* (New York: St. Martin's Press, 1984), p. 137.

[54] World Bank, *Adjustment in Africa: Reform, Results, and the Road Ahead* (Washington, DC: The World Bank, 1994), p. 22.

[55] Ibid., pp. 18, 23.

The Geography of Losers

The most striking aspect of the pattern of overvaluation that occurred in West Africa once the independent governments had control of their currencies was the obvious weakness of two groups defined by their location: foreign business and the rural population. Of the two, it is, of course, much more surprising that foreign business lost out. However, the pattern of exchange controls and overvaluation that came to characterize West African economies after independence did have an impact, as merchant interests feared as early as 1900, on the ability of foreign firms to remit profits back to their home country. D. K. Fieldhouse, in his study of Unilever (the parent of the United Africa Company), noted that West African countries' adoption of exchange controls and other regulations did, to some extent, "put a private enterprise at the mercy of civil servants and politicians."[56]

When the merchant interests had to confront the black successors to the colonial officials head on, they lost out not only in the controversy over how the currency should be regulated but also in the actual allocation of foreign exchange. Businesses' strength could not be translated into leverage that would compete with the advantages derived by leaders from a system that allowed them to gain significant political advantages through the administrative allocation of foreign exchange. In particular, multinational companies, based outside of Africa, could not compete politically because they were not involved in the network of clientelistic politics that soon developed in the capitals around the allocation of foreign exchange. For instance, until 1967, Nigeria allowed free transferability of currency to the sterling zone. After that, the rate at which foreign companies could repatriate their profits was strictly regulated.[57] Ghana's first commission of inquiry into import license malpractices (the Ollennu Commission) described a political process that was almost designed to highlight the weaknesses of big companies, which had a weak presence in West Africa. It noted that ministry of trade officials,

> ignored the procedure and encouraged their friends and favorites to see them in person for licenses and amendment. On the other hand, it was extremely difficult for some importers to obtain import licenses or amendments through the normal channel.[58]

[56] D. K. Fieldhouse, *Unilever Overseas: The Anatomy of a Multinational, 1895–1965* (London: Croom Helm, 1978), pp. 599–601.

[57] Adeoye A. Akinsanya, "State Strategies toward Nigerian and Foreign Business," in *The Political Economy of Nigeria*, ed. I. William Zartman (New York: Praeger, 1983), p . 177.

[58] Commission of Enquiry into Alleged Irregularities and Malpractices in Connection with the Issue of Import Licenses, *Report* (Accra, Ghana: Government Printer, 1964), p. 12.

While many multinational corporations routinely pay bribes, these are usually one-time, large payments for guaranteed contracts such as a kick-back for an arms sale. As the corporate predecessors to today's multi-nationals recognized at the turn of the century, companies based in the United States or Europe, whose West African operations are usually a small part of overall company earnings, are less willing, and less able, to engage in the kind of continual, highly personalistic politics that went on endlessly in Ghana and elsewhere in West Africa in the 1960s through the 1980s. In contrast, the local elites the multinationals were competing against lived or died on the basis of access to foreign currency. Thus, Ghana's Ollennu Commission noted that import licenses were given out to government institutions, government corporations, and companies that government, or government officials, had special interests in. Those who did not have privileged access through the government had to pay bribes of between 5 and 10 percent of the contract.[59] As a result, "while some firms, big and small alike, were having a raw deal, import licenses were being lavished on some small business enterprises."[60] The Nkrumah government itself noted early on that import licenses were hurting poten-tial overseas investors, who feared that they could not get these licenses.[61] In contrast, the CFA countries received significant inflows of foreign ex-change because foreign firms did not have to confront the kind of prob-lems that import licensing and soft currencies caused them in anglophone Africa.[62]

Multinational corporations were also politically weak because many Af-rican leaders regarded the multinational companies as agents of imperial-ism, and the corporations therefore had even less rapport with the new leaders than they did with the colonial authorities in the 1920s and 1930s. The major threat that multinational corporations could make—that they were not going to invest further—probably did not seem that persuasive to African politicians given that a central plank of many new countries' economic policies was to decrease their dependence on foreign firms and increase the role of the state. In cases where multinational en-terprises have been able to confront African governments, as in the some-what successful circumvention of Nigerian indigenization decrees in the

[59] Commission of Enquiry into Alleged Irregularities and Malpractices in Connection with the Issue of Import Licenses, *Summary of the Report* (Accra, Ghana: Government Printers, 1964), p. 5.

[60] Ibid.

[61] Ghana, *Economic Survey, 1964* (Accra: Central Bureau of Statistics, 1964), p. 17.

[62] D. K. Fieldhouse, *Black Africa, 1945–1980: Economic Decolonization and Arrested De-velopment* (London: Allen and Unwin, 1986), p. 61.

1970s and 1980s, they were highly dependent on local collaborators who could navigate the byzantine politics of the capital.[63]

Thus, once they lost the currency exchange mechanism, which had institutionalized their political strength, multinational corporations found that they could not operate in the particular type of political arena that developed in West Africa after independence. These companies then coped as best they could with the overvalued exchange rate and looked to invest their money elsewhere, where there were more favorable economic circumstances and policies. *Pace* dependency theory and the literature on globalization, the problem of developing countries, at least in the area of exchange rates, is not that multinational enterprises have been too politically powerful but that they have not been strong enough to influence policy.

Of course, the other class of losers in the overvaluation of the exchange rate was producers in the rural areas who exported goods. The dynamics of the bias against rural areas in Africa are now well understood. Although the majority of Africans still live in the countryside, the pricing of a variety of goods and the delivery of social services has been heavily slanted in favor of the relatively small urban population who are closer to the state and can threaten it. Bates assigned much of the blame for small farmers' political weakness to their atomistic nature, given that they are spread across large amounts of land with little communication. However, he also noted that African governments had consistently repressed any attempts to organize the rural majority.[64] Former Nigerian president General Babangida himself noted in his 1992 New Year's speech, "The absence of truly grass-roots commodity-based farmers' associations has also for long hindered small-scale farmers from participating in the policy process. Existing associations were not real apex organizations, making it difficult for government to verify competing claims of clientele."[65] As chapter six indicates, the ability of rural elites to circumvent state actions in the countryside did not extend into power they could deploy in the capital.

Successive nondemocratic African governments viewed the urban population as their main constituency because votes (which would have privileged the much larger rural population) were not important but the fear of a destabilizing urban riot was very real. Such calculations were only natural given the OAU's decision rule that if a state controlled the capital

---

[63] See Thomas J. Biersteker, *Multinationals, the State, and Control of the Nigerian Economy* (Princeton: Princeton University Press, 1987), p. 243.

[64] Bates, *Markets and States in Tropical Africa*, pp. 106–19.

[65] "Babangida's New Year's Address to the Nation," Radio Nigeria Network, 1 January 1992 reprinted in Foreign Broadcast Information Service, *Daily Report: Sub-Saharan Africa*, 7 January 1992, p. 35.

city, it controlled the countryside. Just as international practices defined what control of a country meant, the specific norms the OAU established also determined what security threats were of most concern to an African state.

La Différence

In contrast, the francophone colonies, with the exception of Guinea (which, after the famous "no" in 1958, broke from France in a much more profound manner than the rest of francophone Africa) and, for a period of time, Mali, did not delink from the franc. Rather, after independence fourteen African countries remained in the franc zone through the CFA franc, originally established in 1946. The French treasury guaranteed that the CFA Franc was directly convertible into the French franc at a fifty to one gearing ratio. Two regional banks, the Banque des Etats de l'Afrique Centrale (BEAC) and the Banque Centrale des Etats de l'Afrique de l'Ouest (BCEAO), were established as the instruments of monetary policy. They were originally headquartered in Paris (like the siting of the WACB, a strong signal as to who set monetary policy) but have been based since the early 1970s in Yaoundé and Dakar respectively.

The political price of the CFA currency was to shift much of the decision-making power to the metropole. France exercises a veto over policies related to the CFA and the rules, enforced by France, demand extremely conservative policies, including an emphasis on positive balance of payments and tight control over credit. As a result, "the exchange rate is exogenous to policy."[66] As a result, the francophone colonies are not able to gain a primary advantage of a distinct national currency: the symbolism that the state is a distinct political and economic entity that allows its commitment to retain the value of the money it prints to be tested by domestic and international markets.

The franc tie was retained by the francophone countries, in part because French colonies in West Africa were much poorer and more dependent on aid than their anglophone neighbors.[67] Also the French, because West Africa was much more important to them, were more willing to provide inducements to their former colonies to retain the link to the franc. The French, for instance, made it very clear to Mali that its future aid levels were dependent on it returning to the franc zone,[68] a demand

---

[66] Nicolas van de Walle, "The Decline of the Franc Zone: Monetary Politics in Francophone Africa," *African Affairs* 90 (1991), p. 389.

[67] Hopkins, *Economic History of West Africa*, p. 289.

[68] David Leith Crum, "Mali and the U.M.O.A.: A Case-Study of Economic Integration," *The Journal of Modern African Studies*, 2 (September 1984): p. 469.

that apparently never even occurred to the British as the WACB dissolved. Internal British diplomatic correspondence makes clear that they expected to have no influence on currency matters after independence.[69] Francophone countries, unlike their anglophone neighbors, therefore had profound incentives to retain a common currency that was not congruent with their distinctive national boundaries. However, these incentives came, ironically, not from a desire to maintain pan-African institutions that might ameliorate the damage of territorial balkanization but from a need to stay close to France.

As very small, very open economies, it made sense for the francophone countries to fix their exchange rate to the French franc. The literature on optimal currency areas suggests that open economies will, on balance, gain from the certainty of a fixed exchange rate.[70] The arrangement was especially successful in controlling monetary policy. Francophone countries essentially did not have their own currencies, as their monetary supply was determined by the French treasury. They could not print money and were therefore exceptionally successful at controlling consumer price inflation.[71] The restraint provided by the CFA franc was particularly important because the propensities in the francophone countries were to replicate the same destructive economic policies that occurred in the rest of West Africa. For instance, fiscal policy was not nearly as conservative as monetary policy. Control over fiscal policy was noticeably lax in some francophone countries and governments in the region consistently failed to coordinate their fiscal policies.[72] Guinea, the one country to go off the French franc for a significant period of time, did experience a quick overvaluation of its currency, which made it, "effectively worth nothing outside Guinea and very little inside Guinea."[73] It is therefore not unreasonable to claim that the institutional arrangements governing the CFA were the primary determinant of the relative soundness of francophone West African monetary policy until the late 1980s.

---

[69] See H. Poynton, "The Currency System in West Africa: Memorandum," reprinted in *British Documents on the End of Empire: Ghana*, ed. Richard Rathbone, vol. 1 (London: Her Majesty's Stationary Office, 1992), p. 56.

[70] The literature is reviewed by Williams, *What Role for Currency Boards*, p. 23.

[71] Ibrahim Elbadawi and Nader Majd, "Adjustment and Economic Performance under a Fixed Exchange Rate: A Comparative Analysis of the CFA Zone," *World Development* 24 (May 1996): p. 942.

[72] David Strasvage, "The CFA Franc Zone and Fiscal Discipline," *Journal of African Economies* 6 (1996): p. 134, and Christopher P. Rosenberg, "Fiscal Policy Coordination in the WAEMU after the Devaluation," *International Monetary Fund Working Paper*, WP/95/25, February 1995, pp. 12–4.

[73] Rimmer, *The Economies of West Africa*, pp. 136–8. He is quoting R. W. Johnson "Guinea," in *West African States: Failure and Promise*, ed. John Dunn (Cambridge: Cambridge University Press, 1978), p. 48.

While the credibility provided by the CFA was a benefit for roughly the first twenty-five years of independence, a determination to keep the currency linked to the franc played havoc with francophone economies in the late 1980s and early 1990s. The CFA became overvalued when the (traditionally weak) French currency appreciated after the Plaza Accords in 1985 while the prices for the African commodities declined. As a result, in the late 1980 and early 1990s, the francophone economies suffered tremendously due to the progressive overvaluation of the currency. Output stagnated in the CFA countries between 1986 and 1994 even while expanding by 2.8 percent in other countries.[74] While the price stability of the CFA zone was still impressive, it seemed that the cost in foregone growth had become too great.[75]

However, despite the economic disaster, the Africans and the French seemed committed to the old rate for fear that the CFA would lose the credibility that it had built up over the years if there was a devaluation. Of course, elites in the francophone countries also had their own interests in keeping the exchange rate stable even if their countries were in an economic tailspin. A devaluation would have made affluent Africans far less rich in French franc terms, an important consideration for elites that often considered Paris home and that had found it convenient over the years to export money to France. The CFA value of government debt owed abroad would also have been greatly increased by a devaluation. Indeed, then French president François Mitterand was supposed to have promised his good friend, President Houphouët-Boigny of Côte d'Ivoire, that the CFA would not be devalued as long as the Ivorian was alive. Bowing to the economic crisis and strong pressure from the international financial institutions and non-French donors, the CFA franc was eventually devalued to a gearing ratio of one hundred to one in January 1994, after Houphouët-Boigny died but before he was buried.

The Return to the Market

The currencies of Ghana and Nigeria remained, like most African countries, overvalued until the mid-1980s when the International Monetary Fund required that they not only devalue but also fundamentally alter the currency exchange mechanism in exchange for desperately needed new

---

[74] Jean A. P. Clément et al., *Aftermath of the CFA Franc Devaluation* (Washington, DC: International Monetary Fund, 1996), p. 1.

[75] See, for instance, Shantayanan Devarajan and Dani Rodrik, "Do the Benefits of Fixed Exchange Rates Outweigh the Costs? The CFA Zone in Africa," in *Open Economies: Structural Adjustment and Agriculture*, ed. Ian Goldin and L. Alan Winters (Cambridge: Cambridge University Press, 1992), p. 83.

loans. There had, of course, been devaluations in Ghana and Nigeria (e.g., between 1967 and 1970 in Ghana), but these currency changes were eventually overwhelmed because of unchecked increases in the money supply. In order to enact devaluations that had a lasting effect, both countries attempted in the 1980s to adopt systems that allowed market forces to determine the exchange rate, either through auctions of foreign exchange or through the legalization of private trading of foreign currency. Ghana managed to institutionalize these reforms but the Nigerian devaluations were ineffective because of weak control over fiscal and monetary policy.[76] Many other African countries enacted significant devaluations during the 1980s. As a result, the black markets for foreign exchange, the most obvious symbol of economic distortions across the continent, had largely disappeared by the mid-1990s.[77]

The emphasis on market-driven currency exchange mechanisms was due to the realization that as long as political pressures could affect the money supply and thereby the exchange rate, the overvaluation problem would continue. Even after three decades of independence, there seem to be very few who believe that West African governments can design institutions that could determine the money supply and exchange rates in a way that would not be affected by clientelistic politics. Instead, as was the case in Ghana, the move to market allocation of foreign exchange was done specifically to "depoliticize" currency adjustments by effectively taking the government out of the process altogether.[78] Implicitly, the return to the market suggests that if currency adjustment remains a political question that can be determined by government, foreign companies and other net exporters will lose out in their bid to prevent the currency from being overvalued.

The Currency and State Consolidation

Concentrating on the buffer institution of the currency exchange mechanism yields a dramatic picture of how African leaders produced economic demarcations that eventually coincided with political boundaries. It is certainly not the case, at least in the critical instance of the currency, that the region has become increasingly integrated into the world economy.

[76] On the Nigerian reform program, see Jeffrey Herbst and Adebyao Olukoshi, "Nigeria: Economic and Political Reforms at Cross Purposes," in *Voting for Reform: Democracy, Political Liberalization, and Economic Adjustment*, ed. Stephan Haggard and Steve Webb (New York: Oxford University Press, 1994).

[77] The World Bank, *A Continent in Transition: Sub-Saharan Africa in the Mid-1990s* (Washington, DC: The World Bank, 1995), p. 21.

[78] Baffour Agyeman-Duah, "Ghana, 1982–6: The Politics of the P. N. D. C.," *The Journal of Modern African Studies* 25 (December 1987): p. 635.

In the eighteenth and nineteenth centuries, people conducting business in West Africa used the same currency locally as was circulated internationally. With the same type of money they could purchase locally produced goods or products from, for instance, East Africa. In the early part of the twentieth century, West Africa was a critical consumer for Great Britain's economy. However, the West African Currency Board fundamentally changed the degree to which anglophone Africans were integrated into the world economy by interposing a formally organized buffer mechanism between the local currency and the currencies circulating internationally. The fact that the West African Currency Board's currency was always kept at par with the pound is less important from this perspective than the fact that a state had caused the local currency to be different from the international currencies that were circulating. The importance of the state interposing itself between domestic and international currencies became more obvious after Great Britain created the sterling area and people in anglophone West Africa could only convert their local currency directly into one international currency.

Independent anglophone African states then further interposed themselves between the local West African currencies and the international currencies by eliminating the automatic conversion of local currencies to the pound that the West African Currency Board had maintained. The independent states also established elaborate (sometimes to the point of byzantine) administrative procedures for local people who wanted access to international currency in order to ration foreign exchange. Indeed, postindependence leaders adopted policies that appeared to be inimical to the actors that are supposed to be the embodiment of the integrated world economy: the multinational enterprises. The fact that the currency changes in West Africa were disastrous should not obscure the success that independent leaders had in separating themselves from the international economy. While the francophone countries retained a regional currency, the CFA franc still was a significant barrier between them and the international economy, compared to the far more internationalized currencies in use as late as the nineteenth century. Indeed, one of the reasons that France has been so eager to retain the CFA franc, despite the cost it has sometimes imposed on the French treasury and the distractions it has caused key policymakers, is that the currency is a useful way of retaining French influence in the region to the exclusion of others, especially Americans.

However, eventually, the achievement of separating themselves from the international economy and excluding both multinational enterprises and rural producers from the political process came back to haunt African countries. The anglophone currencies became so overvalued in the late 1970s and early 1980s that exporting became increasingly unprofitable.

Further, the deadweight losses and corruption associated with the administrative allocation of the currency became severe burdens on the economies.[79] Similarly, in the francophone countries, the desire to retain the old gearing ratio caused those countries to enter into the economic equivalent of a death spiral in the late 1980s. The crisis became so severe because the process of setting the exchange rate had become so concentrated in the capital, and net exporters had become politically irrelevant. There was no natural "feedback loop" within the national political system that would have put pressure on the governments to change the economic practices that were destroying them. And, unlike Europe, the decline in tax revenue from less foreign investment and reduced peasant production did not have any immediate security implications. Eventually the economic situation became so desperate that West African countries, and others in Africa, had to declare the equivalent of bankruptcy and allowed the International Monetary Fund and the World Bank to dictate critical reforms. Many of these reforms were adopted, and the elimination of spectacularly overvalued currencies has been arguably the most important achievement of the economic reforms that African countries began adopting in the mid-1980s.

The exchange rate as used by African leaders did bear many similarities to the hard territorial boundaries that African leaders created. Both tended to concentrate power in the capital while disempowering those who were not located at the center of political power. The hard territorial boundaries were sustainable because the international sovereignty regime that African leaders established only demanded that they control the capital and African countries developed mechanisms, discussed in chapter five, to put down emerging security threats. Indeed, to some extent, the hard territorial boundaries made the administrative allocation of foreign exchange possible in the 1960s and 1970s by providing significant incentives to concentrate all political power in the urban areas.

However, the currency regime was not sustainable because African countries were still dependent on multinationals and rural producers for exports, and governments could not compel them to produce. The central irony of the currency exchange mechanism chosen by anglophone African countries was that policies and procedures that gave maximum discretion to the central government, and therefore privileged those who could operate easily in the capital, eventually caused the political reach of the capital to contract. Those who did not benefit from the administrative allocation of foreign exchange either left (multinational businesses) or were forced to engage in smuggling and use other currencies in order to ensure their economic survival (rural smallholders). In extreme in-

[79] See Herbst, *The Politics of Reform in Ghana*, chapter 3.

stances, as in Zaire, prolonged dysfunctional policies by the central government led to economic secession by some provinces who decided to use another currency.

If there had been a different set of interests and, especially, a different international climate that actually rewarded state consolidation, African countries may well have adopted different economic policies. If the array of domestic interests and the state system had been different, the CFA franc might have been counterproductive as a state consolidation strategy because it made government officials less responsible for economic policies. By having a currency linked to the former colonizer, the francophone countries could not use the national coin as a symbol of their independence and their ability to govern their own economies. Indeed, the CFA franc was often seen as a holdover from colonial times. However, the CFA, chosen more for reasons related to France's foreign policy than economic or political rationality, turned out to be, in many ways, a better policy than disbanding the currency arrangements as the anglophones proceeded to do because it allowed the francophone countries to avoid some of the worst problems of currency manipulation. Yet even the CFA caused considerable damage when African countries refused to devalue it in the face of changed economic circumstances.

Conclusion

The warnings of the imperial treasury at the turn of the century turned out to be prescient. Without a strong institutional barrier that removed African state officials not only functionally but also geographically from the control of money supply, the anglophone countries had disastrous exchange rate policies that played a role in the diminishment of state authority after independence. Likewise, business, as many companies predicted at the beginning of the twentieth century, proved to be one of the big losers when maximum discretion was given to local authorities. Certainly, the oft-stated sentiment that independence changed nothing in terms of the relationship between foreign companies and African governments is clearly not true. Unfortunately, the hope of African leaders that adoption of their own currencies in the 1960s would be a symbol of their countries' emergence as strong independent states turned out to be a cruel joke.

Eight

The Politics of Migration and Citizenship

Qui n'a pas été à Kumasi, n'ira pas au Paradis."
  From a popular West African song
  quoted by Kenneth Little, "West African
  Urbanization as a Social Process,"
  in *Independent Black Africa: The Politics
  of Freedom*

THE MOVEMENT of people was central to precolonial politics given the particular understanding of how state power was broadcast. The development, starting in the colonial period, of nominally hard boundaries that were to regulate the movement of people in Africa was therefore a significant development. Since the creation of these hard boundaries, often maligned as irrelevant, there has been a fundamental change in African migration patterns so that, for the first time in the continent's history, people are migrating toward the centers of political power. Simultaneously, the (literal) personification of territorial control in the postindependence period through the development of citizenship laws—which seek for the first time in African history to tie each person to a geographically defined polity—is another development critical to the understanding of state power in Africa. This chapter investigates how changing patterns of migration and the dynamics of citizenship laws both affect and reflect the abilities of African states to consolidate power. These two phenomena are inevitably intertwined because citizenship laws embody the identities that African states have tried to construct on the assumption that populations are no longer mobile.

This chapter argues that, contrary to conventional wisdom, African boundaries have fundamentally changed the nature of population movements across the continent. As a result, citizenship has acquired a salience that is often greater than the ties between ethnic groups separated by a border. However, African countries have not exploited the surprising firmness of their boundaries to develop innovative citizenship regulations that might establish a strong national bond between state and citizen. As a result, a critical opportunity for state consolidation often has been lost.

Migration after Independence

Once many African countries gained independence in the early 1960s, the closing of international borders became an important symbol of sovereignty in what were usually very tenuous states.[1] For the first time, Africans were asked to define permanently who legitimately lived in their societies and who did not, and this process of creating citizenship effectively foreclosed on many opportunities to migrate. The forging of the concept of "foreigner" caused by impending independence led to tensions in the late 1950s and early 1960s in Ghana, Ivory Coast, Sierra Leone, and elsewhere when the new citizens demanded that the increasingly resented migrants be expelled. The long tradition of welcoming strangers was cast aside because it was imperative that these new states, whose understanding of sovereignty was intimately related to their territorial boundaries, give personal meaning to the geographic contours of the state. Of course, the granting of independence to a large number of small states made the assignment of one national identity to each person especially dramatic. For instance, West Africa changed almost overnight from a territory where people could migrate within large colonial blocks to a conglomeration of over a dozen countries, each determined to define with care who could enter their territory.[2] The fragmenting of Africa therefore effectively ended many traditional patterns of migration that had been under threat during the colonial era.

There is still a large amount of migration in Africa. However, movement of people in independent Africa is often temporary and is primarily for individual economic reasons in contrast to past patterns where it was possible for whole communities to escape permanently from their rulers. Samir Amin correctly noted that the fundamentally economic nature of migration in Africa today eliminates the political opportunities that migration previously provided:

> But the modern migrations are periodical migrations of labour, not of people. That is to say, the migrants come into a receiving society that is already organized and structured. There, they acquire a generally inferior status as workers or share-croppers . . . Before European colonization, Africa was the scene of mass movements of peoples. Since then, marked movements of labour have taken place and continue today.[3]

[1] Aristide R. Zolberg, "The Formation of New States as a Refugee-Generating Process," *The Annals of the American Academy of Political and Social Science* 467 (May 1983): p. 28.

[2] See W. T. S. Gould, "International Migration in Tropical Africa: A Bibliographic Review," *International Migration Review* 8 (1974): pp. 353–5.

[3] Samir Amin, introduction to *Modern Migrations in Western Africa*, ed. Samir Amin (London: Oxford University Press, 1974), p. 66.

The most dramatic evidence of the new tenuousness of migration in Africa is the emergence of mass expulsion orders as a legitimate way to treat foreigners. In Ghana, a country that had long-standing stranger communities, the pressure of independence and the need to protect newly defined citizens caused the government to expel two hundred thousand foreigners in 1969.[4] Similarly, Nigeria decided to expel three million aliens in 1983, despite the Economic Community of West Africa's attempts to secure the free movement of people in the region, a glaring reminder of the salience of citizenship laws in Africa and the vulnerability of noncitizens.[5]

Refugees and the New Territorial Realities

It could be argued that the presence of a large number of refugees in many parts of Africa is evidence that the exit option is still viable for many people on the continent. However, now when people attempt to leave their country of origin in large numbers, they are no longer able, as was the case in the past, to settle in a new area as strangers. In contrast to other parts of the world, few governments in Africa view refugees' migration as permanent and most expect refugees eventually to return to their country of origin. Most refugees are not even allowed to penetrate into the interior of asylum countries, and there is usually a concentration of displaced people around the international boundaries.[6] For instance, thousands of refugees from Ethiopia remain in camps in Sudan with the idea that they will some day return to their homes, and this concession is seen as a great kindness by the Sudanese. Not so long ago, many of these people would have simply been able to move into Sudan and find an area to live in, far from the unhappiness that drove them from their old homes. Liisa H. Malkki correctly terms the camps a "technology of power" that offers authorities a new way to control Africans, especially in light of the tradition of migration.[7] Similarly, when fighting broke out in Guinea Bissau in 1998, the Senegalese army was able to keep most of those fleeing the fighting from entering Senegal.[8]

Refugees can be seen as Africans who have resorted to the traditional

[4] Margaret Peil, "Ghana's Aliens," *International Migration Review* 8 (1974): p. 367.

[5] Olajide Aluko, "The Expulsion of Illegal Aliens from Nigeria: A Study in Nigeria's Decision-Making," *African Affairs* 84 (October 1985): p. 539.

[6] John R. Rogge, "Refugee Migration and Resettlement," in *Redistribution of Population in Africa*, ed. John I. Clarke and Leszek A. Kosinski (London: Heinemann, 1982), pp. 39–40.

[7] Liisa H. Malkki, *Purity and Exile: Violence, Memory and National Cosmology among Hutu Refugees in Tanzania* (Chicago: University of Chicago Press, 1995), p. 236.

[8] "Senegal's Cold Shoulder," *Electronic Mail and Guardian*, 1 July 1998. Found at: http://www.mg.co.za/mg/news/98july1/1jul-senegal.html.

exit option but who have collided with the new political realities that make permanently leaving their home countries extremely difficult. The presence of such a large number of displaced people and the accepted idea that they should remain in camps or under the control of the host government until they can be repatriated demonstrates just how extensively African governments have been able to solidify their borders against mass protest migrations. Certainly, one of the reasons that Africa has the largest number of refugees in the world[9] is that the speed at which boundaries have become consolidated has overwhelmed people seeking, as their ancestors did, to vote with their feet. Again, Africa's territorial boundaries have enormous political significance, even if they do allow some people through.

The Move to the Cities

The dramatic changes in the opportunities to migrate might not be nearly as important if almost all internal migration within African countries was not to the cities. The present mass movement to the cities constitutes a second, *independent* factor contributing to the disappearance of the traditional exit option. The economic opportunities in the urban areas resulting from profound centralization and the anti-rural policies of many governments have conspired to produce the highest rates of urbanization in the world.[10] Africa's major cities are growing at a rate of 4.9 percent per year while population growth is expanding at a rate of only 2.9 percent.[11] Between 1960 and 1980, the percentage of residents in urban areas doubled in twenty-four of forty African countries.[12] While only 17 percent of Africans lived in urban areas in 1970, by the year 2000 almost 28 percent will.[13] Inevitably, much of the migration to the cities is to the political center. In all but four African countries (Benin, Cameroon, Malawi, and South Africa) the capital is the largest single city and capitals are "almost invariably the fastest growing cities in African states."[14] Africa is still a rural continent compared to other areas of the

[9] Howard Adelman and John Sorenson, introduction to *African Refugees: Development Aid and Repatriation*, ed. Howard Adelman and John Sorenson (Boulder, CO: Westview Press, 1994), pp. ix–x.

[10] World Bank, *World Development Report 1997*, p. 231.

[11] World Bank, *African Development Indicators 1996* (Washington, D.C.: The World Bank, 1996), pp. 7, 333.

[12] J. Gus Liebenow, *African Politics: Crisis and Challenge* (Bloomington: Indiana University Press, 1986), p. 182.

[13] Richard Sandbrook, *The Politics of Basic Needs: Urban Aspects of Assaulting Poverty in Africa* (London: Heinemann, 1982), p. 40.

[14] Ieuan Ll. Griffiths, *The Atlas of African Affairs*, 2nd ed. (London: Routledge, 1994), p. 162.

world (with all the political problems this population structure entails) but there are more people resident in the centers of political units than at any point in the continent's history.

However, population movements to the urban areas, notably the capital, produces a particular type of state consolidation. While migration may cause more people to come directly in contact with the state and they may be more vulnerable to the security apparatuses of the state, such inward movements of people do nothing to help the state consolidate its authority over distance. Inward migration may actually aggravate the problem because African leaders may feel less of a need to create the necessary infrastructure to extend the geographic reach of the state if the people are coming to them. In addition, irrespective of current migration problems, the problem of extending power over distance will not be solved by migration because, by world standards, a very significant share of the population of almost every African country will remain in the rural areas.

Citizenship as a Boundary Mechanism

What the diminishment of the exit option does provide is an extraordinary opportunity for African states to tie people to geographic entities. Therefore, citizenship laws are critical to examine because these regulations explicitly tie populations to unique, territorially defined polities. Citizenship rules are especially important as boundary mechanisms: they determine who is and who is not a citizen and therefore attempt to give meaning at the level of the individual and the community to the cadastral boundary lines originally created by the Europeans.

Of course, laws regulating nationality are only one aspect of citizenship. The literature on citizenship has been vitally concerned with both the legal and emotive ties between people and their geographically defined states.[15] However, the laws themselves are what can best be examined in the African context where public opinion polling of any type is almost nonexistent. Also, the nationality laws themselves are critical in defining the shape of the nation. As Dominique Schnapper notes, "The state constitutes the nation, in the full sense, by giving it body and by ordering the social system around it . . . The institutions of the state anchor the nation in historical continuity."[16] Since, as chapter four notes, the purely emotive ties between populations and African states are not

---

[15] See, for example, Dieter Fuchs and Hans-Dieter Klingemann, "Citizens and the State: A Changing Relationship?" in *Citizens and the State*, ed. Hans-Dieter Klingemann and Dieter Fuchs (Oxford: Oxford University Press, 1995).

[16] Dominique Schnapper, *Community of Citizens: On the Modern Idea of Nationality* (New Brunswick, NJ: Transaction Publishers, 1997), p. 97.

obviously strong in most cases, the nationality laws themselves can be understood as reflecting critical aspects of the citizenship ideal in Africa.

Due to the weakness of African states and the seemingly porous nature of their boundaries, the conventional wisdom is that "In Africa, ethnic identity runs thicker than national citizenship, reflecting the fact that the continent's national borders were put in place a mere hundred years ago by colonialists who drew lines on maps without reference to the people in them."[17] In fact, after independence in the 1960s, citizenship laws became salient very quickly. William F. S. Miles and David A. Rochefort report in their careful study that Hausa villagers on the Nigeria/Niger border "do not place their ethnic identity as Hausas above their national one as citizens of Nigeria or Niger and express greater affinity for non-Hausa cocitizens than foreign Hausas."[18] Thus, citizenship laws seem, as N. J. Small wrote, to, "articulate a sense of nationhood in a territory that has political unity but little else."[19] The mistake that many have made is comparing the salience of African boundaries to others in the world. Rather, the correct analogue is to African boundaries in the past that, as discussed previously, were not designed to regulate the movement of people. Given the history of shared sovereignty and the primacy of exit until the eve of independence, the imposition of citizenship on each and every African was a revolutionary event.[20] Citizenship therefore had an immediate importance that should not be overlooked simply because the borders are weak.

The Political Impact of Citizenship Laws

Unfortunately, the study of the comparative effects of citizenship has been inadequate. Most of the debates surrounding "constitutional engineering" in new democracies have focused on electoral laws (e.g., proportional representation versus district-based systems) or around the design of national political structures (e.g., prime ministerial versus presidential systems).[21] While these subjects are inherently important, the

[17] Barbara Crossette, "Citizenship is a Malleable Concept," New York Times, 18 August 1996, p. 3.

[18] William F. S. Miles and David A. Rochefort, "Nationalism Versus Ethnic Identity in Sub-Saharan Africa," American Political Science Review 85 (June 1991): p. 401.

[19] N. J. Small, "Citizenship, Imperialism, and Independence: British Colonial Ideals and Independent African States," part one, Civilisations 27 (1977): p. 18. See also Reinhard Bendix, Nation-Building and Citizenship (New York: John Wiley and Sons, 1964), p. 74.

[20] T. O. Elias, "The Evolution of Law and Government in Modern Africa," in African Law: Adaptation and Development, ed. Hilda Kuper and Leo Kuper (Berkeley: University of California Press, 1965), p. 189.

[21] See, for instance, Joel Barkan, "Elections in Agrarian Societies," Journal of Democracy

failure to examine citizenship laws systematically, given their particular relevance to poor nations, is inexplicable. The only area of the world where significant scholarly attention is being devoted to citizenship laws is western Europe, where the influx of migrant labor and flows of people from former colonies to the metropoles has forced rethinking and reexamination of laws regarding nationality.[22]

However, the current European experience is not a very good guide to citizenship politics in Africa. Historically, citizenship laws in Europe became more salient as states began to exert their sovereign identities and to devote considerable attention to regulating domestic social relations.[23] Citizenship laws reflected a "national self-understanding that was deeply rooted in the national past and powerfully reinforced at a particular historical conjuncture."[24] Thus, Germany insisted on citizenship only via descent in part to exclude Polish and Jewish immigrants in the Prussian east from the new polity.[25] However, as European states matured and became more confident of their sovereignty (to the point of creating the European Union), citizenship became less salient. In western Europe, human rights are now enjoyed by many within a polity, even though they may not formally be citizens and there is no longer a clear demarcation between citizens and noncitizens.[26] Thus, Turkish guestworkers may enjoy the privileges of the French polity even if they are not citizens[27] because France is no longer willing to make a dramatic distinction between citizens and nonnationals. International human rights conventions have fur-

---

6 (October 1995): pp. 106–16, and Juan Linz, "Presidential or Parliamentary Democracy: Does it Make a Difference?" in *The Failure of Presidential Democracy*, ed. Juan Linz and Arturo Valenzuela, vol. 1 (Baltimore: Johns Hopkins University Press, 1994).

[22] See David Jacobson, *Rights across Borders: Immigration and the Decline of Citizenship* (Baltimore: Johns Hopkins University Press, 1996); Rainer Bauböck, ed., *From Aliens to Citizens: Redefining the Status of Immigrants in Europe* (Aldershot, U.K.: Avebury, 1994); Mark Gibney, ed., *Open Borders? Closed Societies?: The Ethical and Political Issues* (New York: Greenwood Press, 1988); Jacqueline Bhabha and Sue Shutter, *Women's Movement: Women under Immigration, Nationality and Refugee Law* (Staffordshire, U.K.: Trentham Books, 1994).

[23] Maxim Silverman, "Citizenship and the Nation-State in France," *Ethnic and Racial Studies* 14 (July 1991): p. 335.

[24] Rogers Brubaker, "Immigration, Citizenship, and the Nation-State in France and Germany," in *The Citizenship Debates: A Reader*, ed. Gershon Shafir (Minneapolis: University of Minnesota Press, 1998), p. 152.

[25] Ibid., p. 151.

[26] Virginie Guiraudon, "Citizenship Rights for Non-Citizens: France, Germany, and the Netherlands," in *Challenge to the Nation-State: Immigration in Western Europe and the United States*, ed. Christian Joppke (Oxford: Oxford University Press, 1998).

[27] Yasemin Nuhoğlu Soysal, *Limits of Citizenship: Migrants and Postnational Membership in Europe* (Chicago: University of Chicago Press, 1994), p. 141.

ther diminished the salience of national citizenship in western nations by stressing the universality of a range of rights and responsibilities.[28]

However, African nations are still extremely insecure about their sovereignty because they do not exercise authority across their territories. Indeed, African nations jealously guard their sovereignty because it is so critical to the exercise of power and have consistently refused to implement arrangements like the European Union's that diminish the authority of states. As a result, citizenship in Africa will continue to be critical in the years to come as states have yet to become confident enough about their sovereignty to begin to diminish the significance of citizenship, one of the few badges of status and privilege that sovereignty allows them to allocate. Only strong states can afford to voluntarily relinquish sovereignty.

Jus Soli and Jus Sanguinis

Fortunately, there is a significant and rich historic debate over the nature of citizenship laws that can at least structure the analysis of nationality laws in new states. When citizenship laws were first developed in England in the early seventeenth century, largely to resolve inheritance disputes, the simple rule was *jus soli*: those born in the territory were citizens, irrespective of the nationality of their parents. However, relatively soon, a fierce counterattack was launched suggesting that tying citizenship to territory of birth was arbitrary and did not allow for consent. In particular, Locke argued that since men are born free, "a Child is born a Subject of no Country or Government."[29] Rather, Locke argued that children should be considered the citizens of the country of their fathers until they became adults and could then choose their own citizenship. Similarly, de Vattel argued in favor of *jus sanguinis*—citizenship through descent irrespective of the location of birth—by suggesting that, "in order to be of the country, it is necessary that a person be born of a father who is a citizen; for, if he is born there of a stranger, it will be only the place of his birth, and not of his country."[30] Peter H. Schuck and Rogers M. Smith have similarly questioned the American practice of automatically granting citizenship to all those who happen to be born in the country.[31]

---

[28] Jacobson, *Rights across Borders*, p. 10.

[29] John Locke, "The Second Treatise," in *Two Treatises of Government*, ed. Peter Laslett (Cambridge: Cambridge University Press, 1988), p. 347. A similar argument was made by J. J. Burlamaqui in his *The Principles of Natural and Politic Law*, trans. by Nugent, vol. 2, 5th ed. (Cambridge: Cambridge University Press, 1807), p. 30.

[30] Emmeric de Vattel, *The Law of Nations* (Philadelphia: T. and J. W. Johnson, 1861), pp. 101, 162.

[31] Peter H. Schuck and Rogers M. Smith, *Citizenship without Consent: Illegal Aliens in the American Polity* (New Haven: Yale University Press, 1985), p. 91.

The high hurdles posed by *jus sanguinis* are attractive to those who want to promote a heightened sense of nationality. Citizenship laws based on *jus sanguinis* are often designed to retain at both a factual and a symbolic level, to keep a people or *volk* together and to prevent certain groups from becoming citizens even if they were born within the national territory. Thus, Germany did not, until recently, grant citizenship to Turkish workers who were born in the Federal Republic's territory but did allow ethnic Germans who have lived outside the fatherland for generations, and who may have no immediate family ties to, and even extremely limited knowledge of, modern Germany, to become citizens. Similarly, *jus sanguinis* is the guiding principal in Indonesia and Malaysia in order to limit the wealthy, but highly resented, Chinese minorities in both countries. Jakarta and Kuala Lumpur changed their citizenship laws from the (Dutch and British, respectively) practices of *jus soli* in order to limit Chinese influence, given widespread concern in both countries over the upliftment of the Indonesian and Bumiputra majorities.[32] Other countries, including Israel, Hungary, and Poland, use *jus sanguinis* rules to grant citizenship to their diasporas in order to encourage their fellow ethnics to return.[33]

However, the inevitable cost of allocating citizenship based on criteria more complicated than location of birth is to exclude individuals and whole groups who are physically located in a state but who cannot claim descent from ancestors who were nationals. Partially as a result of new citizenship regulations, there are two hundred and twenty thousand ethnic Chinese who are stateless in Malaysia and eight hundred thousand who have no citizenship in Indonesia.[34] Many have criticized the phenomenon in western countries of significant guest worker populations who do not have claims to citizenship rights, an explicit attack on *jus sanguinis*. For instance, Michael Walzer, while agreeing that countries have the absolute right to draft any immigration policy, has argued that naturalization must be available to "every new immigrant, every refugee taken in." Walzer argues that to exclude from citizenship people with whom the territory is shared is "a form of tyranny."[35]

[32] Ko Swan Sik and Teuku Moh Rhadie, "Nationality and International Law in Indonesian Perspective," in *Nationality and International Law in Asian Perspective*, ed. Ko Swan Sik (Dordrecht, Netherlands: Martinus Nijhoff Publishers, 1990), p. 143. See also, for Malaysia, Visu Sinnadurai, "Nationality and International Law in the Perspective of the Federation of Malaysia," in the same collection, pp. 314–21.

[33] Mary Kaldor, "European Institutions, Nation-States, and Nationalism," in *Cosmopolitan Democracy: An Agenda for a New World Order*, ed. Daniele Archibugi and David Held (Cambridge: Polity Press, 1995), p. 85.

[34] Arturo G. Pacho, "Political Integration through Naturalization: A Southeast Asian Perspective," *Asia Quarterly* 4 (1980): pp. 242–3.

[35] Michael Walzer, *Spheres of Justice: A Defense of Pluralism and Equality* (New York: Basic Books, 1983), p. 62.

There is, then, a clear tradeoff between allegiance and inclusion. Citizenship regulations that pose high barriers to entry may generate more intense levels of national identity because states are able to screen potential citizens to see if they meet whatever set of desired characteristics leaders believe are central to national identity. The result will almost always be some number of people who are in the polity but not of the polity because the location of their birth was not enough to qualify them for citizenship. In turn, those countries that do not have as high barriers to entry will not face as poignantly the problem of groups who are legally but not geographically excluded from the polity. Those states will, however, find it more difficult to define national identity and how it relates to citizenship because they have have chosen to manage their naturalization process in a far less active manner.

Citizenship in Africa

Due to the colonial origins of Africa's boundaries there was, from the dawn of independence, a strong attraction to the pan-Africanism that would make the inherited boundaries less salient. However, only a few African countries even attempted to implement the pan-African ideal and develop novel ideas of understanding citizenship. For instance, Malawi extends citizenship to Mozambicans north of the Zambezi River[36] because former president Hastings Banda tenaciously held on to the idea of a greater Malawi, which would include substantial parts of its lusophone neighbor. Guinea Bissau also extends citizenship to all citizens of Cape Verde, given the close ties between the two countries.[37] Similarly, Somalia grants citizenship to all ethnic Somalis in Kenya and Ethiopia (so-called "unredeemed Somalis").[38] Some other innovations are associated with wars of national liberation. For instance, both Guinea Bissau and Mozambique grant citizenship to anyone who fought for independence during their wars of national liberation.[39] On the other hand, Ertirea has

[36] Malawi, *Malawi Citizenship Act,* 1966, para 15, as found in the UN High Commissioner for Refugees CD-ROM *REFWORLD,* 5th ed., January 1998.

[37] Guinea-Bissau, *Code de la Nationalité,* 22 May 1976, article 5, as found in the UN High Commissioner for Refugees CD-ROM *REFWORLD,* 5th ed., January 1998.

[38] "Any person living beyond the boundaries of the Republic of Somalia but belonging by origin, language, or tradition to the Somali Nation may acquire Somali citizenship by simply establishing his residence in the territory of the Republic." Haji N. A. Noor Muhammad, *The Legal System of the Somali Democratic Republic* (Charlottesville, VA: Michie Co., 1972), p. 302.

[39] Guinea-Bissau, *Code de la Nationalité* article 1c and Mozambique, *Constitution,* 30 November 1990, article 20 as found in UNHCR CD-ROM, *REFWORLD,* 5th ed., January 1998.

denied citizenship to Jehovah's Witnesses, in part because they did not participate in that country's war for independence against Ethiopia.[40]

More ambitious efforts to go beyond the traditional European notions of the territorial state were rejected. For instance, when Félix Houphouët-Boigny tried in 1964 to gain "dual nationality" for citizens of other countries of the Organisation Commune Africaine et Malgache, the idea had to be discarded because of highly unusual public opposition to the Ivorian leader's initiative.[41] While African leaders repeatedly note that their political practices and norms must be different from European practices (a premise that is also fundamental to this book), their states have shown little imagination or ability in moving away from Eurocentric notions of who qualifies for entry into the polity. More generally, citizenship laws have tended to reinforce territorial boundaries. In both the physical and human boundaries that define states, parochial national interests quickly triumphed over pan-African aspirations.

There is, however, still considerable variation regarding how African states regulate citizenship. Despite Verzijl's claim that it would be "love's labour lost to attempt to collect from the statute books of the present-day sovereign States all the laws relating to the acquisition and loss of their nationality,"[42] I have coded the relevant aspects of citizenship laws for almost all African countries.

Of the forty countries I can code, fourteen trace citizenship primarily by place of descent and twenty-six determine citizenship in the first instance by ancestry (see the appendix). However, the dividing line between *jus soli* and *jus sanguinis* is, in fact, somewhat ambiguous. Many of the countries that trace citizenship by ancestry allow those born within the territory to apply for citizenship after a certain period of time, and all countries that assign citizenship to those born within the borders also provide for citizenship by descent when nationals have children abroad. The critical difference between the two groups, and the deciding factor in the classification, is that the *jus soli* states grant citizenship automatically to those born within the territory while those born inside *jus sanguinis* states still have to apply for citizenship. Naturalization usually depends on the approval of government officials who may deny citizenship on the basis of residency requirements, criminal records, or an inability to demonstrate integration into the community by failing, for instance, to learn

---

[40] "Eritrea Strips Jehovah's Witnesses of Citizenship," *Reuters*, 10 March 1995.

[41] Robert J. Mundt, "Côte d'Ivoire: Continuity and Change in a Semi-Democracy," in *Political Reform in Francophone Africa*, ed. John F. Clark and David E. Gardinier (Boulder, CO: Westview Press, 1997), p. 196.

[42] J. H. W. Verzijl, *Nationality and Other Matters Relating to Individuals*, part 5 of his *International Law in Historical Perspective* (Leiden, Netherlands: A. W. Sijthoff, 1968), p. 31.

the language. Not surprisingly, *jus soli* countries have lower hurdles to citizenship than countries that determine citizenship in the first instance by ancestry.

Unfortunately, it was not possible to establish with statistical certainty that particular laws actually affect naturalization as it is practiced on a daily basis. African countries do not publish statistics on naturalization, reflecting the sensitivity of the issue, the general opaque workings of many home affairs (or equivalent) ministries, and the weak statistical bases. A thorough review of international statistical sources and publications by individual African countries revealed that no Africa country appears to publish naturalization data on a regular basis. Studies in Europe have found that propensity to naturalize is closely connected to citizenship policies.[43]

However, the importance of citizenship laws can sometimes be dramatic. In the early 1990s, Zaire changed its citizenship laws in anticipation of new elections and required Tutsis to prove that they had Zairois ancestry dating back to 1885, instead of 1960 as was initially the case, to become citizens.[44] These communities, estimated to include between four hundred fifty thousand and six hundred thousand people, had lived in Zaire for a generation and eventually came into armed conflict with the "original" inhabitants (who were Zairois) of the region over nationality disputes. Forty thousand people died in conflicts prompted at least partially by citizenship laws in 1993.[45] The fighting that broke out in eastern Zaire in 1996 and that eventually led to the overthrow of Mobutu was also at least partially prompted by Tutsis who wanted above all to be Zairois citizens but, having been denied that opportunity, were forced to form alliances with the Tutsi government in Rwanda.

Correspondingly, those countries with more inclusive citizenship laws have scored some notable successes in uniting their populations. For instance, Tanzania extended citizenship to tens of thousands of Rwandan refugees,[46] thereby significantly reducing the possibility that the refugees will become a separate, alienated population, and opening the possibility that they could be absorbed by the already significant Hutu communities in Tanzania. Ironically, it was also migrants from Rwanda who were at

---

[43] Gérard de Rham, "Naturalisation: The Politics of Citizenship Acquisition," in *The Political Rights of Migrant Workers in Western Europe*, ed. Zig Layton-Henry (London: Sage Press, 1990), p. 184.

[44] Human Rights Watch/Africa and Fédération Internationale des Ligues des Droits de l'Homme, "Zaire: Forced to Flee: Violence against the Tutsis in Zaire" *Human Rights Watch* vol. 8, no. 2 (1996), p. 7.

[45] Jean-Baptiste Kayigamba, "Haven for Killers in the Making," *Inter Press Service*, 29 May 1996.

[46] Dar es Salaam Radio, "Comment," 11 December 1980, quoted by British Broadcasting Corporation, *BBC Summary of World Broadcasts*, 12 December 1980.

the heart of the fighting in eastern Zaire because they were unable to become citizens. Efforts by the Moi government to grant citizenship to large communities of Tanzanians who had long been resident in Kenya will remove at least one potential ethnic conflict.[47]

In general, African citizenship laws bear a close, but not absolute, connection to the practices of their colonizers at independence. Table 8.1 displays those countries that adopted their colonizer's citizenship laws and those that have changed practices since independence. In many countries, the colonial inheritance has been exceptionally powerful. All of the francophone countries follow the French practice of relying principally on citizenship through descent. Anglophone countries have also been influenced by the old British practice of granting citizenship to anyone born in the territory.[48] However, as with most everything else, the colonial connection is less salient in anglophone Africa than among the francophones. Other countries have also been influenced by their own colonial traditions. In Zaire, for instance, the old Belgium practice of establishing tiers of citizenship continued long after the former metropole changed its citizenship practices.

As a result, African states have not fully realized the potential gains provided by the decreasing importance of exit. As opposed to European states, where citizenship rules were carefully designed to reflect the national experience and mold the polity, African states have often not actively managed their citizenship regulations. The luck of the colonial draw, to a considerable degree, still determines what citizenship regulations an African state has. Perhaps this continuity in boundaries between peoples is not surprising, given that the inherited territorial boundaries have also been embraced by African leaders. As a result, African states have lost numerous opportunities to increase the salience of national identity. The reason for the failure to develop more nuanced and appropriate citizenship regulations can be found in the logic developed in chapter four: African states, unlike those in Europe, do not face a set of immediate security challenges that make tying the population to the political center a necessity. Ironically, while citizenship remains a highly contested issue in Africa compared to developed countries, it remains an untapped resource for state-builders.

Of those countries that have changed their citizenship regulations, there has been a clear drift to *jus sanguinis* from *jus soli*. Such a change

---

[47] Kenya Broadcasting Corporation, "Kenyan Citizenship Now Open to Long-Stay Tanzanian Residents," 29 March 1991, reprinted in British Broadcasting Corporation, *BBC Summary of World Broadcasts*, 1 April 1991.

[48] The British, who had been a prime example of *jus soli*, changed their laws in 1981 to prevent some born within the UK from gaining citizenship. de Rham, "Naturalisation: The Politics of Citizenship Acquisition," p. 163.

TABLE 8.1
Patterns of Citizenship Rules Compared to Colonizer at Independence

Retained colonial practice	*Changed colonial practice*
Anglophone Countries (the U.K. was a *jus soli* state)	
Gambia	Botswana
Kenya	Ghana
Lesotho	Malawi
Nigeria	Sudan
Sierra Leone	Zambia
Swaziland	
Tanzania	
Uganda	
Zimbabwe	
Francophone Countries (France was a *jus sanguinis* state)	
Benin	
Burkina Faso	
Cameroon	
Central African Republic	
Chad	
Congo	
Côte d'Ivoire	
Gabon	
Guinea	
Mali	
Mauritania	
Niger	
Senegal	
Togo	
Lusophone Countries (Portugal was a *jus soli* state)	
Angola	
Guinea-Bissau	Mozambique
Former Belgian Colonies (Belgium was a *jus sanguinis* state)	
Burundi	
D.R.O.C.	
Rwanda	

Note: Ethiopia and Liberia were not colonized. Somalia did not exist until it received independence when Italian-controlled Somalia and British-controlled Somaliland were merged. Somalia's laws do resemble Italy's *jus sanguinis* regulations. Equatorial Guinea received its independence from Spain and its laws resemble its colonizer's *jus soli* regulations. Eritrea and Namibia received their independence from, respectively, Ethiopia and South Africa.

Source: see appendix.

may reflect debates over national identity in a few countries. However, as noted below, it at least sometimes appears that *jus sanguinis* is not the appropriate policy for many African countries given their domestic political circumstanaces. Even when changes have been made, the *jus sanguinis* regulations do not reflect much of an African character; instead, they read largely the same as similar regulations in Europe. Thus, even countries that have managed their citizenship regulations have sometimes foregone the opportunity that European countries often exploited: to have citizenship laws both reflect and mold very particular notions of national identity.

Instead, the appeal of *jus sanguinis* in certain situations may be purely tactical because this method for citizenship determination is often convenient for leaders who want to keep others from challenging their rule. Given how recent both African countries and African borders are, many try to make a case that a particular leader is a "foreigner," and these accusations take on particular salience during elections. Thus, some Ghanaians believe that Jerry Rawlings is not really Ghanaian because his father was Dutch; it is commonly said that Museveni is not a Ugandan because he is a Tutsi, or that Frederick Chiluba of Zambia is really from the Congo. If citizenship is not determined solely by location of birth, these accusations can become credible. Thus, in May 1996, the parliament of Zambia completed work on a new constitution that prevented Kenneth Kaunda, previously president of the country from 1964 to 1991, from running for president again because he is now considered to be a foreigner by the ruling Movement for Multiparty Democracy. The bizarre finding that Kaunda (whose parents were migrant Malawian missionaries who settled in what was then Northern Rhodesia in the 1920s and who was born in what is now Zambia) is not a citizen when he, in fact, has an excellent claim to be the father of modern Zambia, illustrates the power of citizenship laws to undermine challengers.

Equally instructive is the case of Alhaji Shugaba, who brought a famous case against Nigeria regarding citizenship. Shugaba's father was a member of the Bagarmi group born in what is now Chad, although neither Chad nor Nigeria existed when his father was born. His father was conscripted into the Sultan's army and finally settled in Madigurui (in what is now Nigeria) in 1911. His father married Shugaba's mother, who was from Madigurui where Shugaba was born. Shugaba rose to be an important member of the Great Nigeria People's Party and majority leader of the Borno State House of Assembly (Borno is a Nigerian state that borders Chad and Cameroon). In 1980, in what would become a ploy that would recur in other African countries, the political foes of Shugaba managed to get him declared an alien and he was deported because his father was not Nigerian. In the end, Shugaba managed to convince the courts that he was Nigerian (because of his mother's nationality), but the case is a cautionary tale of how citizenship laws can be manipulated for political purposes.[49]

Citizenship and Demographic Realities

Given the inherent tradeoff between allegiance and inclusion, it is important to develop an analytic perspective to indicate what effect different citizenship regulations will have. An important element of the relationship between citizenship regulations and state consolidation is the demographic reality that leaders face. As citizenship is to be the legal and emotive tie between citizen and state, the political geography of a country has an enormous impact on how particular citizenship regulations play out in a given country. However, there is no perpetual recontracting of citizenship regulations. Rather, as demonstrated above, citizenship regulations in individual African states are highly dependent on the colonial heritage. Therefore, it is critical to understand both the demographic realities leaders face and the (at least somewhat exogenously determined) citizenship regulations that they operate under.

Using the typology of states developed in chapter five, *jus soli* regulations appear to be most appropriate for countries with unfavorable geographies. No set of regulations is likely to create a strong allegiance to these states, given how distant they are from a large percentage of the citizenry due to both the distribution of their populations and their failure to build an adequate infrastructure to overcome their geographies. These countries will also have, as chapter five indicates, growing (due to migration) urban areas that are far from the capital and that may be in competition with the political center. However, regulations that demand something greater than location of birth to enter the polity are likely to produce large numbers of excluded groups, given that the people far from the state's center will often be ethnically distinct from groups closer to the core. In such remote areas, citizenship may be one of the few things that the state can provide. Exclusion therefore risks producing extreme alienation. Indeed, the Tutsis in eastern Zaire, when their citizenship was revoked, became the nucleus of the revolt against Mobutu.

---

[49] The Nigerian law required that those in the country before independence have either a parent or a grandparent who is Nigerian in order to be considered citizens. See Arthur V. J. Nylander, *The Nationality and Citizenship Laws of Nigeria* (Lagos: University of Lagos, 1973), p. 112. The Shugaba case is discussed at some length by O. Adigun, "Nationality and Citizenship: The Legal Problematic of Transborder Ethnic Communities in Nigeria," in *Borderlands in Africa*, ed. A. I. Asiwaju and P.O. Adeniyi (Nigeria: University of Lagos Press, 1989), pp. 275–6.

TABLE 8.2
Citizenship and Political Geography

	Jus Soli	*Jus Sanguinis*
Countries with Unfavorable Geographies	Low Allegiance/Low Exclusion	Low Allegiance/High Exclusion
Hinterland Geographies	Low Allegiance/Low Exclusion	High Allegiance/Low Exclusion
Countries with Favorable Geographies	Low Allegiance/Low Exclusion	High Allegiance/Low Exclusion

Source: see appendix.

Table 8.3 lists countries by type of political geography and by citizenship status. As is evident from the table, most of the countries with unfavorable political geographies also have *jus sanguinis* regulations. As a result, most African countries with unfavorable political geographies will not find that citizenship regulations aid them in the critical task of establishing some lowest common denominator of national identity. Instead, citizenship regulations, as they currently stand, may actually make the job of establishing a common identity more difficult because these states have established fairly demanding tests for naturalization, despite the fact that they cannot actually offer much to their citizens.

In countries where the political geography is favorable and the infrastructure allows the state to have greater contact with a relatively high percentage of the population, *jus sanguinis* regulations at least have the potential to develop a set of allegiances to the state based on a relatively well-defined sense of nationality. In those countries, as noted in chapter five, the state is likely to be relatively close to the population, either because the country is small in absolute terms or because of a favorable political geography. Relatively high hurdles to citizenship can therefore be matched with a relatively extensive state presence, and it will therefore at least be possible to begin the process of establishing a coherent national identity. Inward migration will continually make these countries' political geographies ever more favorable as the capital cities will continue to grow, helped by the fact that it is unlikely that there will be cities that compete with the capitals. The costs of exclusion are likely to be relatively low because a country with favorable political geography is more ethnically homogenous and has few distant lands inhabited by groups that do not have much of a relationship to those resident in the core. In fact, as table 8.3 indicates, only eleven of the nineteen countries that might benefit from *jus sanguinis* regulations have them. Again, the colonial experience appears to be far more important in determining citi-

TABLE 8.3
Citizenship and National Design (Countries in boldface are *jus sanguinis*)

Countries with Difficult Political Geographies	Hinterland Countries	Countries with Favorable Political Geographies	Countries with Ambiguous Geographies
Angola	**Chad**	**Benin**	Cameroon
D.R.O.C.	**Mali**	**Botswana**	Côte d'Ivoire
Ethiopia	**Mauritania**	**Burkina Faso**	**Ghana**
Mozambique	**Niger**	**Burundi**	Kenya
Namibia		**C.A.R.**	**Malawi**
Nigeria		**Congo-Brazzaville**	Uganda
Senegal		Equatorial Guinea	**Zambia**
Somalia		**Eritrea**	
Sudan		**Gabon**	
Tanzania		Gambia	
		Guinea	
		Guinea Bissau	
		Lesotho	
		Liberia	
		Rwanda	
		Sierra Leone	
		Swaziland	
		Togo	
		Zimbabwe	

Source: see appendix.

zenship laws than the particular circumstances of African countries. At least in this set of countries, *jus sanguinis* regulations have the potential to help establish relatively coherent national identities while not bearing the intense political costs incurred by excluding significant groups.

Similarly, in hinterland countries, citizenship regulations are more likely to have effects closer to countries with favorable rather than unfavorable geographies. While these states are large, their population distributions cause them to be in many ways similar to much smaller states. Migration tends to make their political geographies even more favorable over time, relative to other large countries. They also have a large percentage of the population around the core and will have relatively few people in the hinterlands who might potentially be excluded by relatively strict citizenship laws. As all of the hinterland countries are former French colonies, their inherited *jus sanguinis* regulations serve them well.

Demographic Patterns, Citizenship, and State Consolidation

As was the case with the exchange rate mechanism, a detailed examination of the effects of population movements and citizenship patterns suggests a radically different understanding of Africa's integration with the international political and economic systems. Over the last century, Africa has moved from a continent where migration across putative boundaries was a time-honored tradition to a continent where geographic boundaries have a real effect on migration potential. At the same time, citizenship has evolved over the last century from the precolonial situation, where Africans were often in territories where there were multiple sovereign powers (and they therefore could potentially "belong" to several different types of political units), to being subjects in one of a few large colonial blocks, to being citizens in one of several dozen uniquely defined geographic entities. Far from African countries becoming more integrated into the international political and economic systems as part of the now much-discussed process of globalization, states have gained greater control over population movements compared to the past and, via citizenship laws, there are extremely serious attempts to tie people and communities to specific countries. The citizenship regulations that African countries have chosen almost uniformly make it more difficult for citizens to cross boundaries because the old traditions of shared allegiance to different political powers have been discounted and the new regulations enhance the authority of the territorial state by assigning it the sole right to determine who is a citizen and who is not.

As Africans have not, in general, actively attempted to manage their citizenship regulations, and those that have have sometimes done so for tactical reasons, naturalization procedures and the operational codes implicit in the different approaches to citizenship have not been used in the best way possible to promote national consolidation. Many countries with favorable political geographies and those with hinterland geographies have, largely due to historical accident, the necessary regulations to develop well-defined national identities without excluding large numbers of people. Since these countries also have the most extensive road systems, they have the physical and legal framework, by African standards, to begin to develop coherent national identities. They still may be far worse off than most poor countries in the rest of the world, but their relative standing in the continent is good. On the other side, countries with unfavorable political geographies often have regulations that seem generally inappropriate for their national designs. That these countries face the most difficulty in consolidating power suggests that citizenship regulations, once again largely inherited, are a further obstacle to the broadcasting of power.

Conclusion

Two of the great ironies of African politics over the last four decades is that states did not consolidate their rule over their territorial expanse, and that the populations cooperated by migrating toward the centers of political power. Both developments came about in part because of the extraordinary salience of African boundaries: leaders found that the boundaries were hard enough to prevent outside intervention, and so did not feel compelled to consolidate their authority in the outlying areas, while potential migrants found that the boundaries had significantly changed their calculations regarding the benefits of exit. However, some countries will benefit from the migration more than others. Tragically, those countries with the most difficult political geographies have yet to demonstrate the imagination to change regulations regarding entry into their polity to reflect the realities of power and state presence in their countries. As a result, both their physical and legal infrastructures are inappropriate for the tasks they face and they are unable to take full advantage of the historic change in the nature of African migration.

Appendix

Country	Jus Sanguinis?	Country	Jus Sanguinis?
Angola	No	Lesotho	No
Benin	Yes	Liberia	No
Botswana	Yes	Malawi	Yes
Burkina	Yes	Mali	Yes
Burundi	Yes	Mauritania	Yes
Cameroon	Yes	Mozambique	Yes
C.A.R.	Yes	Namibia	No
Chad	Yes	Niger	Yes
Congo	Yes	Nigeria	No
Côte d'Ivoire	Yes	Rwanda	Yes
D.R.O.C.	Yes	Senegal	Yes
E.Guinea	No	Sierra Leone	No
Eritrea	Yes	Somalia	Yes
Ethiopia	Yes	Sudan	Yes
Gabon	Yes	Swaziland	No
Gambia	No	Tanzania	No
Ghana	Yes	Togo	Yes
Guinea	Yes	Uganda	No
G.Bissau	No	Zambia	Yes
Kenya	No	Zimbabwe	No

Sources: The primary source for the annex material was: UN High Commissioner for Refugees gopher site "REFWORLD" location: gopher://iccuc2.unicc.org:70/11/un-hcrcdr/legal.m/refleg.m. The CD-ROM published by the UNHCR in January 1998 under the same name was used to update information. Some material was also taken from the individual country reports in the *International Encyclopedia of Comparative Law* (Tübingen: J. C. B. Mohr, various years); Stanislas Melone, ed., *Droit des Personnes et de La Famille*, vol. 6 of *Encyclopedie Juridique de l'Afrique* (Paris: Les Nouvelles Editions Africaines, 1982); and from United Nations, *Laws Concerning Nationality*, St/Leg/Ser. B/4 (New York: United Nations, 1954).

Individual country information was also derived from:

Jean-Bernard Blaise and Jacques Mourgeon, *Lois et Décrets de Côte d'Ivoire* (Paris: Librairies Techniques, 1970).

Jacques Venderlinden, *Introduction au Droit de L'Éthiopie Moderne* (Paris: R. Pichon, 1971).

Tudor Jackson, *The Law of Kenya* (Nairobi: Kenya Literature Bureau, 1986).

Arthur V. J. Nylander, *The Nationality and Citizenship Laws of Nigeria* (Lagos: University of Lagos, 1973).

Muhammad N. Noor, *The Legal System of Somalia* (Charlottesville: Michie Co., 1972).

Douglas Brown and Peter A. P. J. Allen, *An Introduction to the Law of Uganda* (London: Sweet and Maxwell, 1968).

Part Five

CONCLUSION

Nine

The Past and the Future of State Power in Africa

> Our ship of state is today sinking! A few are
> manipulating the system to their advantage, but
> our intellectuals, our women, our youth, the
> masses are being flushed down the drain. All our
> systems, educational, economic, health, are in a
> shambles. Yet we persist in our national
> obtuseness . . . No . . . To be, we have to think
> . . . Nigerians must think deeply. We must shun
> the simplistic solutions now being proffered.
>   Ken Saro-Wiwa, *A Month and a Day: A Detention Diary.*

IT IS NOW possible to review the patterns of state consolidation in Africa over the last several hundred years. In and of itself, a review of the trajectories of states is valuable because many of the fundamental features of African politics have become more understandable. Perhaps more importantly, a deep understanding of how states have progressed in Africa allows for the development of alternatives that might address some of the pathologies from which Africa suffers. Those concerned about the future of Africa must take the admonition of Ken Saro-Wiwa—murdered by the regime of General Sani Abacha because he demanded fundamental reforms in the way Nigeria treats minorities in outlying areas—to think about the future of states with the utmost seriousness. The question of how, finally, to ensure that there are viable states across Africa is one of the great political and humanitarian challenges that the world faces in the twenty-first century.

The Evolution of State Power

There are, as would be expected, important continuities and discontinuities in patterns of state consolidation in Africa across the centuries. The fundamental continuity is that almost all leaders have had to confront the common problem of low population densities, which have made it expensive to control people as distance from the capital increases relative to areas with higher population densities. Allowing for different historical contexts and variations in technology and political norms, precolonial, colonial, and postindependence leaders also developed remarkably similar strategies in the face of a sparse and unforgiving physical setting: gaining clear control over a core political area, defined as either the capital or the critical urban areas and those rural areas with critical economic assets (e.g., mines and plantations), and then ruling over outlying areas in a varied manner depending on the degree to which infrastructure could be developed and the extent to which armies and police forces could be deployed. Thus, as in the past, power still radiates outward from the core political areas and tends to diminish over distance.

The most important discontinuity in the building of African states is in the role of boundaries and the state system. In the precolonial period, boundaries were defined according to how far a state could extend its power. As a result, boundaries reflected the nature of state power in precolonial Africa: confused, fragmented, and constantly changing according to the varying fortunes of the different political units in a given neighborhood. The fundamental change that colonialism wrought was to forge a system of territorial boundaries that were, in and of themselves, consequential and, at about the same time, create a state system that showed the utmost respect for those boundaries. While many colonial leaders ruled core and periphery areas in a manner similar to their precolonial predecessors, their boundaries no longer reflected how far power could be broadcast but rather, how far leaders believed their power should extend. The African successors to the colonialists adopted the European position on colonial boundaries; indeed, they created a new state system, based on the Addis rules, that was dedicated to reinforcing the salience and viability of the received boundaries. The relatively well-defined and consequential boundaries created are no longer a good mirror of state power, which tends to continue to be fractured, weak, and contested.

At the same time, postindependence leaders adopted a series of other boundary mechanisms, including national currencies and citizenship regulations, that served to increase the salience of the national boundaries. So much of what is written about globalization is wrong when applied to Africa, precisely because leaders have actually constructed more institutions to mediate the pressures from international markets and crossnational flows of people compared to any time in the past, especially the precolonial period when African countries were much more closely integrated into the world economy and when migration was much easier. Far from the nation-state melting away in the face of pressures for globalization, national boundaries, broadly defined, are, in a number of ways, more relevant than ever before. Indeed, despite the enormous emphasis on global political and economic forces in the literature, this study has demonstrated that the geographic and demographic facts on the ground are still critical to understanding political processes in Africa.

Boundaries have therefore been critical to the consolidation of African states since 1885. These boundaries are, as many have pointed out, arbitrary, porous, and sometimes do not have an immediate physical presence in the territories they are supposed to demarcate. Many people do cross the borders in search of opportunity, ranging from peasants who graze their cattle on both sides of the Zimbabwe/Mozambique border to professionals who migrate from Ouagadougou to Abidjan in search of a better job. However, these observations largely miss the point. The boundaries have been singularly successful in their primary function: preserving the territorial integrity of the state by preventing significant territorial competition and delegitimizing the norm of self-determination. As a result, weak states have been able to claim sovereignty over sometimes distant hinterlands because no other state could challenge their rule. At the same time, the currency and citizenship practices have further differentiated African states from one another, although they have not necessarily furthered the consolidation of power within the boundaries.

Therefore, an enormous investment has been made in frontiers themselves in order to make them strong enough so that African states do not feel an immediate need to control the distant hinterlands. This path was not an arbitrary choice by the colonial and postindependence leaders. Rather, they were responding to a physical environment that made the extension of power very difficult and to a state system that allowed them to create boundaries that reflected their ambitions. As a result, the pattern of African state consolidation in terms of taxes, nationalism and the desired characteristics of the design of the state is radically different from that of Europe.

The fundamental problem with the boundaries in Africa is not that they are too weak but that they are too strong. It is not that they are artificial in light of current political systems but that they are too integral to the broadcasting of power in Africa. It is not that they are alien to current African states but that African leaders have been extraordinarily successful in manipulating the boundaries for their own purposes of staying in power rather than in extending the power of their states. To say that the boundaries have been a barrier to state consolidation in Africa is largely a non sequitur. The states, to a certain extent, are their boundaries.

Thus, chapter five showed how the scale of countries—a fundamental question of national design—had very different returns in Europe compared to Africa. Since there are few incentives to control the hinterland, it is not surprising that large countries have often failed to broadcast power across their entire national territory. As a result, indicators of power—whether they be roads or the ability to disrupt traditional land tenure practices—tend to be low for large countries. It is striking that, at the turn of the twentieth century, no large African country can be said to have consolidated control over its entire territory.

State Failure

The path of state consolidation that leaders in Africa chose was viable for most of the twentieth century. The ambitions of the colonial rulers were so modest that it did not matter in many ways that the state had only limited ties to the majority of the population outside the cities because the fundamental colonial goal of preserving order was met. The tremendous euphoria surrounding independence and the success that African leaders had in delegitimating claims of self-determination initially masked the incompleteness of state consolidation.

However, eventually the other shoe dropped. The contradiction of states with only incomplete control over the hinterlands but full claims to sovereignty was too fundamental to remain submerged for long. As a result, many of the pathologies that now are so apparent in Africa began to emerge: leaders who steal so much from the state that they kill off the productive sources of the economy; a tremendous bias in deference and the delivery of services toward the relatively small urban population; and the absence of government in large parts of some countries.

The problem of state failure, where leaders cannot even govern their core areas, is becoming more apparent as African states travel further from the grand unifying moment of independence. The turning point was when Yoweri Museveni took power in Uganda in January 1986. This was the first time that power had been seized in Africa by a leader who had gone back to the bush and formed his own army. It was a literal instance of the hinterland striking back. Of course, rural-based movements should come as no surprise given the documented inability (in chapters five and six) of African countries to extend their writ of authority into the distant rural areas. However, previous military takeovers had originated in the national army and were essentially palace coups. Since 1986, inspired (and sometimes supplied) by Museveni, armies created to compete against national forces in Rwanda, Zaire, Ethiopia, Liberia, Sierra Leone, Somalia, Congo-Brazzaville, and Chad, have challenged African governments and have sometimes been able to take power. Other long-standing internal threats, notably in Angola and Sudan, demonstrated in the 1990s that they could not be defeated and remained extremely dangerous.

Unlike the situation in the 1960s, when the state had all of the guns, these movements are able to procure weapons on the international market, especially after central European countries began to dump their stocks when the Cold War came to an end. At the same time, the hot wars in the Horn of Africa and southern Africa left large numbers of weapons that could be bought cheaply. Rule by the center in these countries was so weak that there was space for challengers to form large and sophisticated rebel armies. When the fighting broke out, the state had so atrophied that a military solution to even the relatively feeble challenges sometimes posed was not possible. Emblematic of the decline in public order is the rise of private security outfits (such as the South African-based Executive Outcomes) that help governments control their territories.

In some countries, state failure has meant that no one has been able to take charge. In Somalia, in January 1991, the Siad Barre government was overthrown but no other group was powerful enough to succeed it. There was a complete collapse of order. At various points in the torturous history of the Liberian civil war, there was no government that could claim much of a writ of authority beyond or even within the capital city of Monrovia. Similarly, in the final years of the Mobutu regime in Zaire, the nominal government did not exercise control over large parts of the country. In central Africa, the failure of the Zairian state led to regional war as Uganda and Rwanda sought repeatedly to impose governments on Kinshasa that would respect their security concerns. They largely failed to do so but, by having their proxies operate so brazenly in eastern D.R.O.C., they showed just how difficult it was for Kinshasa to broadcast authority. As a result, fundamental questions of order permeate African politics and tend to dominate other issues such as political liberalization and economic reform.

The human toll resulting from the inability of African leaders to preserve order has been extraordinary. Of the fifteen "complex emergencies" declared by the United Nations Department of Humanitarian Affairs, eight (Angola, Central African Republic, Congo-Brazzaville, the Great Lakes, Liberia, Sierra Leone, Somalia, and Sudan) are in Africa.[1] In such situations, populations have been subject to horrific abuses as warlords and teenagers with machine guns terrorize and extort the unarmed. Economic systems have become so fragile that any meteorological disruption has the potential to cause disaster. Many of these emergencies have compelled both citizens of the countries affected and outsiders to, at least implicitly, acknowledge that state consolidation has failed and that external intervention is necessary.

---

[1] See the UN Department of Humanitarian Affairs web page, found at: http://www.reliefweb.int.

African State Consolidation in Perspective

The analysis of state-building in Africa highlights important contrasts
with the conventional European model but should not be considered
exotic. The factors that are critical to the African stories of state consolidation—political geography, domestic political calculations by leaders,
the role of boundaries, and nature of the state system—are all factors that
are commonly invoked to explain the rise of European states. There is no
need to suggest that there are social or psychological variables—such as a
unique role for ethnicity—that need to be understood in order to plot
the trajectory of African states. However, in Africa, domestic and international political factors combined to produce a radically different state
trajectory than was found in Europe, or in some other parts of the world.
For instance, the presence of low population densities made the establishment of fixed territorial boundaries especially desirable to African leaders who would otherwise have faced great difficulty in gaining sovereign
control over all their citizens. Indeed, precisely because the internationally accepted vision of sovereign states with fixed borders is so at
odds with how power is often deployed in Africa, leaders are especially
dogmatic about retaining the inherited states, even while proclaiming the
need for indigenous solutions elsewhere. Higher population densities in
Europe were part of the reason that territorial boundaries were not respected there but were, instead, fought over because land was relatively
more valuable and therefore was worth sacrificing men and treasure to
control.

Therefore, state consolidation in Africa, and elsewhere in the developing world, should be integral parts of the great comparative project of
describing state trajectories. Indeed, creating a truly comparative model
of state-building would go a long way to putting Europe in its place as
one of the great locations of state-building but as not the only example.
That would be an important advance and would allow us to understand
that some phenomena said to be worldwide, notably "globalization," are
either not present in other parts of the world or play themselves out very
differently.

This analysis has also demonstrated the futility of the division between
comparative politics and international relations. Finding a salient boundary between these two subdisciplines of politics is obviously pointless
when, as this study has pointed out, political geography and domestic
political calculations are, in fact, intertwined with the state system. Scholars who study the developing world, in particular, have largely come to
understand that domestic politics cannot be understood without at least
examining the international political and economic context in which

states act. However, many international relations scholars have been less open to the idea that domestic politics also affect the designs of state systems. This methodological bias is not inadvertent; rather it came about because of the failure to study international relations outside of Europe. In particular, the realist international relations model of the state system being largely exogenous—imposed on individual leaders and not open to easy modification—has its origins in European history, especially the long periods of war the continent experienced. Anarchy can be seen to be largely disassociated from the domestic politics of countries. However, not all state systems are anarchic and some are therefore open to greater manipulation by states. Thus, the process of broadening the study of state systems to include those outside of Europe should also bring about a greater willingness to incorporate comparative politics into the grand theorizing of international relations.

Finally, this study has demonstrated the importance of placing even very young states in a deep historical context. Again, emphasizing the broad historical continuities and discontinuities in politics is not new in the study of Europe but is in Africa and elsewhere, where it is assumed that the arrival of European national structures marked a new moment that made the past irrelevant. Ironically, it has been African leaders, among others, who have been at the forefront of abandoning their own history because they desperately cling to the European-style states that are today the determinants of the perquisites of power. However, as profound social forces with deep historical roots come into increasing tension with these new state structures, the past must be recovered.

The Future of State Power in Africa

However, state-building cannot be considered a "merely academic" issue in Africa. Given how poor the record of state consolidation has been in Africa and the amount of human suffering that failed states cause, it is imperative to ask whether there are alternatives to the trajectory of state consolidation that began in Berlin in 1885. Unfortunately, despite spectacular state failures in Chad, D.R.O.C., Liberia, and Somalia, as well as the more pervasive, and perhaps as pernicious, routine atrophy of institutions in other countries, there has not been a profound debate about alternatives to existing states. The intellectual triumph of the nation-state detailed in chapter four is still very much apparent. In particular, the UN since 1945 has basically been a decolonization machine: its primary purpose has been to proclaim as quickly as possible that every country is able to rule itself and to keep reiterating that claim irrespective of the facts on the ground. For instance, even though it was obvious to all concerned that Somalia had collapsed by December 1992 when the U.S./UN intervention force was being planned, no one seriously considered trusteeship or other legal concepts other than continuing the fiction that Somalia was still a sovereign nation-state.

Also, the now-burgeoning literature on failed states focuses largely on preventing crises so that states with poor track records can continue to exist, or on discovering methods to put the failed states back together. For instance, I. William Zartman, while admitting that a case can potentially be made for changes in the nature of nation-state, still argues that:

> It is better to reaffirm the validity of the existing unit and make it work, using it as a framework for adequate attention to the concerns of its citizens and the responsibilities of sovereignty, rather than experimenting with smaller units, possibly more homogenous but less broadly based and stable. . . . In general, restoration of stateness is dependent on reaffirmation of the precollapse state.[2]

Few ask if it would be better to try to redesign at least some African states rather than simply trying to prevent disaster and then attempting to resurrect them after profound failure. Thus, there has been little discussion of alternatives to even postgenocide Rwanda, despite the obvious structural problems of that country and despite the fact that continued rule by the minority Tutsis is obviously not viable. Similarly, despite the fact that the wars that broke out in the late 1990s in Central Africa were regional in nature and due, at least in part, to the problematic design of D.R.O.C., few suggestions were even made that peace could only come about if the boundaries were changed. The international community acts like creditors who, having seen their investment lost by a company without a viable business, seek to reinvest in the same company after bankruptcy has been reached but without demanding a restructuring that would protect their investment. Saro-Wiwa's challenge to think deeply has yet to be met.

The attachment developed by Africans and others to the current state system is extraordinary, given that even the parties to the 1885 Berlin Conference noted explicitly that they reserved the right to change principles "as experience may show to be expedient." The feeling of the conference was that rules demarcating the continent could not be permanent because "possibilities and new requirements will probably reveal themselves, and the time may arrive when a wise foresight will demand the revision of a system which was primarily adapted to a period of creation

---

[2] I. William Zartman, "Putting Things back Together," in *Collapsed States: The Disintegration and Restoration of Legitimate Authority*, ed. I. William Zartman (Boulder, CO: Lynne Rienner, 1995), p. 268.

and of change."[3] However, Africans chose to keep the states that the Europeans demarcated and ignored the warning that future developments would cause basic principles to be questioned.

The turn of the century is an especially appropriate time to revisit the question of alternatives to the nation-state in Africa. The dramatic failures of some states and the poor performance of many others has diminished the attachment that many in Africa automatically felt toward the new nation-states in the 1960s. Two entire generations have now been born in Africa who do not remember the relief many felt at the dawn of independence when the decision to retain the old boundaries meant that there would not be widespread violence of the type that had engulfed the Indian subcontinent in the late 1940s. Instead, these generations, now the vast majority of people in Africa, have lived under states that have failed to deliver the goods in terms of economic well-being, political order, or freedom. Since the genocide in Rwanda in 1994, there has been an emergence of interesting new debates across Africa that call into question previous assumptions about sovereignty. For instance, West African countries did not accept the overthrow of the democratically elected government in Sierra Leone of Ahmad Tejan Kabbah in 1997. There is no consensus on how far neighbors should interfere in the affairs of individual countries and still widespread support for the sovereignty of already existing states. Still, a new window of opportunity has opened as many Africans begin to question some of the practices that have been enshrined since 1963.

At the same time, the norms of the international community are in tumult. It is clearly recognized that the previous stress on sovereignty above all other considerations is now outdated. As former UN Secretary-General Boutros Boutros-Ghali famously noted, "The time of absolute and exclusive sovereignty, however, has passed; its theory was never matched by reality."[4] More generally, the flux induced by the end of the Cold War opens up the possibility for new organizational forms. Already, "Kurdistan" in northern Iraq, "Kosovo," the new type of political organization that is now forming in the West Bank and Gaza, the power-shar-

---

[3] General Act of the Berlin West African Conference, Article 36 and Annex 3 to Protocol no. 9 of the General Act, both reprinted in *The Scramble for Africa: Documents on the Berlin West African Conference and Related Subjects, 1884/1885*, ed. R. J. Gavin and J. A. Betley, (Lagos, Nigeria: Ibadan University Press, 1973), pp. 278, 300.

[4] Boutros Boutros-Ghali, *An Agenda for Peace 1995* (New York: United Nations, 1995), p. 44. However, indicating the analytic limits of the UN, the secretary-general also noted that the increase in UN membership caused by the new states in central Europe and the former Soviet Union "reconfirms the importance and indispensability of the sovereign State as the fundamental entity of the international community" (p. 41).

ing agreement between Ireland and the United Kingdom, and the "one country, two entity" creation in Bosnia are challenging the complete monopoly of the nation-state. That these creations were largely brokered by the great powers, previously among the most conservative forces in the international community, suggests more space for alternatives than has been the case in the past.

As donors redirect their aid from Cold War proxies to countries that are achieving some successes with their economic and political reform, it is only natural that those countries that are failing spiral further downward. Somalia entered its particularly sharp downward trajectory in part because it could no longer play the U.S. off against the Soviet Union in order to receive more aid. The decline in aid is not only a short-term problem. More generally, it has been precisely those states—including Chad, Ethiopia, Liberia, Sudan, and Zaire—that received large amounts of largess during the Cold War that have often faced the most severe problems with state failure. The artificially high external resource flow received due to the global strategic competition had the effect of masking the fundamental problems the state faced and delaying the point at which leaders had to adjust. When the aid associated with the Cold War ended, these states simply collapsed.[5]

The shift in external funding toward reformers represents a fundamental break with the practice of the last one hundred years, which saw international actors offer support to the African state system, first through the creation of colonies, then by the enshrinement of sovereignty, and finally by the provision of financial resources without regard to domestic economic or political performance. In Charles Geshekter's words, the intravenous tube that has been vital to so many African countries is finally being removed. It is thus hardly surprising that so many African states have failed since the Berlin Wall fell.

Some still suggest that alternatives to the nation-state will not develop because the international system has been so conservative in recognizing the viability of alternatives. Thus, Robert H. Jackson argues, "There is little evidence to suggest that the rules of this sovereignty game will not continue to be generally observed in the future as they have been in the past."[6] However, as Hendrik Spruyt has argued, it is not the case that change in the nature of the constitutive units of the international system has always taken place in a slow, incremental manner. Rather, there are

---

[5] For instance, from 1962 to 1988, six countries—Ethiopia, Kenya, Liberia, Somalia, Sudan, and Zaire—accounted for most of U.S. foreign aid to Africa. Five of those six can now be considered failed states and Kenya has been a tremendous disappointment. Michael Clough, *Free at Last?: U. S. Policy Toward Africa and the End of the Cold War* (New York: Council on Foreign Relations, 1992), p. 77.

[6] Jackson, "Sub-Saharan Africa," p. 154.

long periods of stability followed by periods of sudden, chaotic institutional innovation. In such a manner did the sovereign state become the dominant institution in Europe.[7]

This study has repeatedly shown that state systems do not simply emerge from the minds of international lawyers but are, rather, the result of brutal political calculations about how it is possible to extend power within individual states. While there might be considerable inertia within state systems, there is no reason to believe that a yawning gulf between the legal theories and the facts on the ground can exist indefinitely. It is only a matter of time before, finally, Africans try to reconcile actual existing states with how power, according to their state system, is exercised.

Now that so many of the props that supported the state system in Africa have been eliminated, the stage for revolutionary change has indeed been set. The only question that remains is if African states and the international community will be able, proactively, to adjust to the changed conditions or if, even in the face of persistent state failure and the accompanying human tragedy, participants and will be satisfied with selective and self-interested changes in the old order. The wars in central Africa in the late 1990s demonstate that state failure is becoming so pervasive that some states may attempt, on an ad hoc basis, to impose their own solutions, especially as their security is threatened by chaos in neighboring states. However, these ad hoc solutions to the failings of the continental state system will inevitably be extremely problematic. For instance, the Rwandan solution to the crisis in central Africa is to extend its internal order—dominated by the Tutsis—to the region. For obvious reasons, this solution is not attractive to others and, as a result, the rebellion that Rwanda fostered to try to overthrow Laurent Kabila in 1998 failed to capture Kinshasa, a city far from the center of Tutsi power. If the continental state system is to be fixed, its problems must be addressed holistically and in a way that addresses the realities of power, not the fantasies of particular leaders.

Some legitimately ask why alternatives to African states should be sought when state failure is not a uniquely African problem. Of course, alternatives should also be pursued for political units elsewhere that are obviously dysfunctional. However, it is also true that the mismatch between how power is actually exercised in some parts of Africa and the nature of the states is often particularly dramatic. Africa's low population densities would have required particularly nuanced and dynamic political institutions for states to consolidate authority over distance. Instead the continent is notable for how artificial and static its boundaries have been since independence. That is why, although state failure does occur else-

---

[7] Spruyt, *The Sovereign State and its Competitors*, pp. 186–7.

where, it occurs most often and most dramatically in Africa. A review of alternatives to at least some African states is therefore particularly appropriate. Those who oppose such a review must explain why they believe that the current situation is unquestionably satisfactory. This book has suggested that such a blanket apology for the structure of African states is unlikely to be persuasive.

Alternatives within the Current International State System

The overarching goal of developing alternatives to African states should be to increase the congruence between the way that power is actually exercised and the design of units. Many of the reasons for state failure can, as noted above, be traced in the end to a fundamental gap between how states govern territory and what the boundaries and state system suggest they should control. Alternatives must therefore work to reduce, in a variety of ways and depending on the situation, the salience of some of the current boundaries. These proposals will be especially relevant to the countries with the most difficult geographies, identified in chapter five, because they confront the greatest problems in broadcasting power. However, some of the alterantives may also be relevant to other African countries. Therefore, it is important to develop a menu of policy options that clearly recognizes the differences between countries in Africa, even if many of their problems have a common origin.

Reform of state institutions must be guided by one other proposition: alternatives must, in the end, come from the Africans themselves. No alternative to the nation-state is going to be forced on Africa, especially given the history of colonialism that began with the Berlin Conference. Indeed, the current hollowing out of the state system created at Berlin and confirmed in Addis will finally allow an African imprint on the continental state sytem after a century when foreign forms have had a monopoly on national political organization.

Breaking the Intellectual Log-Jam

Thus, the first step toward developing new alternatives would be to provide the intellectual space necessary for Africans to present alternatives by stating that the international community is not blindly wedded to the current state system. In and of itself, this would be a revolutionary act that would help to break the intellectual logjam that devotion to the status quo has caused. Given the state of African universities, the international community might have to go further and provide small amounts of resources for individuals and think tanks that might actually want to analyze alternatives to the nation-state. However, once it is clear that there is at least some fluidity in the state system, African alternatives will not be long in coming. For instance, some leading politicians in Sudan are demanding that the people of Southern Sudan be able to "exercise their fundamental rights of reviewing the experience of the single sovereign state."[8]

Ironically, given the amount of time that African leaders devote to preaching the need for "African solutions to African problems," those who are committed to thinking of alternatives to the western-designed states of Africa may be in considerable jeopardy. Some of those proposing changes in the state system, and, by obvious implication in their own countries, like the martyred Saro-Wiwa, may risk the wrath of their leaders despite the fact that greater flexibility in national design has a strong resonance with the African past. Advocates of change in national design should be provided with protection much like that the international community currently provides democrats urging liberalization in their own countries.

To further the development of alternatives to the current state system, the international community and African countries can also begin to understand African problems on a regional basis without regard to country boundaries. Despite seemingly endless rhetoric about the regional nature of many of African problems, most reports and analytic works still use the existing nation-states as their unit of analysis. Studies of southern Africa, for instance, are organized around the member countries of the Southern Africa Development Community (SADC). The intellectual framework continues to be dogmatically based on the current maps because in many cases, multilateral agencies such as the United Nations and the World Bank—constituted solely by sovereign countries—are conducting or funding the analysis. These agencies find it hard to work on any set of assumptions other than that the current boundaries will continue indefinitely because the UN system itself is the source of the sovereignty that African leaders jealously guard.

Donors can accelerate the process of designing new alternatives by using some of their aid for regional integration to promote alternatives and projects that really do treat sections of Africa as regions, as opposed to groupings of countries. This would be in contrast to current practices where foreign aid further reifies African practices of thinking about regional problems by using existing countries as the unit of analysis. For instance, aid to southern Africa helps reinforce the southern African state

[8] Alfred Taban, "Letter on Self-Determination," *Reuters*, 12 November 1995, p. 1. The quotation is from an open letter sent by five leading politicians, including former vice president Abel Alier, to the government of Sudan.

system because the SADC has, more than anything else, been used as an aid platform to garner more funds from the international community than would have been possible if each country had to ask for assistance by itself. The fact that the U.S. closed its aid missions in Lesotho and Swaziland (for budgetary reasons) and allocated assistance to those countries from a regional center could be the first step in communicating a message to these countries, especially Lesotho, that the nature of their states, especially in the postapartheid era, will have to be rethought. Such a prompt would be useful because the Lesotho government refuses to entertain the idea of incorporation inside South Africa, despite the fact that it is surrounded by its neighbor and that, with only 10 percent arable land, there is little reason to believe that it is viable. Instead, the government in Maseru dreams of taking parts of the Free State back from South Africa.[9] Projects with a true regional scope and that allocate funds to recipients irrespective of the country they are in would be a further useful step in not only promoting development but in establishing a new intellectual framework.

Decertifying Old States

A further step that the U.S., and other countries, can take is to formally recognize that some states are simply not exercising physical control over parts of their country and should no longer be considered sovereign. It is critical that the U.S., and other countries, at least tentatively move away from the notion that once a state achieves membership in the General Assembly, it is sovereign forever, no matter what happens within its boundaries. For instance, the U.S. government decertifies countries (effectively reducing their eligibility for U.S. aid) that are not attempting to stop the production and transshipments of narcotics. Indeed, the U.S. legislation goes further and demands that countries prevent and punish the laundering of drug-related profits and "bribery and other forms of public corruption which facilitate the production, processing or shipment" of drugs. Thus, Nigeria was decertified under General Abacha in part because it did not investigate any senior officials alleged to be involved with drugs.[10] The U.S. is effectively arguing that these countries are not executing their sovereign responsibilities in regard to the enforce-

---

[9] Violet Maraisane, "Lesotho: Southern African Nation Ponders its Future," *Inter Press Service*, 14 December 1995.

[10] The relevant U.S. laws are cited in U.S. House Committee on Foreign Affairs *International Narcotics Control and United States Foreign Policy: A Compilation of Laws, Treaties, Executive Documents, and Relevant Materials*, December 1994, p. 31. The presidential message decertifying Nigeria can be found on p. 543.

ment of their own laws. It would seem reasonable that a similar decision could be reached if a state is not exercising other aspects of sovereign control, including the failure or inability to project authority and to provide basic services in large parts of its territory. During the Mobutu era, the U.S. should have recognized Zaire for what it was, or was not, and decertified it as a sovereign nation. It would certainly be no more difficult to ascertain that a state is not governing over parts of its own country than it is to determine that senior officials are involved in drug trafficking but are not being prosecuted.

Decertification would be a strong signal that something fundamental has gone wrong in an African country and that parts of the international community are no longer willing to continue the myth that every state is always exercising sovereign authority. Concretely, decertification might trigger the initiation of new efforts at finding other leaders who are exercising control in parts of the country. Decertification would also be a signal that a country should not be accorded the usual privileges of sovereignty, including such prestigious appointments as a rotating position on the Security Council. It is puzzling that the U.S. strongly opposed Libya's attempt to gain a seat on the Security Council (because of its support for international terrorism) but seemingly had no problems with Zaire being on the United Nations' most powerful body, despite that country's obvious dysfunctional nature.

Whatever the concrete measures taken, decertification would provide some avenue out of the current impasse where there is no status to accord a country other than sovereignty irrespective of domestic realities. Decertification should be a rare step that would only be used as a last resort. Making decertification relatively difficult would also make its signal that much more powerful when it was used. Decertification would also have the advantage of correctly stating that the U.S., or other important actors, understand that some countries are not sovereign even if it is not clear as to what they are. Decertification could thus be a halfway house for countries that are at some later point able to reconstitute their sovereign authority. Alternatively, decertification could be the first step in recognizing that a state has died, if it ever lived, and that something else has to take its place.

It is an irony that the states that the United States does not recognize (including Cuba, Iraq, Libya, and North Korea) are, by any measure, states. The problem with those countries, according to United States, is that their states have far too much control over their societies. In turn, African states that have little control over their societies continue to be recognized as states. Decertification would provide a way out of this ridiculous situation while not immediately categorizing those countries that have weak states with pariah countries like Libya or North Korea.

Recognizing New Nation-States

After forty years of assuming that the boundaries of even the most dysfunctional African states are inviolable, another important initiative, and the logical next step after decertification, would be to consider the possibility of allowing for the creation of new sovereign states. Opening the possibility for new states to be created would challenge the basic assumption held by African leaders and the international community that boundaries drawn haphazardly during the scramble for Africa a century ago should continue to be universally respected. At the same time, allowing for more dynamism in the creation of African states would help recapture a critical insight from the precolonial period: political control has to be won, not instituted by administrative fiat.

The primary objection to recognizing new states in Africa has been the basis for selection. Given that there are very few "natural" boundaries in Africa that allow for the rational demarcation of land on the basis of ethnic, geographic, or economic criteria, the worry is that recognizing new African states will lead to a splintering process that would promote the creation of ever-smaller units while entailing seemingly endless political chaos. Thus, Gidon Gottlieb argues against the creation of new states because he fears "anarchy and disorder on a planetary scale."[11] The very real costs of new nation-state construction, especially the almost inevitable mass movements of people with all the suffering that such movements usually entail, is another important consideration for those who argue that Africa's boundaries must be preserved at any cost.

However, at some point, the reality of disintegrating, dysfunctional African states stands in such contrast to the legal fiction of sovereign states that experimentation with regard to new states is in order. The argument that once new states are recognized, descent down the slippery slope of microstate creation is inevitable gives the international community, and especially, Africans, no credit to discern the specifics of situations on a case-by-case basis. To say that new states should be recognized does not mean that criteria for state recognition cannot exist. It simply suggests that the criteria have to be created and that the dogmatic devotion to the current boundaries be discarded. The inevitable disruption caused by state creation will also have to be balanced against the profound harm that existing states (that know that they cannot go out of business) do to their populations every day.

The allergy against creating new states should also be tempered by the analysis in chapter five that suggests that smaller states, given the particu-

---

[11] Gidon Gottlieb, *Nation against State* (New York: Council on Foreign Relations, 1993), p. 26.

lar political geography of Africa, actually have certain advantages in consolidating power. The evolving international economy also may make it possible for small states to prosper in a manner that challenges traditional notions of the commercial advantages of national size. This does not mean that all will automatically go well in small states, but it is hard to see that the creation of smaller units is inherently bad. Given how poorly large states have performed, the burden of proof is certainly on those who want to retain the national design of these states.

The new type of state disintegration that parts of Africa is undergoing opens the way to a better and more constructive appreciation of the right to secession. While there may be full-fledged civil wars in the future, the more likely path for secessionists to take is simply to exit a disintegrating state. Somaliland (the part of Somalia that was ruled by the British before independence and that declared itself independent after Mogadishu was left without a government when Siad Barre fell in 1991) is more Africa's future than Eritrea: the province that simply goes its own way because the central government, if there is one, lacks the ability to even contest the secession. Similarly, while eastern Democratic Republic of the Congo will not secede, it is clear that Rwanda and Uganda will be required to exercise a certain amount of control throughout this region as Kinshasa's writ has attenuated and Kigali and Kampala face real security threats across their western borders. This type of secession is different from what occurred in former Yugoslavia. In Yugoslavia, there were, arguably, at least some federal institutions that could still have mediated the conflict, but the Slovene and Croatian decisions to secede (and the international recognition of those declarations) destroyed whatever hope there might have been of the crisis being managed from Belgrade.[12] Correspondingly, the Yugoslav break-up has also been extremely bloody because the old order's army was still functioning and could be appropriated by one of the warring parties. However, in many cases where African states are collapsing, the central institutions that might have mediated the conflict atrophied long ago. Similarly, many armies of failed states suffer from the same institutional weaknesses as the rest of the government and are not viable fighting forces.

An innovative criterion for recognition that is relevant to the particular circumstances of Africa's failing states would be: does the break-away area provide more political order on its own than is provided by the central government? The international community would thus be asking an extremely relevant question that goes to the core of the problems of state consolidation in Africa because the test would center on whether

---

[12] Susan L. Woodward, *Balkan Tragedy: Chaos and Dissolution after the Cold War* (Washington, DC: Brookings Institution, 1995), p. 144.

the broadcasting of power and boundaries could be made more coincidental. Such a hurdle would necessarily rule out many attempts at secession that were not of the utmost seriousness. The long-term aim would be to provide international recognition to the governmental units that are actually providing order to their citizens as opposed to relying on the fictions of the past. The development of such a realistic, nuanced perspective would acknowledge what is happening on the ground while avoiding the anarchy that Gottlieb and others fear. Such a criterion would also be more relevant to granting sovereignty that actually mattered, rather than a putative nation's commitment to human rights, a market economy, or the Nuclear Non-Proliferation Treaty, three of the many criteria suggested by Morton H. Halperin and David J. Scheffer that new states should have to meet to be recognized by the international community.[13] However, these qualifications, while highly desirable, reflect the assumption that physical control of the hinterland is not an issue. In fact, in Africa, control of outlying areas is the critical problem.

This is not to say that granting the right to secession to at least some groups that are able to establish order within their own areas would be without its dangers. Clearly, any signal from the international community that its commitment to the territorial integrity of African states is being reduced could result in considerable instability and uncertainty, and would be met by voracious opposition on the part of many African states, which have grown dependent on the post-WWII understanding of sovereignty. However, as noted above, the reality on the ground in some African countries is that sovereign control is not being exercised by the central states in outlying areas and that subnational groups are already exerting authority in certain regions.

By recognizing and legitimating those groups, the international community has the opportunity to ask that they respect international norms regarding human rights and also has a chance to bring them into the international economy. For instance, the World Bank and the International Monetary Fund offered no assistance to Somaliland because it did not have a recognized status, despite the fact that the government in Hargeisa was at least providing some services to its citizens.[14] A less dogmatic approach to sovereignty would allow the international community to adjust to reality and to begin to help a substantial number of people. If the new subnational arrangements are ignored, they will continue to be more like institutionalized protection rackets than states that guard the rights of their citizens. At the same time, local rulers who are actually

[13] Morton H. Halperin and David J. Scheffer, *Self-Determination in the New World Order* (Washington, DC: Carnegie Endowment for International Peace, 1992) pp. 84–93.

[14] John Drysdale, *Whatever Happened to Somalia?* (London: HAAN Associates, 1994), p. 147.

exercising elements of sovereign control will continue to focus on informal trade, often involving drugs, guns, and poached animals to survive, rather than beginning initiatives to promote more routine economic development that would aid all of the people in their region. The international community thus faces the choice between ignoring successful secessionist movements and thereby forcing them to remain semicriminal affairs or trying to help create new state institutions. The fact that some African states will dissolve will be the reality, no matter which policy stance is adopted.

Alternatives to the Sovereign State

Far more revolutionary would be for at least parts of Africa to be reordered around some organization other than the sovereign state. While such reforms would be a dramatic change for international society, their adoption would be a welcome acknowledgment of what is actually happening in parts of Africa where many states do not exercise exclusive sovereignty over their territories. Discussing alternatives to the current understanding of sovereignty is perfectly legitimate because sovereignty is not an innate attribute of a state but something that is conferred by international society and that is based, as chapters two, three, and four demonstrate, at least partially on how leaders hope to govern. New thinking regarding competitors or supplements to the sovereign state would also recognize that the particular moment in world history when the entire planet's history is being ruled by one type of political organization does not have to be permanent and is not necessarily desirable.

Once again, it will primarily be up to the Africans to come up with alternatives to the nation-state. However, the international community can play an important role in at least signaling that the atmosphere has changed and that there is at least the possibility of alternatives to the sovereign state that could be accepted. Alternatives to the nation-state are being developed now; it is simply a question of whether the international community will recognize them. For instance, the anarchy of Somalia has prompted some scholars to finally discuss alternatives to the old, failed political order.[15]

Certainly, an important area to explore would be experiments that account for the diminishing control that some African governments exercise over distance. In areas far from the capital, other actors, including

[15] See the report by consultants from the London School of Economics and Political Science, *A Study of Decentralised Political Structures for Somalia: A Menu of Options* (London: London School of Economics and Political Science, 1995).

traditional leaders and local "warlords" who have moved into the vacuum created by the collapse of the local branches of the state, may exercise substantial control, provide security, and collect taxes. Understanding that in some of the failed or failing states in Africa, rural communities already face a complex situation where sovereign control is only exercised partially, if at all, by the central government would be an important return to reality and an abandonment of the fictions of international law. These situations differ from the criteria discussed above for recognizing new states because no obvious authority exercises clear control over a defined piece of territory. Unfortunately, this situation is probably much more likely in collapsing African states than the appearance of a new force that can actually exercise sovereign authority over a defined piece of territory.

Having recognized the confused situation on the ground in some African countries, an important innovation would be to loosen the institutional framework governing international organizations. It would be particularly useful to encourage the participation by subnational units, be they potential breakaway regions or simply units such as towns or regions that have been largely abandoned by their own central government, in, at first, technical meetings and later directly in organizations such as WHO, UNICEF, and UNDP that provide resources directly for development. Such a sharing of sovereignty would be a reflection of who is exercising authority on the ground, just as shared sovereignty during the precolonial period was an acknowledgment that no one state exercised absolute power in a particular region. Correspondingly, the messy diplomacy of the precolonial period, where units had complex relations with other types of units, is, in some ways, more appropriate than the current practice of states only having diplomatic relations with other states.

Participation in technical and service delivery organizations by actors (e.g., traditional leaders or "warlords") who currently exercise authority and may deliver services but are not sovereign is appealing because international acceptance can be calibrated to the actual power being exercised. Thus, if a region's schooling has become largely dependent on the leadership and funds provided by a traditional leader, that ethnic group might develop some kind of formal relationship with the relevant UN agency. Of course, care would have to be taken that the new leaders were able to exercise their authority for a sustained period of time. Also, the international community would be free to make judgments about the degree of assistance based on human rights concerns just as it does now, in a limited sense, for countries that seek aid. Such a stance might, in at least some circumstances, be more helpful to the people of a region than pretending the old political arrangements still work. If the government of a country objects to losing authority, it should, as was the case in the precolonial period, be forced to prove that it can actually govern the region.

Breaking the institutional logjam in the critical international institutions that actually provide services would probably be more important than having the General Assembly or other highly political organizations begin to recognize subnational ethnic groups.[16] Because it is the source of sovereignty, highly visible, and political, recognition by the General Assembly is probably the last step for a region or group of people breaking away from their old nation-state. In the indeterminate position that at least some regions of some African countries will occupy, focusing on service delivery is probably more important than grand politics. Indeed, the suggestion about joining the General Assembly comes out of a study solely concerned with alleviating ethnic conflict, rather than the more general set of problems of the dysfunctional nature of African states and their particular type of disintegration.

The actual diplomacy of integrating nonstate actors into what were previously clubs of sovereign nations would, of course, be difficult. However, in a variety of circumstances, the international community has proved adept at adapting to diplomacy with something other than the traditional sovereign states. As Reno demonstrates, foreign companies have not been reluctant to negotiate with informal authority in Liberia and Sierra Leone, and are willing to make a deal with anyone who has real, as opposed to theoretical, control over a territory.[17] Similarly, while the international community does not, in general, recognize Taiwan as a separate country, the vast majority of countries still manage to have normal commercial relations with Taipei and, at times, what looks suspiciously like diplomatic relations only slightly hidden. Once the sovereignty issue has been addressed, it should not be that hard for technical agencies to actually begin relating to those units that are actually providing services. Such a measure would also be a logical, if still revolutionary, departure from current practices, which tacitly allow nongovernmental organizations to cross borders during humanitarian crises without devoting much attention to the niceties of sovereignty.

The international community should also explore alternative means of providing some sort of recognition to some subnational communities that are not necessarily organized territorially. For instance, Hans Brunhart, Liechtenstein's minister of foreign affairs, has put forward an initiative that stresses the importance of every community having some level of autonomy within the nation-state and of increasing some communities'

---

[16] This is Gottlieb's suggestion, *Nation against State*, p. 39.

[17] See William Reno, *Corruption and State Politics in Sierra Leone* (Cambridge: Cambridge University Press, 1995), pp. 128–82.

abilities to act vis-à-vis the central state. In particular, the initiative provides communities, defined in a variety of ways, the means to appeal to the international society if the central government reneges on agreements it has made to devolve certain powers to the local level.[18] While this proposal may not necessarily be ideal for African countries, it does recognize that the international community's fixation with the nation-state has been inappropriate. By providing international recourse to groups that have not previously been recognized, the proposal provides an example of the new thinking necessary if there are to be alternatives to dysfunctional nation-states. In Africa, providing recourse to ethnic communities that have been treated poorly by the nation-state is particularly important given the inability of many states to fully govern in the rural areas and their common recourse to brute force outside the cities to assert their power.

Conclusion

The African model of state consolidation has prevented much of the continent from experiencing the brutality of interstate war that so mars much of the human experience during the last one hundred years. However, it also appears that this particular avenue of state-building leads to a dead end for a significant number of countries. The African model—where states are born easily but do not die—is dramatically at odds with traditional western accounts of state-building. It is time for scholars who have avoided non-European paths toward state consolidation to begin to take the African examples, and the examples of other regions with low population densities, into account in order to develop a truly comparative account of how states develop. At the same time, leaders in Africa and elsewhere should end their state of denial and accept that serious thinking must begin regarding alternatives to at least some of the political arrangements that were initially demarcated by the Europeans. If they do not, the response to the ever more serious political and humanitarian challenges to state failure in Africa will inevitably be too little, too late.

[18] Hans Brunhart, "Statement at the Forty-Seventh Session of the General Assembly," 23 September 1992, p. 3.

Index